TRANSCENDENCE

TRANSCENDENCE

HEALING AND
TRANSFORMATION
THROUGH
**TRANSCENDENTAL
MEDITATION**

DR NORMAN E. ROSENTHAL

HAY HOUSE

Australia • Canada • Hong Kong • India
South Africa • United Kingdom • United States

PUBLISHED AND DISTRIBUTED IN THE UNITED STATES OF AMERICA BY:
Penguin Group (USA) Inc., 375 Hudson Street, New York, New York 10014, USA

FIRST PUBLISHED AND DISTRIBUTED IN THE UNITED KINGDOM BY:
Hay House UK Ltd, Astley House, 33 Notting Hill Gate, London W11 3JQ.
Tel: +44 (0)20 3675 2450; Fax: +44 (0)20 3675 2451. www.hayhouse.co.uk

PUBLISHED AND DISTRIBUTED IN AUSTRALIA BY:
Hay House Australia Ltd, 18/36 Ralph St, Alexandria NSW 2015. Tel.: (61) 2 9669
4299; Fax: (61) 2 9669 4144. www.hayhouse.com.au

PUBLISHED AND DISTRIBUTED IN THE REPUBLIC OF SOUTH AFRICA BY:
Hay House SA (Pty), Ltd, PO Box 990, Witkoppen 2068. Tel./Fax: (27) 11 467 8904.
www.hayhouse.co.za

PUBLISHED AND DISTRIBUTED IN INDIA BY:
Hay House Publishers India, Muskaan Complex, Plot No.3, B-2, Vasant Kunj, New
Delhi – 110 070. Tel.: (91) 11 4176 1620; Fax: (91) 11 4176 1630. www.hayhouse.co.in

Copyright © 2011 by Norman E. Rosenthal, M.D.

Grateful acknowledgment is made for permission to reprint an excerpt from "Little
Gidding" in *Four Quartets*, copyright © 1942 by T. S. Eliot and renewed in 1970 by
Esmé Valerie Eliot. Reprinted by permission of Houghton Mifflin Harcourt
Publishing Company.

Transcendental Meditation® and TM® are protected trademarks licensed to Maharishi
Foundation USA, a nonprofit educational organization.

Book design by Lucy Albanese

The author of this book does not dispense medical advice or prescribe the use of any
technique as a form of treatment for physical or medical problems without the advice
of a physician, either directly or indirectly. The intent of the author is only to offer
information of a general nature to help you in your quest for emotional and spiritual
wellbeing. In the event you use any of the information in this book for yourself, which
is your constitutional right, the author and the publisher assume no responsibility for
your actions.

A catalogue record for this book is available from the British Library.

ISBN 978-1-84850-775-3

Printed and bound in Great Britain by TJ International, Padstow, Cornwall.

For

Josh, Liana, and Ari

CONTENTS

FOREWORD

Mehmet C. Oz, M.D.

LET ME RETURN to my surgical roots and cut to my conclusion: Dr. Norman Rosenthal's *Transcendence: Healing and Transformation Through Transcendental Meditation* is a profoundly important book on a topic that you need to know a lot more about. Moreover, it has been written by an eminently qualified expert: an internationally respected psychiatrist and twenty-year senior researcher at the National Institute of Mental Health, who first described seasonal affective disorder and pioneered the use of light therapy.

So, why is this book so incredibly valuable?

Stress wears us down, drains us of the joys of life, fuels countless diseases and disorders, and is slowly, or rapidly, killing us. Cardiovascular disease, obesity, diabetes, as well as digestive disorders, anxiety, and depression, are often caused or exacerbated by stress. You know these grim realities—and hopefully you are already doing something to neutralize stress, such as eating better and exercising more. But there is something you may not be doing, but which you really must do, beyond exercise and diet. And that is promoting your own mental resilience: developing your natural, innate ability to overcome mentally the mounting pressures and demands that pervade our lives. Stated bluntly, you must promote mental resilience or lose the fight against stress—and suffer the consequences.

Dr. Rosenthal's *Transcendence* brilliantly addresses the importance of mental resilience—and much more. It reveals, in a most readable and enticing fashion, the need to access—through a simple, time-tested meditation technique—the silent core of our own Being; and it recounts the unprecedented, scientifically documented, wide-ranging benefits that naturally ensue.

I have known Dr. Rosenthal and his work for more than ten years, and am happy to count him as a respected colleague and one of my panel of experts to whom I turn for advice about the mind—in sickness and in health. I have always admired Dr. Rosenthal for his ability to tackle the most challenging emotional problems we all face. In *Transcendence*, Dr. Rosenthal addresses his clinical and literary skills to the subject of Transcendental Meditation as a promising technique for helping a wide range of people both physically and emotionally.

As a cardiovascular surgeon, I am familiar with the ability of TM to reduce high blood pressure, the so-called silent killer. In many controlled studies, simply but elegantly described in *Transcendence*, we learn that this blood pressure reduction is not only statistically significant, but clinically significant as well. This is reflected in the ability of TM to greatly reduce cardiac mortality in people at risk for heart disease. But *Transcendence* takes us far beyond the physical benefits of TM, and advances a persuasive argument that TM may help people with a wide range of emotional conditions—including anxiety, depression, attention deficit disorder, and addictions—as well as veterans experiencing post-traumatic stress disorder. The list may sound overblown, but Dr. Rosenthal makes his case well by offering gripping stories of emotional transformation, backed up by impressive research and logical explanations for how TM may provide such varied benefits.

There are chapters on the potential value of TM in inner-city schools, prisons, and shelters for the homeless that make for fascinating reading, and offer genuine hope for people trying to make their way in these difficult environments. In one of my favorite chapters in *Transcendence*, we learn how TM can help even highly successful people live fuller and richer lives. Finally, there is an explanation for how TM might improve the level of harmony, both within ourselves and the world outside.

Dr. Rosenthal is one of those rare professionals who are able to mix authority and accuracy with riveting stories that read like a novel. In *Transcendence*, he has given us all a gift that will enlighten, entertain, and perhaps even transform. This will become the go-to book for those searching for the wisdom within meditation.

Mehmet C. Oz is the Emmy Award–winning host of The Dr. Oz Show *and vice chairman and professor of surgery, New York Presbyterian–Columbia University.*

Part I

TRANSCENDENCE

INTRODUCTION

My Journey Back

> We shall not cease from exploration
> And the end of all our exploring
> Will be to arrive where we started
> And know the place for the first time.
>
> —T. S. ELIOT

HOW OFTEN HAVE you set out upon some course of exploration—
perhaps a relationship, a journey, or a field of study—then put it aside
for a time, only to find the experience quite different when you return?
The Greek philosopher Heraclitus said you can never step in the same
river twice, because the second time you have changed, and therefore
the experience is different. That is how it was for me and Transcendental Meditation (TM).

The first time I ever heard of TM, I was a medical student in Johannesburg, South Africa. It was the early seventies, and at that time, even
in apartheid South Africa, the world of the young was rustling with
promises of change. Anything seemed possible. The Beatles had gone
to India to learn TM from its modern-day founder, Maharishi Mahesh
Yogi. This quest for exotic wisdom was embodied for me in the words
of the rock musical *Hair*, "I've been to India and saw the yogi light."

I was intrigued. What *was* transcendence? What was the yogi light, and how might I find it?—without actually going to India (which was not in the cards either financially or logistically). I was drawn to the promise of an alternative type of consciousness, one that embraced all human beings and the universe to boot, yet involved no mind-altering drugs.

Happily, it turned out that the practice of Transcendental Meditation had already reached the far shores of Africa, so a fellow medical student and I headed off to a small house in the suburbs that doubled as a TM training center. I was reassured to discover that Transcendental Meditation is in no way a religious practice. No one asked me to buy into any belief system. Instead, I learned that TM is simply a technique of the mind that can be practiced by people of any religion or of no religion at all. The technique goes back thousands of years and was taught to Maharishi Mahesh Yogi by his own teacher in the Himalayas. Maharishi extracted the TM technique from its religious context and distilled it to its essence, which he believed could be of value to people of all creeds in many situations.

Maharishi brought the technique first to India (in 1955) and then to the rest of the world, including the United States, which he first visited in 1959. Although for many Westerners Maharishi is most widely known for his contact with the Beatles in the 1960s, that was only a small part of his career. He was the founder and leader of the worldwide Transcendental Meditation program for over fifty years and devoted his life to sharing his insights and knowledge both in his writing and his public appearances. He also promoted scientific testing of the technique, to help bring meditation into the scientific mainstream.

As part of our TM instruction, my friend and I were each given our own mantra (a sound-word-vibration). Then, over several days, we were taught how to think the mantra as we sat in quiet relaxation. We were to practice for twenty minutes twice a day. Although I found it very soothing, I did not feel any lasting effect—which in retrospect is hardly surprising, since I seldom practiced. In the busy life of a medical student, TM slid down my priority list, then off. It was replaced by studies, dissections, autopsies, and eventually patients, the most rewarding part of a medical education. Add in my rudimentary attempts at a social life, and no time seemed left in the day.

The brain in all its wondrous mystery has always intrigued me, so I became a psychiatrist. I immigrated to the United States in 1976, embarked on a psychiatric residency at Columbia Presbyterian Hospital, and in 1979 moved to the National Institute of Mental Health (NIMH) in Bethesda, Maryland, to become a researcher and pursue a clinical practice in psychiatry. There I soon had the good fortune to encounter Herb Kern, a patient whose moods varied remarkably with the seasons:[1] In the summertime he was a happy, creative scientist, but as the days grew shorter, he invariably fell into a deep depression. Herb theorized that his seasonal shifts of mood might be related to seasonal changes in the length of the day. He visited the NIMH during one of his depressed phases and became the first patient whom my colleagues and I treated by expanding the length of his day, using bright artificial light. Within three days of starting treatment, he bounced out of his depression!

The idea of seasonal mood changes driven by day length struck me as important because I myself, after moving north from South Africa, had experienced such changes, though not as severely as Herb. Perhaps many people had such seasonal mood changes, I thought—and research over the years has shown it to be so! Over the next several years, my colleagues and I went on to describe a syndrome we called *seasonal affective disorder* (SAD), and also to develop a novel treatment for the condition—exposure to bright light.[2] I describe the story of this discovery in my book *Winter Blues*.

Although light therapy for SAD is now routinely prescribed in all the darker parts of the globe, such as the northern United States and

Europe, at the time my research began many colleagues thought the idea was strange, even humorous. I had to put up with a lot of teasing, and I am greatly indebted to my senior colleagues at NIMH for supporting a young researcher with his outlandish idea.

From that early research experience, I took away several important lessons: to listen carefully to my patients; to be open to new observations; to follow my intuition—even if it took me down untrodden paths; and *never* to ignore the importance of the obvious, such as light and dark. All these lessons are relevant to this book, because after thirty-five years they brought me back to Transcendental Meditation, that brief fad of my medical school days, and the experience was totally different. I now know meditation to be something that can transform people's lives. And I mean *transform*, as in "He or she is a different person."

This realization first dawned on me several years ago when I began to treat Paul, a young aspiring writer and filmmaker who suffered from severe bipolar disorder. Like me, Paul had learned TM, then let it lapse.

Some years later, when Paul was in his early twenties, his illness struck. His first manic episode was, in his words, "The beginning of a five-year roller coaster through hell—two psychotic manias that landed me in prison, a transfer to a mental hospital, a cocktail of drugs that caused me to gain forty pounds and evaporated all my emotions, followed by the misery of the bipolar depressive phase that stripped me of all capacity for pleasure and left me suicidal." At that point, even though Paul was on a combination of medications, as well as a rigorous program of healthy living, here's how he describes the way he felt:

> Despite all these efforts, after two years of being stable
> since the end of my depression, I was still not happy. I wasn't
> really *unhappy*, but I didn't laugh, feel good, or have much

emotion. I was basically just getting by, keeping my head above water. I resigned myself to the idea that I would never be happy—I mean *truly* happy.

Paul tried to start meditating again, but irregularly. That changed, however, after a pivotal experience, which he describes as follows:

> While working on a documentary, I met a man who was a big meditator. Somehow the subject of bipolar disorder came up, and it turned out that this man had a severe case. Yet he told me that for the last twenty years he had been really happy ninety percent of the time. I was amazed, but I believed him. I could see it in his face and his eyes—that he was really happy and wasn't lying. It was then that I decided to do TM twice a day every day. Of course, I would miss here and there, but I resolved to do it regularly.
>
> Ever since then, things got better over time. The positive effects took a couple of months to set in noticeably. When they did, they came gradually, progressively, stronger and more profound as time passed. It is now four years since I have been meditating regularly and I'm better than I've ever been. Just like the man I met that day in San Francisco, I'm not just happy, I'm *really* happy ninety percent of the time.

When I told Paul that I had once practiced TM, but had let it lapse, he said, "You should start meditating again, Dr. Rosenthal. You'll see. It'll make a great difference." He made this suggestion several times and I nodded my head, all the while wondering how I would fit two twenty-minute sessions into an already packed day. Perhaps it was the earnestness of his repeated suggestion that prompted me to act. Or maybe it was my recollection of how, over the years, I have learned at least as much from my patients as they have ever learned from me. It was at that time that I met Bob Roth, a highly experienced teacher, who checked my meditation technique and set me on the right course. Unlike the young medical student I was in Johannesburg, I now realize that no new skill can be acquired without practice, so I have been faithful to the twice-a-day regimen. As a reward, I have acquired in TM a valuable tool for stilling my mind and quieting the fight-or-flight responses so often triggered by the stress of modern life.

Transcendental Meditation does more than merely correct symptoms, however. After a few years of practice, it has allowed me to enter a place inside my mind that is difficult to describe with any better word than *transcendence*. It is a blissful state that encompasses elements of serenity, peace, and acceptance, but also exhilaration and a sense of new possibilities, both for now and for the future. I don't mean to imply that I always feel this way—far from it. I will say, though, that I cannot remember a time when I have felt happier or more at peace with myself and my surroundings.

In the past few years, since I have been meditating regularly, I have recommended TM to a number of my patients, many of whom have reported excellent results. You will read about them in this book, together with the experience of other clinicians and researchers intrigued by TM. My colleagues and I are excited, not only at TM's potential to relieve various forms of human suffering, but also at how much we can learn in the process. Transcendence turns out to be an excellent window into the mind and the brain.

A great deal of clinical research has been done on TM. For example, we now know that when people practice TM, their blood pressure drops. They show higher blood levels of a soothing hormone called *prolactin*, as well as more coherent brain wave patterns, which are associated with good mental functioning. New evidence even suggests that TM may improve longevity and lower medical costs by reducing hospital stays and doctors' visits. Even people who are not in physical or psychological distress can be helped. TM has been shown to help "normal" people reach their full potential and live in greater harmony with one another.

All this research is now moving into the practical realm. Already, ambitious new outreach programs are using TM to help groups of people under particular stress, including inner-city schoolchildren struggling to cope with life amid the clamor of crowded and violent schools; veterans with post-traumatic stress disorder; homeless and formerly incarcerated men trying to adapt to life in the workaday world; and Native Americans, who are battling high rates of diseases like diabetes. This ancient tradition has many potential untapped uses, including some that you can identify by reading this book.

In addition, TM training is becoming easier to find as professionally trained TM teachers are available in most parts of the world.[3] As I will discuss later, neither this nor *any* book can teach the technique of TM, which is learned individually from a teacher. As with other courses of study, a fee is charged to cover costs of instruction and administration. Do not be deterred, however. Loans, scholarships, and grants are available to ensure that anyone who wants to learn meditation can do so.

As a person who has witnessed the mental and spiritual anguish of many hundreds of people, I have to say that the potential clinical power of this technique is amazing. It offers the promise to transform the lives of millions who suffer. At the same time, I hope the practice will not be confined to spiritual seekers or to people so afflicted that they come to medical attention. It can also relieve stress and maximize the potential that resides within each and every one of us. If Transcendental

Meditation were a drug, conferring so many benefits with few, if any, side effects, it would be a billion-dollar blockbuster.

I am *not* suggesting that TM be considered as a stand-alone treatment for emotional disorders, especially when an effective standard of care already exists. But when it comes to the brain and mind, the fact is that no single treatment works every time for any given set of symptoms. We often have to try several different medications or treatment approaches before we find the right mix. I *am* suggesting that TM should be part of that mix, especially when conventional approaches prove unsatisfactory. You will meet in this book many people who fall into that category, people for whom TM has provided additional help they could find nowhere else. Indeed, for a few people, TM has done the job all by itself. I am thinking, for example, of a physician described in chapter 6, "Helping the Spikes and Valleys," whose depression during medical school responded to TM after failing to respond to conventional treatment. This man has stayed well without antidepressants for the past thirty-five years, and to this day he continues to meditate twice a day.

You may wonder, as I did many years ago, whether twenty minutes twice a day is too much time to commit. I now view it very differently. Soon after starting to meditate regularly, TM became for me—as it is for most people—a pleasant and peaceful retreat. I see it as an investment in my well-being and physical health. Finally, to my initial surprise, it makes me more efficient during the rest of my day—and others agree. As one Wall Street broker told me, far from detracting from his ability to get things done, his regular meditation practice actually gives him *more* productive time.

In this book I will explore four major themes related to TM, represented in the four parts of the book: Transcendence, Healing,

Transformation, and Harmony. These sections deal respectively with (1) the curious and wonderful state of consciousness called *transcendence*; (2) the physical benefits of TM that scientific research has confirmed; (3) its psychological impact, seen in research and the stories of real people whose lives it has transformed; and (4) the way TM promotes harmony at multiple levels—within the mind, between mind and body, between people, and within society.

Although I am excited by the relief TM offers those suffering from physical and emotional disorders, there is a great deal more to the practice. I hear all the time from both patients and friends about their desire to move beyond the humdrum and the ordinary. People have a certain yearning. It's not that anything is wrong with their lives—they just want something more, something larger than their daily routine. I have come to believe that for myself and many others, this need can be met by delving deep into the self and discovering the ocean of consciousness within.

In the course of my exploration, I have talked with people from many walks of life who have made these journeys of transcendence and have been transformed in the process. I have spoken to inner-city schoolchildren, veterans with post-traumatic stress disorder, people with addictions, formerly homeless and incarcerated men, and those suffering from emotional illnesses, and have been impressed by the impact of TM on their lives. I have also spoken to successful artists—including movie stars and filmmakers—as well as scientists and business executives, and have arrived at the same observations. I can only conclude that this technique can improve the lives of a broad sweep of people, and I look forward to sharing what I have learned with you.

Some of you may find this preview of the benefits of TM—this seemingly simple technique—exaggerated and hard to believe. I don't blame you. It has taken me quite a while to come to these conclusions myself. But as a psychiatrist and scientist with over thirty years of clinical and research experience, I have found that once in a great while, something comes along that truly surprises—TM is one such thing. I have examined the data—the literature, my patients, and myself—and am persuaded that something rather special is going on here. I encourage you to read the stories of the people in this book, as well as all the research behind my conclusions—and judge for yourself.

1

A RETURN TO THE SELF

Aspects of Meditation

The Brain—is wider than the Sky—
For—put them side by side—
The one the other will contain
With ease—and You—beside—
The Brain is deeper than the sea—
For—hold them—Blue to Blue—
The one the other will absorb—
As Sponges—Buckets—do—
                                        —EMILY DICKINSON

WHEN I THINK of Dickinson's image of the brain as wider than the sky or deeper than the sea, it conjures up for me, as it does perhaps for you, a sense that our minds harbor an untapped vastness, of which we use only a small part. I believe that when we meditate, we venture into this vastness almost as astronauts or divers do. We explore a universe that is both uncharted and familiar.

Many available forms of meditation exist, involving techniques that vary from concentration on the breath, an image, or a sound to walking and other forms of movement. This book deals only with Transcendental Meditation (TM) for several reasons. First, it is the method that I have practiced myself with excellent results. Second, I have observed its many positive effects on the lives of patients, friends, and colleagues. Third, it is an easy form of meditation to learn and practice. And finally, there is an astonishing amount of research on its physical and psychological benefits.

By my latest count, there have been 340 peer-reviewed articles published on TM,[1] many of which have appeared in highly respected journals. For those unfamiliar with scientific publishing, "peer-reviewed" means that each article is subjected to scrutiny by independent reviewers who are authorities in their field. Even if the reviewers deem the article worthy, they typically suggest changes; only after these recommendations have been addressed does the paper get published. As a researcher who has been both reviewer and reviewee, I can vouch for the large amount of work that goes into this process.

I have nothing bad to say about other forms of meditation, all of which have their proponents. What is important to realize, however, is that they all use different procedures, which meditation experts Fred Travis and Jonathan Shear have sorted into three fundamental categories: *focused attention, open monitoring,* and *automatic self-transcending.*[2] In each category, what the meditator is asked to do is different, and each produces a distinctive change in brain wave patterns.

In the *focused attention* styles of meditation, the meditator holds the mind's eye on something in particular, such as an image (perhaps a picture of a flower) or a profound emotion (such as loving-kindness toward other human beings). If other thoughts intrude, attention is directed back to the focus. In *open monitoring* techniques, which include Buddhist-type mindfulness meditation, the meditator learns to observe the breath, or whatever thoughts and feelings may arrive, without reacting to them—in order to become more aware of internal patterns. Transcendental Meditation falls into the third group, which Travis and Shear have called *automatic self-transcending,* so named because effortlessly thinking the mantra repetitively takes you beyond the mantra and into another state of consciousness,[3] which I will discuss in greater detail later.

Given the different brain wave patterns produced by each type of meditation, it makes sense that each type has its own unique effects on both the brain and the meditator. The benefits observed for one type may or may not apply to another. For example, in the Tibetan Buddhist tradition of loving-kindness-compassion meditation, increased activity has been reported in those areas of the brain that are important for regulating emotions.[4] These changes are more prominent in experienced than in novice meditators, which suggests a more stable regulation of emotions in the veterans, even when they are not meditating.

Mindfulness Meditation, on the other hand, has been shown to increase the activity of neurons not only in certain emotional areas of the brain,[5] but also in frontal regions, which are responsible for decision making and other executive functions. You might expect these changes to increase the meditator's ability to focus attention.

In Transcendental Meditation, however, there is a more global effect. For example, characteristic brain wave patterns (which I will discuss shortly) are seen in many different parts of the brain (though primarily in the frontal areas) during a TM session itself but also after the session is over. Knowing that, you might expect the meditator to maintain a broad perspective on things even outside of meditation sessions and not to be entirely preoccupied by the activity of the moment.[6] (You can find more information about the different categories of meditation and their associated characteristics and EEG changes in the notes section.)[7]

Each form of meditation could make for a fascinating study in its own right. In this book, however, I address only TM, about which there is more than enough to say to fill all its pages.

LEARNING TO MEDITATE

Transcendental Meditation is always taught one-on-one, at least initially, by a teacher who is a longtime meditator trained not only to instruct new students and provide follow-up, but also to customize the approach for each student. Initial instruction has seven steps: two lectures and a personal interview with a certified teacher, then four teaching sessions on four consecutive days. Each session lasts about ninety minutes. Ideally, the fledgling meditator then follows up with the teacher, perhaps weekly for the first month and monthly thereafter. These thirty-minute "checking" sessions give students a chance to ask questions and make sure their technique is still on track, so they will derive the maximum benefit.

During the training, each student is assigned a specific mantra or sound, with instructions on its proper use. There is a set number of mantras, and the TM teacher selects one for each student based on certain criteria. Mantras are particular soothing sounds, known by experience gathered over centuries to bring on transcendence (of which more later). The mantras used in TM derive from the Vedic tradition of ancient India. Another important aspect of the mantra is that it has no specific meaning to the meditator, which is important. Think about it: If your mantra were "apple pie," every time you started to meditate your mouth would water, which would hardly promote a transcendent experience.

Here is another crucial but little known point: The mantra alone is not enough. It is the "vehicle" for effortless, inward movement of the mind, but it is not a "magic bullet." Using the mantra properly—effortlessly, without concentration or deliberate control of the mind—is as important as the sound itself.

Students are asked not to reveal their mantras to others. My colleague Bob Roth, who has taught thousands of people to meditate, says that in his experience, when students compare their mantras, the resulting confusion and self-consciousness can inhibit learning and the easy flow of proper meditation. I don't regard my mantra as some deep dark secret, but not discussing it helps me maintain a sense of privacy and specialness about it.

Most meditators I have encountered respect the value of keeping their mantra private. Former Beatle Ringo Starr told filmmaker David Lynch about an incident related to this topic, which involved himself and George Harrison many years ago. Here's how Ringo describes it:

> I remember [Maharishi teaching me that first meditation] so well, with an apple and a white handkerchief. And he gave me a mantra, *my* mantra. And I made a promise not to tell anyone else my mantra. And then, after that, George and I were in a room, hinting about telling each other. What can you do? We were in our twenties! We got really close but we never said it. But when we got really close, I was sick; I mean I was breaking this promise. So anyway, I've never entertained the idea of telling anyone what it is. And if I talk to anyone, you know, I say I got my mantra "milk bottle," and that's how you do it.

Even though I am about to tell you what it is like for me to meditate, please be aware that my story will not substitute for a qualified teacher. Learning meditation is like learning yoga, martial arts, or the piano—you need a teacher, not just a book. In my experience, ongoing contact with the teacher—as well as the relationship between student and teacher—can be critical to a successful outcome.

In order to derive the full benefit of meditation, two sessions per day of twenty minutes each are recommended. Good times for these sessions are shortly after waking and in the late afternoon before supper, but there is room for flexibility. Some of the more common questions that arise about meditation are addressed in an appendix at the back of this book (see page 261).

WHAT IS IT LIKE TO MEDITATE?

Although there is no such thing as a "typical" TM session, certain qualities pervade every meditation: deep relaxation, inner peace, and (sometimes) a highly enjoyable shift in consciousness. To start, I settle down in a comfortable chair in a quiet room, turn off the phones, dim the lights, and prepare for my journey. That's ideal, though, really, you can meditate anywhere. Bob Roth, who has been meditating for forty years, has had wonderful sessions, for example, in airplanes or the backs of cabs. When he was a student working at an ice cream shop, he used to sneak into the broom closet to meditate.

After I close my eyes, I use the mantra in a way that allows my mind to settle into quietude. There's no effort, no need to concentrate or control my mind. In daily life my mind is generally very busy, constantly rustling with plans, memories, the events of the day—all the miscellaneous flotsam and jetsam that the mind throws up, often without rhyme or reason. As I continue to meditate, all that mental noise quiets, and I welcome the silence.

At certain points during any session, I may experience transcendence—a feeling that I have gone beyond time and space. I am not thinking of anything in particular. Rather, transcendence is an experience of unfocused bliss, which may last for seconds or minutes. It comes and goes mysteriously and cannot be forced. It is a gift of the meditation, one that comes on its own through effortless, innocent practice.

So singular is this state that I am devoting the next chapter to telling you more about it and have named this book *Transcendence* to honor its importance.

EMERGING FROM MEDITATION

It is important to come out of a meditative state gradually. An experienced meditation teacher will tell you to give yourself a few minutes before emerging fully. I try to enjoy those last few minutes as I would the tail end of a pleasant dream. A gentle transition will promote a sustained calm after the session ends, while emerging abruptly can feel startling or disruptive. One of my patients, a young man whose job required that he leave his cell phone on at all times, routinely developed a headache if it rang during one of his sessions.

Tim Page, a Pulitzer Prize–winning music critic and a longtime meditator (thirty-five years and counting), also emphasizes the importance of coming out of meditation smoothly. Here's how he describes it—naturally, in terms of music:

> There's a silence at the beginning of a piece of music and a silence at the end. And the silence at the end is the result of a journey, and it's charged with whatever has happened to you during the journey. It's a much more profound and meaningful silence than the one at the start. For me, meditation is deepest when I'm coming out and I'm withdrawing from it. Just as a diver will get the bends if he surfaces too quickly, so I will get the psychological bends if I come out of

> meditation too quickly. If I'm in a deep meditation and all of
> a sudden I have to spring into motion, it's irritating, exasper-
> ating, and puts me in a bad humor.

The two silences that Tim reports are different because the meditation session has changed the brain in some way—just as a piece of
music or any experience can do. As we will see, when the brain is af-
forded the experience of meditation on a regular basis, the resulting
changes can be cumulative and dramatic.

WHAT HAPPENS IN THE BODY AND BRAIN DURING MEDITATION?

When a person attains transcendence, both body and brain undergo
predictable changes that have been carefully studied by Fred Travis,
director of the Center for Brain, Consciousness, and Cognition at Maharishi University of Management in Fairfield, Iowa. Over the past
twenty years, Travis has shown, for example, that transcendence brings
with it a special way of breathing. The breath slows down so much
that sometimes when watching others in this state, you almost wonder
whether you should give them a shake. Happily, they will soon enough
take a long, slow breath, then once again appear to stop breathing.[8]

Experiments on people practicing TM show that brain waves
change during transcendence in a highly significant way. As you probably know, brain waves are patterns of electrical activity that arise
largely in the outer layers of the brain, the cerebral cortex. To measure
them, researchers place electrodes at particular points on the scalp.
The electrodes sense brain activity and the resulting readout is called
an electroencephalogram (EEG). Below you can see two examples of

these readouts. On the left you see alpha waves, a slow frequency of 8 to 12 cycles per second that occurs when a person is relaxing with eyes closed. On the right are beta waves, which run 13 or more cycles per second; they reflect an alert and focused state of mind. In daily life, people generate sporadic alpha waves, but during meditation they become significantly more numerous.

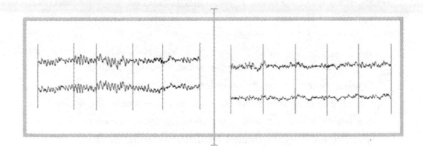

The panel on the left shows the slower alpha waves; the panel on the right shows the faster beta waves. The two separate tracings in each panel represent five seconds of EEG from electrodes placed at two different points on the scalp.

Even more interesting, at least to me, is that the TM practice increases brain wave *coherence*, which is an area of growing interest among neuroscientists. All the different parts of the brain generate brain waves in several frequencies. These brain waves are said to be coherent when waves of a given frequency from different parts of the brain are in step with one another, as shown below on the left. Compare that to the right-hand panel, where coherence is lacking—the waves are out of step.

The panel on the left shows brain waves (mostly alpha) that are highly coherent across different leads. Notice how the readouts from the different electrodes line up. In other words, the waves are highly correlated across the different leads. Contrast that with the brain waves (mostly beta) in the panel on the right, where there is a low level of coherence; in other words, the waves are not highly correlated across the different leads.

Brain wave coherence is generally a good thing: It correlates with high levels of intelligence and competence—which makes sense, when you consider that the normal brain contains literally billions of nerve cells connected at trillions of synapses. To produce a train of thought or execute an action, all the cells have to function as a unit, just as soldiers in a battle need to advance in a coordinated way.

Even novice meditators show these brain wave changes, starting within weeks (or even days) after they begin to meditate. By two months, their brain waves during meditation are indistinguishable from those of meditators who have been practicing for decades. Travis regards this as confirmation that TM is a technique that is easily learned. Where you do see EEG differences between novices and seasoned meditators is when the people are awake but not meditating. In seasoned meditators, more brain wave coherence can be seen through-out the day.[9]

You may well wonder, though, whether the increase in brain wave coherence really makes a difference. The simple answer is yes. For example, Travis and colleagues conducted a study on twenty top-level Norwegian managers who had excelled in management over many years as evidenced by expanding their business or turning around a failing business.[10] They compared these managers with twenty skilled knowledge workers, such as accountants or engineers, who had no management responsibility but were matched for age and gender. They found that the managers showed greater EEG coherence than the workers. Likewise, in a study of thirty-three athletes, they found that elite athletes showed greater EEG coherence than their less success-ful competitors.[11] They concluded that EEG coherence reflects brain efficiency.

Travis's EEG studies also help explain *how* transcendence, experienced repeatedly, may boost competence—it has to do with which particular parts of the brain are involved. During transcendence, the EEG shows increased coherence in alpha frequency and the lower part of the beta frequency in the prefrontal areas of the brain (just behind the forehead). This important region regulates emotions and impulses, evaluates the relative importance of things, and is crucial for decision making. While the alpha frequency corresponds to a state of relaxation and inner reflection, the lower beta frequency is involved in focusing and decision making. The EEG appears to be telling us that TM spreads a great wave of calmness across the brain, while organizing the prefrontal brain regions in a way that improves focus and decision making. Travis finds that after people have been meditating for a while, the EEG becomes more coherent throughout the day, which may account for the growing benefits of TM practice over time.

THE GIFTS OF MEDITATION

Throughout this book I will be describing the gifts that can come to you with meditation. Among others, these include better health, a longer life, self-actualization, *and* personal transformation. Even as I write this list, it seems unbelievable. Yet I have read the articles and examined the data, and am impressed by their detail and consistency. Many of these gifts, as you can imagine, take months or years to arrive. At this point, however, I'm happy to tell you an amazing fact: There are gifts that we can receive from just a single session of meditation.

That makes sense because it is literally true that every experience we have changes the brain. Here's how it works: During any experience, large groups of nerve cells fire all at the same time. In the process, the bonds connecting the firing nerve cells are enhanced. If the experience repeats, so does the firing, and the connections tighten further. As neuroscientists are fond of saying, "Nerves that fire together, wire together."

This fundamental fact about the nervous system explains how any and all experiences form neural circuits and "rewire" the brain. If the firing is powerful enough, even a single experience can be engraved deeply into the brain, as we see in post-traumatic stress disorder. But in general, the more an experience repeats, the firmer the wiring. That's why, as the old adage states, practice makes perfect. Aristotle pointed out, "We are what we repeatedly do." Good (or bad) habits shape who we are. That is how the benefits of meditation can be fortified through repetition and can change us in important ways.

What benefits might you expect, then, from a single session of meditation? For some people even their first session can be an epiphany. David Lynch, in his book *Catching the Big Fish,* compares the experience of his first TM session to cutting an elevator cable and falling into bliss. William Stixrud, a clinical neuropsychologist and longtime meditator in the Washington, D.C., area, says that even in his first meditation session, he felt sure he had finally discovered an antidote to his chronic and disabling anxiety.

So, breakthroughs can come very fast—but don't count on it. Many people need a few months of regular meditation before the benefits kick in. That's how it was for me. Happily, I was able to persevere, thanks in large measure to my coach, Bob Roth, who was tireless in helping me stick to my routine and practice the technique properly.

After a month or two, finally, I *got* it. For a brief moment, I felt what it was to transcend, and I knew I could do it again. It was a threshold experience, much like the ecstatic day when I realized I could swim, that I could actually take my feet off the bottom of the shallow end and paddle around without sinking; or when I realized—this was before the era of training wheels—that I had pedaled half a block with no one holding on to the bike. In all these cases I needed to persevere before I saw any payoff.

Having surmounted that initial barrier, however, I now find that many benefits can occur each time I meditate. I can't wait to find out how things will be after ten or twenty years. People tell me it just gets better. Here are the four gifts of a single TM session as I experience them after just a few years of practice.

1. The Art of Being

> Just to be is a blessing; just to live is holy.
>
> —ABRAHAM JOSHUA HESCHEL

When I first came across these words from the philosopher Abraham Joshua Heschel, they struck me as very wise, but they described an experience that was unusual for me. Like many others in America and Europe, I was constantly in motion, always doing something. Why,

I wondered. Did I feel some need to keep proving that I was worth something? Was solitude scary? Was I afraid I'd miss out on something? Certainly I saw all those dynamics around me; in my patients and friends, and more so in recent years. Now that smart phones are ubiquitous, many of us seem constantly plugged into the Net—surfing the web, e-mailing or texting. It's as if we're feeding off some giant electronic placenta, getting a constant stream of messages, news updates, advertisements for discounted products, jokes, cute cat pictures, and "friend"ings (not to mention phone calls and voice mails). Living this way, there's always something to react to.

By the time I returned to TM, however, I had become increasingly convinced that in my attempt not to miss out on anything—by being continually plugged in—I was in fact missing out on something very important: the art of being. I agreed in principle with Abraham Joshua Heschel that "just to be is a blessing," but I had forgotten—or never learned—how to just be. When my wife saw me meditating regularly, she remarked, "It's a miracle that you are even able to sit still for twenty minutes twice a day, regardless of what is happening during your meditation."

As meditation began to take hold, however, my inner world began to quiet—for me, this was the first gift of meditation. It has given me a technique that allows me to be by myself, very calm and happy, at least twice a day. Now I can explore my inner world without distraction, a gift I experience with every meditation session.

2. A Vacation Home Inside My Head

For a long while I was obsessed with finding a home in the country, a place with beautiful views of the mountains. I would rush out on weekends with a real estate agent in tow, looking at this or that piece of property. Nothing seemed quite right, the search was exhausting, and I came home empty-handed. I regard that as a lucky break because now I have no need for such a retreat. I have two vacations every day without having to bother about the commute, maintain a property at a distance, or deal with any of the other headaches of being a landowner. I find the afternoon meditation particularly energizing, and others have reported the same effect. It's almost as though you've wiped clean the slate of the day's burdens and are ready to start afresh and enjoy the evening.

As with most wisdom, I've since discovered that this particular insight is not new. Marcus Aurelius, emperor of Rome in the second century AD, wrote the following in his classic *Meditations*.

> Men seek retreats for themselves in country places, on beaches and mountains, and you yourself are wont to long for such retreats, but that is altogether unenlightened when it is possible at any hour you please to find a retreat within yourself. For nowhere can a man withdraw to a more untroubled quietude than in his own soul.[12]

3. Release of Stress

A patient I will call Jerry, a busy executive, spends his days rushing from one high-stakes meeting or teleconference to the next. There are always large sums to be lost or gained, people to be placated, deals to be negotiated. As he was suffering from anxiety and panic attacks even on appropriate medications, it was clear to me that Jerry needed some additional assistance, and I recommended Transcendental Meditation. One year later, he feels a great sense of relief. TM has even enabled him to discontinue his antianxiety medications. Often, during his meditation sessions, he becomes aware of his stomach grumbling. As he puts it, "It's as if my stomach is saying to me, 'Thank you for giving me a break in my day and relieving me of stress for a while.'"

Jerry's excellent result is not unusual. Meditators often say they feel a gentle release of stress during TM sessions, either physically or psychologically. I often feel that, too. As part of deep relaxation, concerns or unpleasant memories, which sometimes take the form of physical pains or tension, may come and go of their own accord. I don't argue with them, worry about them, or try to analyze them. I just let them come and go. After a session in which such experiences have arisen, I emerge feeling somehow lighter and easier. The issue is still there, but it has lost its charge.

What is happening during a TM session that can provide this type of relief? To me, it makes sense to compare it to "systematic desensitization," a technique pioneered some fifty years ago by the South African behavior therapist Joseph Wolpe. While still in South Africa, I treated a former patient of his who had a morbid fear of animal dander. Poring through Wolpe's tomes of notes, I read about how he had encouraged his patient to relax on a couch. Then, once she was relaxed, he exposed her to animal dander—at first in small doses, then, over weeks, in larger amounts, all the while making sure that she stayed relaxed. Wolpe reasoned that it was impossible to have two contradictory feelings at the same time, in this case relaxation and morbid fear.

Perhaps TM works in a similar way. If neurons that fire together wire together, then perhaps when they *don't* fire together, connections in the nervous system may loosen. In the process, fears and worries may to some extent dissolve in a sea of calm.

Often, when a TM session releases the excess emotion around an issue, it puts things into perspective. I feel better about the problem and am able to take the right action—yet another gift of TM.

4. Pearls on a String

Sometimes during a TM session an insight will simply arrive, unbidden, like a basket of fruit left on the doorstep. For example, I was once bogged down in chores that I didn't feel like doing when, in the midst of a session, a message arose from somewhere deep inside: "If you want to get something done, you can't wait until you feel like doing it." This may seem like a very simple insight to you, and I agree, but it was one that my normal waking mind had failed to deliver. Most of us have gaps like that, life lessons we've somehow missed (or forgotten). My life has gone more smoothly since that realization.

Another time, while meditating, I experienced regret over a poor business decision I had made. Regret morphed into shame and sadness. I just let the feelings come and go until eventually, from a quiet place within, came the realization that I had made the best decision I could at the time, so it wasn't fair to regret it now on the basis of hindsight. I had previously been aware of the philosopher Søren Kierkegaard's famous aphorism that life is best understood backward, but must be lived forward. But when a variant of this same insight came to me during meditation, in relation to my own issue and in words selected by my own mind, somehow the lesson stuck, and I forgave myself.

A colleague tells me that once, during meditation, an insight arrived in the form of a single sentence that represented a complete solution to a problem she was having with a construction crew. Later she reflected on the insight in the light of common sense, and it *still* looked good. So she acted on it—and readily solved the problem. A good question to ask yourself about insights that emerge during TM sessions is: Do they make good sense once you have emerged into the light of day? Quite often they do.

David Lynch cautions against going into meditation with the expectation of revelations or creative inspiration, and other meditators agree. Insight while meditating is not a primary goal of TM. Yet Lynch himself had a revelatory TM experience. On one occasion, important insights that arose while he was meditating helped him craft *Mulholland Drive* into the highly polished movie that it is. He writes, "Like a string of pearls, the ideas came. And they affected the beginning, the middle and the end."

As a scientist I wonder whether meditation yields such insights because it increases coherence in both alpha and beta wave bands. Besides being involved in calm reflection, the alpha frequency is thought to correspond to expectancy or wakefulness. In addition, the alpha band coordinates and organizes faster brain wave frequencies, including the beta frequency, which corresponds to active thinking and focus. Travis agrees that the presence of *both* alpha and beta coherence probably explains the insights that sometimes emerge from meditation. That would make sense, especially as the EEG coherence during TM is strongest in the prefrontal cortex, which is critical to evaluating choices and making good decisions. As a meditator, however, I am simply grateful for such insight whenever it comes, and I acknowledge it as one more gift of meditation.

In the next chapter I will discuss what is arguably the *most* valuable gift to come out of a single meditation session: transcendence.

2

THE MIND WITHIN THE MIND

What Is Transcendence?

> Our normal waking consciousness . . . is
> but one special type of consciousness, whilst
> all about it, parted from it by the filmiest
> of screens, there lie potential forms of con-
> sciousness entirely different.
>
> —WILLIAM JAMES[1]

> There is something beyond our mind which
> abides in silence within our mind. It is the
> supreme mystery beyond thought. Let one's
> mind . . . rest on that and not rest on any-
> thing else.
>
> —MAITRI UPANISHAD[2]

ACCORDING TO ANCIENT Vedic writings, there are four forms
of consciousness—waking, sleeping, dreaming, and a fourth that they
call *turiya*, or transcendence. What is transcendence? Where do you
normally encounter it? How can you lift the filmiest of screens, to use
the words of the eminent American psychologist William James, and
gain access to it? And once you experience transcendence, what good
will it do you? These are some of the questions I will attempt to answer here.

I first encountered transcendence in an unexpected place, at the National Institute of Mental Health, after my friend and colleague Thomas Wehr saw *Quest for Fire*, a movie about prehistoric human beings. We'd both been studying the biological effects of light and dark for some time, so the movie set him wondering what life was like before modern indoor lighting. Specifically, how did people sleep during the long winter nights? Even though indoor lighting has been available for thousands of years, the soft glow of an oil lamp or the focused glare of a gas lamp hardly brought to the night the intense illumination of today—so bright it's visible from space. Wehr wondered, could modern lighting have altered life in some fundamental way?

To find out, Wehr asked sixteen research participants to spend their nights lying quietly in bed in a completely darkened room for fourteen hours at a stretch—roughly the equivalent of a December night in Washington, D.C.[3] He wanted to re-create the way our ancestors presumably must have spent long winter nights in their caves or huts. For the other ten hours of the twenty-four-hour day Wehr's participants were exposed to ordinary sunlight and artificial lighting as they went about their usual daily activities. Wehr compared his subjects' sleep patterns after four weeks of long nights with the patterns seen when the same people were asked to lie in the dark for ten hours each night (the approximate duration of a June night in Washington, D.C.).

The results were intriguing. During the long winter nights, a clear pattern emerged: People settled into two separate periods of sleep, one toward the beginning of the night and one toward the end. As for the period of wakefulness in between, which lasted on average about two hours, several participants, as they lay in their beds, described a tranquil attentiveness, accompanied by a crystal-clear consciousness. As we will see, this description is very similar to the transcendent states described by people practicing Transcendental Meditation.

Subsequently, it turned out that descriptions of the night as being broken into two distinct periods of sleep separated by a few hours of wakefulness go back many hundreds of years. References to the "first sleep" are found from the age of Homer up to the dawn of the modern era, according to A. Roger Ekirch, who has written a book on the subject.[4] Ekirch says that the two sleep periods were roughly the same length, with people waking after midnight before entering their second sleep. Written descriptions of a mystical state of mind in the interval between the two sleeps, widely known as The Watch, sound like the state of calm attentiveness reported by the people in Wehr's study. For example, in his tale "The Haunted Mind," Nathaniel Hawthorne comments on this middle-of-the-night consciousness as follows:

> If you could choose an hour of wakefulness out of the whole night, it would be this. Since your sober bedtime, at eleven, you have had rest enough to take the pressure off yesterday's fatigue. . . . You have found an intermediate space, where the business of life does not intrude; where the passing moment lingers, and becomes truly present; a spot where Father Time, when he thinks nobody is watching him, sits down by the wayside to take a breath.[5]

Robert Louis Stevenson wrote about awakening outdoors one night on a trip to the French highlands: "In my whole life I have never tasted a more perfect hour of life." Reflecting on "the light and living slumber of the man who sleeps afield," Stevenson wrote:

> There is one stirring hour, unknown to those who dwell in houses, where a wakeful influence goes abroad over the sleeping hemisphere and all the outdoor world are on their feet. It is then that . . . homeless men, who have lain down with the fowls, open their dim eyes and behold the beauty of the night.

At what inaudible summons are all these sleepers thus recalled in the same hour to life? Do the stars rain down an influence, or do we share some thrill of mother earth below our resting bodies? Even shepherds and old country-folk, who are the deepest read in these arcana, have not a guess as to the means or purpose of this nightly resurrection. Towards two in the morning they declare the thing takes place; and neither know nor inquire further.[6]

More recently, wanting to discover firsthand how it must have felt during The Watch, author Jeff Warren headed off to northern Canada, where he lived in a cabin during the winter of 2004. His experience was remarkably similar to those reported by the people in Wehr's study. After nine long nights, Warren found that his sleep did indeed break into two periods—with a period of altered consciousness in between. Here's how he describes his personal experience of The Watch in his book *The Head Trip.*[7]

I woke and couldn't tell whether or not I was still dreaming. My limbs were heavy, my head was sunk deep into the pillow and my whole body was buzzing. . . . The heaviness in my body didn't go away—it continued on and on, a marvelous languor that lasted for over two hours and finally drew me back down into one last early-morning dream.

Again, we will see that this "marvelous languor" resembles some descriptions of the state of transcendence.

What role might The Watch have played in the course of evolution? Wehr has suggested three hypotheses: First, since different members of the tribe would presumably be in The Watch at different times during the night, someone would be awake and vigilant at most hours—a valuable defense against marauders or predators. Second, just before they wake into The Watch, people are usually in a period of REM sleep, that important phase of sleep when dreams occur. They would presumably have plenty of time to review their still-fresh dreams— a potentially valuable source of information—while lying awake between sleeps. Finally, the state of tranquil attentiveness and crystal clear consciousness, so similar to a state of transcendence, might have a value of its own—for example, to relieve stress and improve decision making. Certainly, a major theme of this book is that transcendence is valuable.

Only since the last century, with the ubiquitous presence of electric light, have people slept in one solid block of time. In the process, we have lost access not only to transcendental experiences that our ancestors apparently enjoyed every night, but also to the freshness of our dreams, along with time to process all the useful information they may contain.

As part of his study, Wehr measured blood levels of several hormones via an intravenous line. One of these hormones is prolactin, which is secreted into the bloodstream by the pituitary gland. Prolactin is normally elevated during breastfeeding, and is thought to have a calming effect on the mother—a benefit passed on to the infant. Elevated levels of prolactin have also been found in roosting birds; presumably it also pays for mother birds to be calm and patient while waiting for their eggs to hatch. In the long-night condition, when people in Wehr's study lay down expecting to fall asleep, prolactin levels rose to their nighttime high (double the daytime level) within thirty minutes.[8] Falling asleep did not cause any further rise in prolactin levels. Interestingly, Wehr found that if the people in his study were told that someone would come in to remove their intravenous line within thirty minutes, prolactin levels failed to rise. Wehr concluded that "the nocturnal increase in prolactin secretion seemed to depend on a state of quiet wakefulness in which an individual does not expect to be disturbed and expects to fall asleep." When people expected a peaceful night, the nighttime rise in prolactin lasted throughout the night, including the period of calm alertness between the sleeps.

It so happens that levels of prolactin also increase in the bloodstream after a TM session, but *not* after ordinary relaxation with the eyes closed.[9] Hence, the rise in prolactin appears to signal, and may contribute to, the deep relaxation that occurs during transcendence, but does not occur during ordinary relaxation. These observations suggest that The Watch and the transcendent state of TM may share a common physiology. Also, just as the people in Wehr's study failed to show their normal prolactin rise if they expected a disturbance, so with TM: If a person begins a session while expecting a phone call or some other interruption, however brief and routine, it is very hard to reach transcendence.

Along with the hormonal changes that occur during TM, you may recall that there are also certain brain wave changes (increased alpha power, and increased alpha and beta wave coherence, especially in the prefrontal cortex of the brain) that occur specifically during transcendence.[10] These brain frequency shifts, as well as the experience of transcendence, generally appear within a few months of regular practice. In fact, not even a scientist highly skilled at reading EEGs can tell the scan of a novice meditator from that of a veteran when the EEG is measured during a meditation session. It is when the EEG is measured during the ordinary waking state—outside of TM sessions—that differences between novice and veteran meditators emerge.

In reading the coming chapters about all the beneficial changes that can occur as a result of TM, please bear in mind these brain and hormonal changes, which are probably instrumental in these transformations.

In the ordinary course of a busy Western life, nonmeditators seldom experience much, if any, transcendence. You may, though, have glimpses of transcendence in those moments when you are just waking up. Some people may have a special gift for experiencing transcendence, and it often occurs at high points in a person's life—for example, on one's wedding day or at the birth of a child. Let's consider, then, what it feels like to transcend.

TRANSCENDENTAL FEELINGS

How is it possible to convey a feeling or a state of consciousness if the person you are talking to has not had the experience? The exhilaration of falling in love, for example, or the devastation of grief doesn't easily translate into words. One of the Upanishads, the ancient Vedic writings, struggles with this question:

> Words cannot describe the joy of the soul . . . who is one
> with his own Spirit. Only those who feel this joy know what it
> is. Even as water becomes one with water, fire with fire, and
> air with air, so the mind becomes one with the Infinite Mind.[11]

One curious aspect of this quote is that, even while observing how hard it is to describe transcendence, it does quite a good job of doing just that. We learn that transcendence is a joyful state that involves a sense of integration between oneself and something infinite outside the self.

During a state of transcendence, people commonly lose their sense of boundaries (where you begin and end). One ten-year-old boy whom I interviewed about his experiences with meditation told me that once during a session he forgot where his hands were, only to discover later that they were on the floor propping him up. Besides the loss of boundaries, the sense of time, place, or date may also go missing. As one successful businessman in his mid-fifties said, "Transcendence is timeless. Before I know it, the twenty minutes are up."

During transcendence, there is consciousness *with no specific focus.* By definition, that distinguishes transcendence from a state of waking (when your mind is typically engaged with specific thoughts, feelings, or actions) and sleeping (when you are not fully conscious) or dreaming (when specific things are going through your mind). This idea of being aware but not of anything in particular may seem quite weird until you have actually had the experience. This is how Maharishi described the process of transcending while practicing TM:

> The Transcendental Meditation technique is an effortless procedure for allowing the excitations of the mind gradu-ally to settle down until the least excited state of mind is reached. This is a state of inner wakefulness with no object of thought or perception, just pure consciousness aware of its own unbounded nature. It is wholeness, aware of itself, devoid of differences, beyond the division of subject and object—Transcendental Consciousness.

The emotions most often associated with transcendence are seren-ity and bliss. The word "bliss," as opposed to "joy" or "happiness," is seldom heard in daily life, but it really does capture the calm pleasure experienced during transcendence, a pleasure directed at nothing in particular and at everything all at the same time. In addition, many meditators also have a sense of being connected to something greater or more profound in the universe. For example, one doctor in his late fifties described transcendence as "a touch of heaven," while a psycholo-gist in her sixties whom I interviewed offered the following description:

> During transcendence I experience a feeling of total calm-
> ness and peace. I also experience a knowing that is very
> beautiful. I think this knowing is a result of being connected
> to the absolute aspect of existence. It is as if "I" exist and
> yet there is another "I" which exists and is eternal and to-
> tally without anxiety or involvement in the relative world. It
> is sometimes as if I am witnessing . . . watching myself tran-
> scend into a state of peace and calmness where time doesn't
> exist . . . and yet, if I wanted to pull myself "up" and become
> alert and active, I could at any moment.

Transcendence, however, is not all in the mind; many descriptions hint at a concurrent bodily experience. One young man described transcendence as "a sweet feeling, as though the soul is sucking up some honey." In the words of journalist Tim Page, "I imagine I'm one of the few people who will say this—the sort of all-body tingling that you get in a particular deep meditation reminds me a little bit of the after-glow after an orgasm. It's got that same kind of satisfaction and the same sort of tapping into some kind of deep peace that you sometimes have after that."

TRANSCENDENTAL IMAGES

In order to describe how it feels when a meditator moves from ordinary consciousness to transcendence, Maharishi was fond of using two images from nature: the waves on the ocean, and bubbles in a pond.

If you look at the surface of the ocean, you will see the waves dancing in the sunlight, each wave unique and full of particular detail. That is how the mind is when it is wide awake and jostling with thoughts. Now imagine climbing into a diving bell and descending deeper and deeper, while the ocean around you grows quieter and quieter. Details fade. In a similar way, as the mind goes deeper into meditation, it settles down, moving into a quieter place. The observing self no longer generates details and definitions, but relaxes into a joyful sense of being part of the boundless ocean.

In his image of the pond, Maharishi compared the way bubbles rise in a pond to the way thoughts arise into consciousness from the deep recesses of the mind. In this image, just as the large bubbles on the pond's surface begin as tiny bubbles, compressed deep down in the pond, so our conscious thoughts emanate from their precursors in the primordial soup of the unconscious. During meditation, as one descends into the depths of the pond, it is possible to catch these thoughts at an early stage, before they have expanded. That may account for the creative insights that can arise during meditation.

In descriptions of the process of meditation, images of water abound. Director David Lynch writes, "When you 'transcend' in Transcendental Meditation, you dive down into that ocean of pure consciousness. You splash into it."

Henry David Thoreau, aptly classified as a Transcendentalist philosopher, depicted the boundlessness and clarity of transcendence through the following watery images.

> If with closed ears and eyes I consult consciousness for a moment, immediately are all walls and barriers dissipated, earth rolls from under me, and I float . . . in the midst of an unknown and infinite sea, or else heave and swell like a vast ocean of thought.[12]

> We become like a still lake of purest crystal and without an effort our depths are revealed to ourselves. All the world goes by us and is reflected in our deeps. Such clarity![13]

Rising into the sky is yet another way that people commonly describe transcendence. One twelve-year-old at the Maharishi grade school for children in Fairfield, Iowa, wrote, "When I meditate, it's like I'm floating up to heaven or I'm there already." Another student from the same school told me about an experience his father had on first learning to meditate. After one session, the father was walking around with such a demeanor of floating that a passerby asked, "What's the weather like up there?" The passerby might have detected the calm and happy state that often persists beyond a TM session.

Even though the eyes are closed, perceptions of light may also arise during a session. A colleague of mine, while meditating, has several times seen a light hovering in the center of her visual field, like a pearl glowing on the horizon, accompanied by calm and pleasant feelings. Novelist Victor Hugo made the connection between meditation and light quite specific when he wrote:

> Meditate. All is full of light, even the night.

Light images, in turn, often merge into mystical experiences, as for the seventeenth-century poet Henry Vaughan.

> I saw Eternity the other night,
> Like a great ring of pure and endless light
> All calm as it was bright.

I have often enjoyed the portrayal of light in the paintings of the famous British landscape painter J. M. W. Turner, but only recently, after I had begun to meditate regularly, did it strike me as transcendent. His early works depict landscapes or seascapes—castles, shipwrecks, temples, and battlefields—in meticulous detail. Over time, however, through a succession of paintings, these details fall away and most of what is left are swirls and splashes of light and color. I am reminded of this sequence in connection with my own meditation practice. Sometimes, as I hear my mantra, I have an image of myself standing on a vast and empty beach. I see the sands stretching into the distance, the sea and the sky. Then, gradually, the sea falls away, the beach disappears beneath my feet, the sky becomes abstract, and I enter a state of pure consciousness, alert but focused on nothing in particular, enjoying the boundlessness. I have slipped into the mind within the mind, the mind beyond the mind, and for a few minutes I experience the bliss of the infinite.

I should emphasize that such exuberant experiences—floating, splashing, diving into pure consciousness or visions of light—are by no means routine. Craig Pearson, executive vice president of the Maharishi University of Management, speaks to this point in describing his own experiences with TM, which he has been practicing for the past forty years:

> There's definitely a diving deep within, a settling down of mental activity and deep integration. Do I experience clear, pure unbounded awareness in some of the extraordinary ways I've discovered it described by some of the great people through history? No, I've only had that experience a few times in my life. But there are people who sit around me in the Golden Dome [of the Maharishi University of Management in Iowa] who have that experience on a regular basis. And with continuing practice, these are the kinds of experiences everyone can have.

Fortunately, four-star graphic effects are neither a necessary part of transcendence nor a key to its transformational effects. It is the profoundly relaxed alertness free of specific thoughts, along with the loss of personal boundaries of time or space, that are the essential elements of transcendence. Once people get to that point, which usually happens within the first month or two of learning, they can expect to obtain full benefit if they meditate regularly and in the correct manner. If you see lights or find yourself splashing about in pure consciousness—as you may—it's a delightful bonus.

COSMIC CONSCIOUSNESS: TRANSCENDING IN EVERYDAY LIFE

If two blissful brief vacations from your daily life were all TM offered, that would be reason enough to consider the practice. The greatest rewards of meditation, however, arise from effects that carry over beyond the actual meditative state into your waking life—a state known as *cosmic consciousness*. These effects can appear within days after starting to meditate, usually in the form of calmness and tranquillity that persist for a while after meditating. Within a few months of starting to meditate, people show evidence of increased brain wave coherence in their EEG patterns even when they are *not* meditating. In general, the more years people have meditated, the more transcendent experiences and brain wave coherence pervade their waking hours. Here is how one long-term meditator described this state:

> There is less of a contrast between activity and meditation. Sometimes during the day, with varying degrees of clarity, my awareness is this unbounded wholeness of my Self, quietly accompanying the thoughts and feelings in my daily life.

People who develop this state of consciousness report that they are more centered, grounded, and even-tempered than before they began to meditate. They feel less knocked about by the turbulence of daily life, and also more confident, because they are less dependent on the outside world for a sense of stability, peace, or fulfillment. Being less influenced by the events of the moment, meditators find it easier to avoid impulsive reactions, instead making appropriate responses even in difficult situations.

Fred Travis studied fifty-one TM meditators, chosen because they reported various levels of transcendent experiences in their daily lives.[14] Travis examined EEG recordings taken while the meditators were solving a complex set of computer challenge tests. The results? In those meditators who reported more frequent transcendent experiences during their waking hours, Travis found that EEG tracings showed higher amplitude and coherence in the alpha band width, which is associated with relaxation and inner reflection. These same meditators also scored significantly higher on the computer challenge test.

In the process of writing this book, I interviewed at least twenty-five meditators who have been practicing TM for thirty years or more, and one trait they share is a remarkable ability to stay focused on each particular question and respond appropriately, while at the same time radiating calm. It is as though they operate on two channels simultaneously—one that attends to business, and another that maintains a state of relaxed alertness. That is, as a consequence of meditating over time, they appear to be more or less continuously in a state of transcendence.

REFINED COSMIC CONSCIOUSNESS

As cosmic consciousness grows over time, perceptions become sharper, clearer, and more refined. Craig Pearson of the Maharishi University, whose book *The Supreme Awakening*[15] explores transcendence throughout the ages in both Western and Eastern cultures, says that refined cosmic consciousness "enables one to experience the extraordinary, radiant beauty hiding just beneath the surface of the world around us." He describes people who have had such experiences as follows:

> They're walking along and suddenly it's as if a veil is removed and now everything around them is shining with glorious light, golden light. . . . And it's not just perception, but the heart is overflowing with love.

People reaching this advanced state of transcendent consciousness may describe themselves as experiencing unbounded compassion or being completely enveloped in an indescribable, soft, divine gentleness.

These experiences are often transient at first, and there can be a certain letdown when they pass. The meditator may wonder, "What happened? How do I get that experience back, that beauty of the world around me?" The experienced meditator learns not to expect such experiences, but simply to enjoy them when they occur.

Such refined cosmic consciousness may arise from interactions with nature or art. Here are some examples from people I have interviewed and from my own experience.

Blake was a student in his twenties who had been meditating for a year when he had the experience he describes below:

> I had just finished a run with my dad and I was sitting on the bench outside the house. There is a fairly large oak tree right across the driveway. I was sitting there drinking water and looking at the tree. It was seventy-five degrees, no humidity, a very light breeze. The sun was shining out of a blue sky, and the tree was kind of shimmering in the sunlight, and almost within a breath's time, my consciousness merged with

the consciousness of the tree. It was as if every movement of the leaves of the tree, every tiny little movement, was in perfect harmony. It was as if every thought that I had was in harmony with every tiny movement of the tree. It only lasted for five to ten seconds, but it was the most powerful and perfect experience I have ever had in my life. It was very special. I do not believe this would ever have happened to me had I not been meditating, and although it only happened once, it has stayed with me and had an enduring positive effect on me.

Lyn, a university professor in her fifties, wrote to me about a similar experience, one that occurred after she had been meditating regularly for only a few months:

It was a significant experience for me, because I truly felt transcendence. I was doing my afternoon meditation. I was already physically settling in my earlier meditations, but this particular experience was distinctive in that I felt a deeper settling—the best way that I can describe it, albeit awkward, is that I felt dissociated from my physical being and a sublime and peaceful elevation of my inner essence. I was very deep in meditation and when I opened my eyes to gently come out of the meditative state, I realized that I was not coming fully out of the elevated sense of peace. I felt at one with my surroundings. As I moved, every sensation was enhanced and significant. That sense of remaining in a consciously active meditative state persisted. When I saw a bird, it was more than just seeing the bird—we acknowledged each other. When I described it to my TM teacher, she asked me if I still felt "that way." It was then that I realized that the peaceful sensation—that settled one-ness and interconnectedness with my environment—was continuing even though I was not actually meditating.

Here is an example of refined cosmic consciousness, which I experienced after meditating for about a year, elicited by, of all things, a place mat!

One evening after dinner, I cleared my dish and sat back down at the table, gazing at my place mat. I was in a tranquil frame of mind, probably the residue of my usual late-afternoon meditation. I had purchased the place mat at an art museum in Paris because it was embossed with Monet's *Water Lilies*, which I have always enjoyed. I had looked at the place mat hundreds of times before, so that by now it took on the familiarity of an ordinary thing that blends inconspicuously into its surroundings—until this evening. All of a sudden, the famous picture of a lily pond appeared to me in a totally new way. I looked at the curved bridge that spans the pond and wondered at the perfection of its shape and how the artist had captured the shadows that fall across its railings. All the greenery took on a new vividness as I pondered the different textures of the plants, the cascading branches of the willow, the fronds of fern and the lily pads. The lilies themselves sparkled in the sunlight and the flecks of their petals shimmered on the surface of the water. For many minutes I gazed at this familiar household object as though I were in Monet's own gardens at Giverny on a lazy afternoon in the late summer, when the days are long and it seems as though the sun will never set.

Even though these sorts of experiences do not happen often, they linger in the mind and, to quote Wordsworth, "they flash upon that inward eye/which is the bliss of solitude." I am told that such experiences may eventually progress to an enduring sense of connection with the universe. This sense may be abstract or, if a person is religious in the conventional sense of the word, may be experienced as a direct connection with God.

The continued progression of consciousness also intensifies a connection with your fellow human beings. This type of *unity consciousness* is found at the heart of all religions, though differently expressed: In the Vedic tradition, "We are all one."[16] In the Judeo-Christian tradition we hear, "Love thy neighbor as thyself." And the Sufis say, "You and I are not we but one."

At a 2009 concert to raise funds for teaching TM in inner-city schools, Paul McCartney and Ringo Starr paid tribute to Maharishi, who had taught them to meditate four decades earlier. On the screen was a wide-angled picture of Maharishi and his students, including the very young-looking Beatles, all garlanded with flowers. McCartney explained that the song he and the other musicians were about to sing was based on Maharishi's words to him all those years before: "Come and be cosmically conscious with me."[17] The teacher was inviting the student to join him in the joy of transcendence, not just twice a day, but all day long.

TRANSCENDENCE AND TRANSFORMATION

In the chapters that follow, you will read about people who have experienced many types of transformation after starting to practice TM. There is a strong sense among TM researchers and teachers that transcendent experiences actually *cause* transformation, but how can we determine cause and effect when it comes to the mind?

Sometimes it helps to know the sequence of things. For example, one of my patients felt much less depressed immediately after his family won a big lottery. Now, instead of facing certain poverty, he is financially secure. Cause and effect? Probably. The next story speaks to the relationship between transcendence and transformation. Cause and effect? See what you think.

Nicole's Story

Nicole is a sixty-four-year-old retiree who worked for many years as a manager in a government agency. In her early twenties, Nicole moved to Washington, D.C., from Kansas, where she had been a brilliant student—graduating as valedictorian of her high school class, and magna cum laude from the local university. But no matter how well Nicole did—either at school or in her subsequent highly successful career—she never felt it was good enough. Here's how she describes it:

> I've always gone to other people for the answer to "Am I good enough?" I've always received lots of plaudits—from hundreds of people. It's as though I was building up a résumé, but nothing was enough to convince me that I was OK—no matter how many successes I had—because it was always *their* opinion, not *mine.*

Nicole had been in therapy for a total of forty-two years, which she regards as having been successful, but her central problem of insufficient self-worth was unyielding, even to excellent psychotherapy. At that point she heard about TM from her current psychiatrist, my friend and colleague Tom Wehr, whose ear I had been bending on the subject during our regular lunches.

During her third TM session, Nicole transcended for the first time—a deep, blissful experience, lasting about ten to fifteen minutes. The next day she was on her way to meet with her TM instructor when she had the following experience:

> I was driving from D.C., which I love, listening to one of my favorite groups on the radio—Schooner Fare, singing "Boats of Stone." The Lincoln Memorial was at the edge of my visual field when, all of a sudden, it was as though a pink cloud came over my mind. I had a warm, happy, and pleasant feeling, and said to myself, "Nicole, you have done very well in Washington these past forty-two years. Thumbs up to you!" It was so strong, so deep, so final—uncluttered by detail—like, "This is the last word on the subject."
>
> There was something about the way the realization came to me that was quite unlike any other conclusion I have ever experienced about myself—it was sweeping, global, unqualified. Usually, if I think something nice about myself, it's always followed by, "but you could have done this or that better." This time there was none of that.
>
> Why did it happen just when it did? It might have had something to do with the song, which involves carrying stones to Washington, that connected in my mind with the Lincoln Memorial and the other D.C. monuments that I love. The good, honest work of hewing the stones and bringing them to Washington seemed to mesh with the solid work I had done for all those years. It was as though a realization was lying in wait to answer a question that has burdened me all my life: Am I OK? I am convinced, though, that it took

TM—and especially the experience of transcendence—to unlock that realization and make it available to me. Certainly I couldn't get there by any other means, despite forty-two years of psychotherapy.

When I spoke to her, Nicole had been meditating for five weeks. The realization she had while driving that day—the answer to her lifelong question—has remained unchanged. She continues to feel good about herself, and plans to meditate for the rest of her life.

Part II

HEALING

3

DECOMPRESSION

Managing Toxic Stress

It is not stress that kills us, it is our reaction
to it.

—HANS SELYE

WHEN I WAS a child, my family and I would often visit Kruger National Park, one of the world's great game reserves. The Kruger was recently the setting for a mesmerizing video shot by a lucky tourist, who
put it on YouTube, where it went viral. Called "Battle at Kruger,"[1] the
video shows a herd of buffalo ambling along beside a water hole, unaware that directly ahead several lions are crouching in the tall grass.
The ambush is set. Then you see the moment when the lead buffalo
catches the scent of the lions and pivots, directing the herd to turn on
their heels and flee. A group of lions manages to separate a baby buffalo from the herd and, in a cluster, they fall into the water. The lions
are trying to pull the calf back onto solid ground when, all of a sudden,
a crocodile lunges up from the water and grabs the calf from the other
side. A tug-of-war ensues. Meanwhile, the buffalo confer, regroup, and
come charging back to save their calf and rout the lions. In one rivet-

ing scene, a bull buffalo flings a lion into the air with the point of one horn. The lions flee and the calf, by some miracle still alive, is reunited with the herd.

The whole drama lasts just eight minutes.

This vignette demonstrates how the stress response has evolved over millions of years to work in animals, including humans: A threat is perceived, which triggers a complex set of coordinated responses— physical, hormonal, and emotional. In the wild, the options are flight (the buffalo run away at first), fight (they charge back once they have assessed the situation), or fright (the calf freezes until it can be saved). If you are lucky, the stress response helps keep you alive.

Moving from the wild to the domestic, imagine that you are sitting peacefully at home one night when, all of a sudden, you hear an unusual noise outside, like a twig snapping. You startle, catch your breath, and go on the alert, listening intently. Then . . . nothing more. You know the doors are locked, the security system is on. As you settle down, your muscles relax and your breathing slows. Perhaps it was just an animal passing by in the dark. This is an everyday example of a false alarm—a threat, transient vigilance, relaxation, then back to business as usual.

Whether you are dealing with a false alarm or a life-or-death battle, a good stress response, like a good short story, has a beginning, a middle, and an end. Above all, it is *short*. Unfortunately, stress is often not that way for humans in the twenty-first century. For people today, stress is often prolonged, unremitting, and damaging to our bodies and our minds.

In this section, we will examine just how harmful stress can be and how Transcendental Meditation can mitigate its damage—and even save lives. The scientific data that show this are impeccable. Even so, as you will find throughout this book, I always encourage people to use TM as part of a broad program of healthy living. There are many ways to lessen stress levels and you will need to be the final judge of what works best for you.

But first, it helps to understand how the stress response works. I will keep it to the bare essentials—just a few paragraphs on what you really need to know. For many, this section will be a review.

HOW DOES THE STRESS RESPONSE WORK?

Your nervous system has a specialized subsystem devoted to automatic activities like breathing, sweating, digestion, and the beating of your heart. Thanks to this "autonomic nervous system," you usually don't have to give these basic functions a thought. The autonomic nervous system is further divided into the sympathetic nervous system (SNS), which governs (among other things) an alarm function, the "fight-or-flight response" just described; and the parasympathetic system, which relaxes you.

The sympathetic nervous system is controlled primarily by centers in the brain, particularly the almond-shaped amygdala (named after the Greek word for almond). Under conditions of stress, these "alarm bells" in the brain give orders to the rest of the body by a network of nerves that travel down the spine and emerge between the vertebrae. They influence the entire body from the hairs on your head (which can stand up in terror) to the tips of your toes (which can turn pale in the cold). In between these extremes, through its nerve endings, the SNS affects every other organ in the body by releasing the neurotransmitter chemical norepinephrine (NE)—also known as noradrenaline—to carry out its many different functions. When you are tense or anxious, the SNS nerves release more NE; when you are calm and relaxed, less.

During a stressful event, the SNS nerves have a second important way of putting the body on high alert. They activate a hormonal system, involving the adrenal glands (just above the kidneys), which release into the bloodstream the chemical epinephrine (also known as adrenaline). As you can guess, epinephrine is closely related in structure and function to norepinephrine. Stress also causes the brain to initiate a hormonal cascade that triggers the adrenals to release cortisol and other steroids called *glucocorticoids*. Many of you have probably used some form of glucocorticoids for medical purposes—for example, in ointment for a rash or in a spray for hay fever or asthma. When you use steroids orally, you are generally cautioned to use them only for a certain number of days before tapering them off. That is because glucocorticoids can save your life in the short term, but can kill you in the long term. The same can be said for stress itself when it goes on for too long. Let's examine how that works in practice.

TOXIC STRESS AND THE HEART

By the time you reach age eighty, your heart will have beaten more than three billion times. With each beat the heart sends blood, containing oxygen and nutrients, through a tree of branching arteries to all the tissues in your body. Your arteries are the crucial pipes and tubing that carry your blood under sufficient pressure to reach even the top of your scalp and the toes of your feet. Together, the heart and blood vessels are known as the cardiovascular system. The arteries that feed the heart itself are known as the coronary arteries. In this chapter you will read about the role of stress in cardiovascular disease (CVD). One form of CVD, called *coronary heart disease* (CHD), occurs when the damaged arteries are those that feed the heart itself and therefore too little blood reaches the heart.

The stress-released hormones epinephrine and norepinephrine cause your heart to pump faster, your arteries to constrict, and your blood pressure to rise. The opposite occurs when you relax. In the short run, the stress response helps move more blood to the muscles that may save your life (remember how the buffalo fled from the lions). But pumping these hormones into the system for weeks and months and years at a time can cause surges in blood flow as well as chronic high blood pressure, both of which can damage the delicate linings of the arteries. Likewise, in the short run, the extra release of glucocorticoids can mobilize the glucose you need to deal with a crisis. On the other hand, excessive and prolonged glucose mobilization can result in fat deposits around the belly and diabetes, both known risks for coronary heart disease.

Cardiovascular disease develops over years. In young people, healthy arteries have a clean, smooth lining. Over time, however, the lining can become damaged in a disease process called *atherosclerosis*, which progresses from fatty deposits to a gooplike inflammation that can gum up arterial walls with yellow plaques, depriving the tissues of oxygen. Plaques can harden and calcify. Then the narrowed arteries can starve tissues of blood—either gradually, as they slowly constrict, or suddenly if a piece of goop breaks loose and completely blocks a smaller artery down the line.

Researchers have suggested at least six different ways by which psychological stress can kill you, all of which involve some form of damage to the heart or arteries.[2] Severe oxygen deprivation can lead to tissue death, such as a heart attack or a stroke, depending on whether it happens in the heart or the brain. And that happens often enough to make cardiovascular disease the number one killer and cause of serious disability in the United States and worldwide. In the U.S. more than one in three adults have been diagnosed with CVD and more than one in three will die of either heart attack or stroke.

The costs of CVD are staggering. If you add the amount spent on treating and diagnosing the condition to loss of earnings and productivity resulting from the disease, the total cost of CVD in the U.S. in 2010 is estimated at more than $503 billion.[3] Conventional therapies for CVD—medicines and surgery—have accomplished a great deal, but are not in themselves sufficient. Despite decades of biomedical advances—and billions (or perhaps trillions) of dollars spent on research, diagnosis, and treatment—CVD remains the number one cause of death. For this reason, the American Heart Association and other professional organizations recommend nondrug lifestyle changes as a first line of treatment for people with high blood pressure and as part of a treatment package for those diagnosed with CHD. Cardiologists also urge people to make these changes *before* any evidence of CHD appears.

Although many of the risk factors for cardiovascular disease seem very physical—such as high blood pressure, high cholesterol, and bad diet—a cardiologist friend of mine is fond of saying, "It may be less important what you're eating than what's eating you." Mind and body are intimately connected, so that stress and distress cause CVD both indirectly (distressed people are more likely to smoke, eat unhealthy "comfort" foods, and neglect their well-being) and directly. Yes, sadness, anxiety, anger, poverty, loneliness, and stress at work or at home can directly cause heart and blood vessel disease, which can kill you.[4] Luckily, your mind can also work to your advantage, so that you are by no means helpless in the face of chronic stress.

In this chapter I will discuss the evidence that shows that Transcendental Meditation can lessen the impact of stress on your body, improve your health, and extend your life span. In later chapters, I will talk in more depth about specific types of distress, such as anxiety and post-traumatic stress disorder (chapter 4), attention deficit disorder (chapter 5), depression and bipolar disorder (chapter 6), and drug and alcohol abuse (chapter 7).

To begin, let's take a very short tour of the effects of emotions and stresses on cardiovascular and coronary heart disease.

DYING OF A BROKEN HEART

The king died and then the queen died of grief.

—E. M. FORSTER,
Aspects of the Novel

Novelist E. M. Forster used the example quoted above to distinguish between a plot, in which events are causally connected, and a story, in which one thing simply happens after another ("The king died and then the queen died"). But can people really die of grief?

The answer is yes, sometimes. For example, when 95,000 bereaved people were studied for four to five years, the effect was clear. In the first month after a death in the family, men died at more than double the expected rate and women were three times more likely to die. The good news is that after the first month, death rates among bereaved relatives returned to normal.[5]

But what about persistent sadness or depression? Does that affect the heart? Here the news is not so good. Full-blown clinical (major) depression is a condition with many symptoms that go beyond sadness, such as disturbed sleep and appetite (see note 1 in chapter 6). People with major depression have three times the normal risk for developing cardiovascular disease and heart attacks.[6] Worse yet, it turns out that even milder depressed symptoms, which would not earn someone the diagnosis of major depression, can also damage the heart. There is in fact a direct relationship between the severity of a person's depression and how likely that person is to develop CVD.[7]

A powerful demonstration of the connection between mind and body comes from studies of hope and hopelessness, optimism and pessimism. Many studies support this link.[8] For example, in one study, researchers asked about 2,800 U.S. adults the following question about the preceding month: "Have you felt so sad, discouraged, hopeless or had so many problems that you wondered if anything was worthwhile?" Those who answered yes on that single question had double the risk of developing CHD during the twelve-year follow-up.[9] Paper-and-pencil tests of optimism versus pessimism are often used in research to define optimists (those scoring in the top 25 percent on optimism) and pessimists (those scoring in the lowest 25 percent). In a 2009 report on the Women's Health Initiative, a U.S. study that followed over 97,000 women over eight years, optimists were more than 25 percent less likely than pessimists to suffer or die from coronary heart disease.[10] In a large, seven-year French study of 23,000 randomly selected men and women aged twenty to fifty-four years, optimists were only half as likely as pessimists to suffer strokes.[11] In one study of about 940 Finns, researchers were able to evaluate the progression of arteriosclerosis in the carotid arteries over a four-year interval. Once again, hopelessness accelerated disease progression.[12] I will tell you more about this way of assessing CVD later in this chapter.

Nobody knows precisely how hopelessness works its harmful effects, but when I think of the stress response system pouring out toxic chemicals night and day, the long-term devastating effects seem much less mysterious.

Aside from depression and hopelessness, two other unpleasant and problematic emotional states may also contribute to CHD—anxiety and anger. According to a recent meta-analysis,[13] anxiety is a significant risk factor for coronary heart disease and cardiac death in both men and women.[14] You might be surprised to learn that anxiety in young men can predict the likelihood of their developing cardiovascular problems in middle age. Almost 50,000 Swedish men who had been evaluated for military service when aged eighteen to twenty were followed up thirty-seven years later. Those who had been diagnosed with anxiety in their youth had suffered from more CHD and heart attacks in later life.[15] According to three large studies, people with phobias, who avoid various situations (such as crowds, heights, or travel) out of irrational anxiety, are more likely than normal to experience sudden death.[16]

Anger and hostility can also damage the heart. One of my patients from the Deep South used to say, "I'm so mad I'm fixin' to die." Little did he realize the truth in his declaration. Several studies have linked cynicism, mistrustfulness, and a tendency to get angry to the development and progression of CHD.[17]

WEAR AND TEAR

Chronic stress in its many forms causes wear and tear—literally—to the linings of the blood vessels. Living alone and feeling isolated predict an increased risk of cardiac death—so do poverty, joblessness, crowded living conditions, low social status, and lack of education. And so can your job.[18]

Did you know your job can literally kill you? Well, it can. In Japan they have a condition called *karoshi*, defined as "occupational sudden death," which results from heart attack or stroke due to stress.[19] So great a problem is *karoshi* that the Japanese government has officially recognized the condition and Japanese corporations have regulated the amount of overtime allowed in an attempt to reduce the deaths. Although the historically powerful work ethic in Japan is probably an important factor in this extreme form of death due to overwork, stress on the job is recognized as a risk factor for CHD all over the world. It's not just the demands of the job that matter, however. Workers are particularly stressed when their jobs are demanding *and* they are not free to make their own decisions. Responsibility without control is a killer. In one study of 1,928 male workers followed for six years, this combination of high demand and low decision-making ability, called *job strain,* led to a fourfold increase in cardiac deaths.[20] Also, unsurprisingly, stress on the job ratchets up when the work is hard but rewards are meager.

All types of stress can increase the risk of CHD. Difficult marriages, for example, can be literally heartbreaking, especially among women; so can caring for an ill or disabled spouse. To make matters worse, when sorrows come, as Shakespeare observed, they come not as single spies but in battalions. For example, a person might lose his job, go into debt, be unable to pay the mortgage, and worry about losing his house *and* his health insurance. Such a person might try to cope with his anxiety by starting to smoke, drinking more than he should, and eating foods that are loaded with enticing fats and salt. Unfortunately, such stories are all too common.

Given the many different types of stress that can damage the heart, what can TM do to help? Let's look at one person's story and then at the scientific data that answer this question.

REDUCING HIGH BLOOD PRESSURE

Nick's Story

Nick was a high school senior in Augusta, Georgia, when Vernon Barnes, an assistant professor of pediatrics at the Medical College of Georgia, came to Nick's school to recruit teenagers for a study on

TM and adolescent high blood pressure (hypertension). The researchers screened 5,000 African American students to find the 100 young people with borderline hypertension whom they needed for the study. Nick was surprised to be one of them. An outstanding athlete who played both football and basketball, Nick was buff—the last person you might have suspected of having high blood pressure, which has been called "the silent killer." To his classmates, Nick seemed like the "It Boy" of the school, but at home his life was difficult. He had ongoing conflicts with his mother and had to work several jobs to help make ends meet. In short, he was swamped.

Nick's blood pressure was high enough for four independent doctors to recommend that he start medications for hypertension, but he decided in favor of a nondrug approach. He chose TM—although he initially thought it was "a joke" and "a bunch of bull"—because Vernon Barnes commanded his respect and had persuaded Nick that because he was a school leader, his participation would encourage others to volunteer as well. Within weeks of learning to meditate, Nick noticed an improvement in his stress level and his ability to focus on the many activities he was juggling. His academic performance, though always good, improved and his SAT scores rose by almost 300 points. He became more accepting of his mother's problems and more respectful, even when he still thought he was right. As he puts it:

> TM gave me the opportunity to veer off into a space in my own domain and let a lot of things go that otherwise I would not have been able to let go. I could observe myself better and didn't feel the need to lash out at people like I did before.

Within two months Nick's blood pressure dropped into the normal range, where it has stayed for the past ten years with no need for medication. During that time, he graduated from college and started working toward a master's in nursing. He continues to meditate twice a day every day, and he has encouraged others to learn the technique. He says: "You can't go through a rain forest without a guide. TM has been my guide for the past ten years."

You might have been surprised that this section began with the story of a young man, as one tends to think of hypertension as a disease of older people. In many cases, however, the problem starts in childhood. In addition, hypertension has increased in children and adolescents over the past decade, which appears to correlate with the recent epidemic of obesity.[21] This problem is especially severe among African Americans.[22]

In the study in which Nick participated,[23] one hundred African American teenagers with blood pressures at the high end of normal were randomly assigned to two groups: one group learned TM and meditated twice a day for four months, whereas the other (control) group received health education lectures for a similar amount of time. At the end of the study, the TM group showed a significant drop in blood pressure compared with the control group, an effect that still held four months after the study ended.

If lowering blood pressure were all that TM did, it would be impressive enough, but it did much more: The meditating group also had lower rates of absenteeism, suspensions, and school rule violations than the control group.[24]

Although these effects of TM in the schoolchildren in Nick's study seem so amazingly diverse, I'd like to jump the gun a bit to show you how they make sense. Practicing TM twice a day reduces the stress response via the sympathetic nervous system, and also perhaps by reducing the release of glucocorticoid hormones. When the stress response decreases, so does blood pressure and so do feelings of anger that can cause schoolchildren—or adults, for that matter—to break the rules. Stated positively, reducing the impact of stress helps people focus on their goals. You'll learn more about that in this chapter and subsequent chapters dealing with attention and effectiveness (chapter 5) and the use of TM in schools (chapter 8).

Decreasing blood pressure and improving cardiac health by means of TM has been the long-term passion of Robert Schneider, a physician-scientist who is currently director of the Institute for Natural Medicine and Prevention at Maharishi University. Over the last twenty years, Schneider and his group have obtained tens of millions of dollars in grant money, much of it from the National Institutes of Health, and numerous blue-chip publications have reported his findings. We'll draw on these findings, but I'd like to start by pointing out an important fact: about 30 percent of adults in the United States and other developed countries have hypertension.

Jim Anderson and colleagues from the University of Kentucky published a meta-analysis in which they pooled data from nine published, well-controlled trials that involved a total of 711 people.[25] The people in these studies started with a range of baseline blood pressure measurements: hypertensive, borderline hypertensive, or normotensive (having normal blood pressure). Overall, the researchers found that blood pressure dropped significantly in all groups practicing TM compared to the controls.

As you probably know from having your own blood pressure taken, there is an upper and lower reading, respectively the systolic and diastolic measurements. Anderson and colleagues found an average reduction of 5 points on the systolic and 3 points on the diastolic readings. When Anderson limited his analysis to only high-quality studies or only those in which the people studied had actual, full-blown hypertension, his findings remained the same. According to Schneider, these reductions are not only statistically significant, but also *clinically* significant; he says they might be expected to result in 15 to 20 percent less cardiovascular disease. In his own studies, Schneider has observed that after people with hypertension have been meditating for longer than three months, they need on average 23 percent less blood pressure medication.

Henny Youngman, a humorist famous for his one-liners, used to respond to the question "How's your wife?" with "Compared to who?" Following that same logic, we should ask how TM stacks up against other nondrug interventions in treating hypertension.

To answer that question, Schneider and colleagues conducted a meta-analysis of all published papers on stress reduction and relaxation techniques for high blood pressure (107 studies involving 960 participants).[26] As you might expect, given the results from the Anderson group, Schneider found that TM significantly reduced both systolic and diastolic blood pressure. None of the other treatments, which ranged from simple biofeedback, relaxation-assisted biofeedback, and progressive muscle relaxation to "stress management training," had any impact on blood pressure.

This comparative analysis leads to an important conclusion: Not all "stress reduction" programs are equally good. It occurs to me that competent doctors would never dream of just assuming that all drugs advertised for a certain condition are equivalent. Why, then, do so many doctors not realize that the same applies to nondrug techniques or alternative treatments? Biofeedback, muscle relaxation, monitoring your thoughts or breathing, and using a mantra are very different activities. One would expect their effects on the brain (or blood pressure) to be different as well.

Of course, other forms of meditation or stress management *might* lower blood pressure as well as TM does. But unless and until their advocates conduct controlled studies like those described here, I suggest we go with the data, and recommend Transcendental Meditation above other nondrug techniques for lowering blood pressure and improving cardiac health.

YES, BUT DOES IT MAKE
A DIFFERENCE?

OK, you may say, TM can reduce blood pressure (which is after all just a number), but does it really make a concrete difference? Does it change the amount of atherosclerosis in blood vessels, the size of the left ventricle, or any other factor conducive to heart attack, stroke, and death? Does TM improve longevity?

Let's look at the evidence.

One way to assess atherosclerotic changes in people is to perform ultrasound measurements on the carotid arteries, which carry blood up the neck to the brain. You may have noticed your doctor examining your carotid artery during a physical exam by placing a stethoscope on your neck to listen for a bruit (a hissing noise) that occurs when the artery is narrowed. A carotid bruit suggests that the person may be at risk for a stroke, which can occur if a bit of plaque breaks off in the arterial stream and gets wedged into a smaller artery close to the brain.

Through measurements like these, Amparo Castillo-Richmond, Schneider, and colleagues were able to determine that TM can actually help reverse the progression of cardiovascular disease. The researchers studied 138 hypertensive African American volunteers, a group chosen because American blacks have a higher rate of cardiovascular death than American whites.[27] The researchers randomly assigned people to two groups: TM or health education, both of which were administered over a six- to nine-month period. There were no changes in people's diet, exercise, or drugs during the study. Using a special type of ultrasonography[28] both before and after the study, the research team measured the thickness of the inner lining of the carotid artery (the intima), which indicates how much atherosclerosis is present. In the control group, the intima thickened slightly over the months, suggesting that the disease was progressing. In the TM group, on the other hand, the intimal thickness decreased, suggesting actual improvement. TM beat the control treatment by a statistically significant margin.

Cardiologists agree that atherosclerosis in the carotid arteries correlates with disease in the coronary and cerebral arteries, which respectively feed the heart and the brain. The carotid results thus imply some reversal of disease in those arteries as well, which would be expected by itself to reduce the risk of heart attacks and strokes. For this reason, these findings attracted widespread attention when they were published in *Stroke*, a journal of the American Heart Association.[29]

Another measurement of great interest to cardiologists is left ventricular mass. The left ventricle has to push blood throughout most of the body, whereas the right ventricle only has to push blood through the lungs. Therefore, as blood pressure rises, it is the left ventricle that labors under the growing burden of the extra pressure. In other words, the left ventricle gets a greater workout, to which it responds by growing larger. As the heart continues to strain, the left ventricle continues to grow. When it reaches a certain threshold, mortality doubles, which is why left ventricular enlargement is a major risk factor for heart disease and death.

To evaluate the effects of TM practice on left ventricular size, Schneider and his team randomly assigned 102 African American adults to one of two treatment conditions: Transcendental Meditation or health education (the control group).[30] Using a different type of ultrasound,[31] they measured left ventricular mass before and after seven months of treatment. In the control group, left ventricular mass increased over time, suggesting disease progression, whereas in the TM group, left ventricular size stayed the same.

The results of the two ultrasound studies were similar but not identical. As measured by left ventricular mass, TM prevented heart disease from progressing, whereas in the carotid study, it actually reversed the disease process. These two studies strongly suggest that TM can significantly alter the course of a potentially fatal disease.

THE METABOLIC SYNDROME

A U.S. Supreme Court justice once said about pornography that he couldn't define it, but "I know it when I see it." The same can be said of a syndrome that has become familiar to physicians and even to the general public: the metabolic syndrome. This syndrome is simply a cluster of cardiovascular risk factors that often coexist in a population that eats too much, exercises too little, and is under continual stress. Key elements of the syndrome are high blood pressure, a large belly, high blood sugar, and high blood cholesterol (especially the bad low-density type). Researchers think that a basic cause of the syndrome may be resistance to insulin. Insulin is the hormone that pushes glucose into tissues, including fat cells, where it is converted into fat for storage. When people become overweight or obese, their fat cells, especially those in the belly, become resistant to insulin. When the fat cells are unable to absorb glucose, its levels in the blood rise, which predisposes the patient to diabetes, which in turn can damage blood vessels. How often have you seen an obese middle-aged man who becomes red-faced and short of breath at the slightest exertion, who is under severe stress, and said to yourself, "He is a heart attack waiting to happen"? He probably has metabolic syndrome and, sadly enough, you will often turn out to be right.

In one fascinating study, researchers Noel Bairey Merz and colleagues at Cedars-Sinai Medical Center in Los Angeles conducted a randomized controlled study to assess the impact of TM on various aspects of metabolic syndrome.[32] They randomly assigned 103 people who had suffered heart attacks or undergone cardiac procedures (such as angio-plasty) to either TM or health education, administered for the same amount of time and at the same frequency. Results were significant. After sixteen weeks, those in the TM group showed increased insulin sensitivity (meaning insulin did a better job of pushing glucose into cells), as well as lower systolic blood pressure. In other words, within just a few months, TM was able to improve two elements of the meta-bolic syndrome. Schneider speculates that improved insulin sensitivity may be one aspect of the stress relief that accompanies meditation. That would make sense because less stress means, among other things, lower levels of circulating norepinephrine and cortisol, both of which tend to boost blood sugar.

Bairey Merz's study yielded one further tantalizing piece of infor-mation. After sixteen weeks, the TM group showed a trend toward greater heart rate variability.[33] Since heart rate variability is strongly in-fluenced by the parasympathetic nervous system (which helps us relax), this finding suggests that TM may slow down a runaway fight-or-flight response not only by damping sympathetic activity, but also by increas-ing parasympathetic activity.

LIFE, DEATH, AND OTHER HARD ENDPOINTS

You will have noticed that there are many ways of measuring the im-pact of TM on cardiovascular disease. The factors discussed so far—for example, thickening of arterial walls—are called *surrogate markers* be-cause they stand in for something (the general health of the arteries) that we know affects an individual's health and longevity but cannot by itself be precisely measured. More certain and tragic measures of outcome, called *hard endpoints*, include heart attack, stroke, or—the hardest endpoint of all—death. One problem with using hard endpoints to validate a treatment is that the study may have to go on for many years, and the National Institutes of Health will seldom fund studies for more than five years.

Confronting these difficulties, Schneider and colleagues hit on an ingenious strategy: They would investigate mortality in people who had been part of their earlier controlled studies of TM for hypertension.[34] They investigated the fate of 202 people who had been at least fifty-five years old at the time of the earlier research. The team searched the National Death Index to determine which ones had died in the intervening years, along with their cause of death. The average time lapsed since the original study was 7.6 years, though some people had been studied almost 19 years before. Once the earlier studies ended, the researchers had no further contact with the participants, so there was no way to know whether those who had been taught TM had continued to meditate. Presumably some had not. Nevertheless, compared with the controls, *the TM group showed a 23 percent decrease in all causes of mortality and a 30 percent decrease in cardiovascular deaths*. Both findings were statistically significant. These reductions in death from all causes and from cardiovascular causes are similar to results reported on comparable people who took conventional blood pressure–lowering medications.[35]

Curiously, the researchers found a 49 percent decrease in cancer deaths in the TM group. Even though this percentage seems impressive, it did not reach statistical significance because of the small number of cancer deaths in the total group.

Even as I write about these findings, I find it hard to believe that participating in a TM study can improve cardiac and overall health for years to come. Could this possibly be true, even with no researchers to noodge them and make sure they kept meditating? Apparently so. We know that because, in the tradition of good clinical research, Schneider and colleagues set out to see if they could replicate their findings. In collaboration with colleagues at the Medical College of Wisconsin in Milwaukee, Schneider and his team randomly assigned 201 middle-aged or elderly African Americans (average age was fifty-eight) with established heart disease into two groups (the now-familiar TM versus health education) and followed them for five years.[36] The researchers looked for hard endpoints: heart attacks, strokes, and deaths. In the TM group, there were twenty such events, compared with thirty-two in the comparison group, a statistically significant reduction. The meditators remained disease-free for longer and had on average a 5-point decrease in systolic blood pressure. As Schneider puts it, "This impact on outcome is of the same order of magnitude as that seen with cholesterol-lowering statin drugs and antihypertensive medications, which reduce cardiovascular events by about 30–40% and 20–30% respectively. The relative risk reduction in hard endpoints [a statistic that takes into account both their lower rate and later occurrence] was decreased by 47%—which is all the more impressive when you consider that all patients continued to receive their usual medical care. You realize that TM is as powerful as many of our best drugs, without the side effects."

SO, WHAT'S THE SECRET?

On the face of it, the data seem amazing. How can sitting with your eyes closed and repeating a mantra twice a day cut your risk of serious disease by half? I would be even more amazed, however, had I not myself been meditating for the past several years. The data require explanation, but first a personal perspective.

I often take walks in my neighborhood, where it is a great pleasure to watch the changing seasons, greet familiar neighbors, and watch the wildlife that somehow seems to flourish on the outskirts of the city. But every now and then, cars come whizzing by as though the narrow lanes were racetracks or they were being chased by the police. That is how many of us lead our lives, rushing here and there, gunning our motors and keeping our internal pedals on the metal, regardless of whether there is an emergency or not. The motor in question is our sympathetic nervous system; the gas is the flood of epinephrine, norepinephrine, and corticosteroids; the result is internal stress, of which elevated blood pressure is just one outcome. When we let up on the pedal, these stress hormones no longer course through our system in such profusion. This conclusion is supported by a recent controlled study of almost three hundred college students from the Washington, D.C., area by Schneider and colleagues from American University. In the TM group, improvements in stress levels and emotional coping correlated significantly with improvements in systolic blood pressure.[37]

From a personal point of view, since starting to meditate, I gun my motor less. When that vague sense of urgency rises up in me demanding action, I am more apt to think, "Am I really in such a hurry? Why not enjoy the moment?" In the same way, while I've never been what you'd call "an angry man," I might get too easily riled up if someone offended, cheated, or harmed me. Sure, some anger is OK (I still don't like it when those things happen), but I used to allow myself to ruminate for too long on the injury. Today, if such a train of thought starts up, it just tends to disappear. I always knew I should "just let it go"—and told myself so—but it was easier said than done. Now the angry thoughts just seem to evaporate; my attention drifts to something more enjoyable. Likewise, I have long known (as I'm sure many of you do) the famous Serenity Prayer, which asks for the serenity to accept the things we cannot change.[38] Again, easier said than done.

Since I've started to meditate, however, it's been far easier to follow this advice.

All in all, it is clear to me that somehow my regular TM practice has reprogrammed my autonomic nervous system, and thereby transformed the emotional tone of my life. Noticing this pervasive shift helps me imagine how, over time, calming the sympathetic nervous system could make a big difference in the wear and tear on all its target organs, including the heart and blood vessels.

Personal anecdotes aside, what scientific evidence (beyond a consistent drop in blood pressure) do we have of reduced sympathetic system activity in people who regularly practice TM?

One way to test this question would be to stress a person acutely and measure some output of the sympathetic nervous system, which is exactly what several researchers have done. In one study, for example, David Orme-Johnson, now at the Maharishi University, startled fourteen regular TM meditators and sixteen nonmeditators with loud unpleasant noises (with their consent, of course).[39] To assess reactions, Orme-Johnson measured their galvanic skin responses (GSR), which increase with increased sweating—it's part of the fight-or-flight response, and therefore an excellent measure of activity in the sympathetic nervous system. In fact, the GSR is one of several measures included in a lie detector or polygraph test, because it tracks emotional responses so well. In this case, as you might predict, the meditators showed a quicker return of GSR to baseline levels, indicating that they more readily recovered their equanimity. The nonmeditators, besides recovering more slowly, also had more "false alarms," in which the GSR blipped up again even without any further noises.

In a comparable study, researchers Daniel Goleman and Gary Schwartz at Harvard perturbed both meditators and nonmeditators by having them watch a grisly occupational safety film called *It Didn't*

Have to Happen in which the actors seem to undergo horrific injuries.[40] For example, in one scene, an innocent bystander is killed by a plank driven through his midriff as a result of a worker's carelessness. Once again, measures of sympathetic arousal (GSR and heart rate) settled down more quickly in the meditators.

I could give you other examples, but let me close with just one more, of particular interest because it involves physical pain, something we can all relate to. Knowing that pain responses are amplified by anxiety, Orme-Johnson and colleagues from the University of California at Irvine hypothesized that long-term meditators would respond less to painful stimuli than controls, because they are less anxious and have a more relaxed sympathetic nervous system.[41] To test the idea, the researchers chose twelve people who had been meditating for thirty-one years on average and twelve controls who had simply attended an introductory lecture on TM. To begin, the researchers measured each person's normal baseline activity in brain regions relevant to pain using functional magnetic resonance imaging (fMRI), a noninvasive technique. The subjects then stuck their fingers into painfully hot water while the measurements were repeated. All twenty-four people then rated their level of pain. Although the two groups reported no difference in how painful the hot water was, the meditators paid less attention to the pain, as evidenced by the imaging results. In the second fMRI, the meditators showed 40 to 50 percent less activity in the relevant parts of the brain.[42]

The twelve controls then learned to meditate and took the hot water test again five months later. The results were astonishing: After just five months of practicing TM, their brain responses to pain decreased by 45 to 50 percent—in other words, to the same level as the long-term meditators.[43] These results are highly encouraging, as they suggest that you don't have to meditate for thirty-one years in order to relax your sympathetic nervous system.

One important point about the pain studies: All these people were tested when they were *not* meditating. Their pain responses are yet one more demonstration, like the blood pressure findings, that the benefits of TM persist throughout the day.

OTHER STRESSES, OTHER CURES

Because cardiovascular disease is the world's number one killer, it is logical that the impact of stress on CVD has been widely studied. It also makes sense that TM researchers have focused on the power of TM to reduce hypertension, heart attack, and stroke. It is important to remember, though, that stress affects *many* organ systems and promotes *many* other types of disease. Stress can even speed up the aging process.

For example, the stomach and intestines are prime targets for stress. Even though we now know that stomach ulcers are caused by the *Helicobacter pylori* bacterium, not everyone infected will get ulcers; stress still plays a role, as it does in irritable bowel syndrome.[44] That's no surprise, given that both the sympathetic and parasympathetic systems are powerful regulators of gastric and intestinal function.

The immune system is also highly sensitive to stress. Did you know, for example, that stress makes you three times more likely to catch cold after being exposed to the cold virus? Also, there are many viruses that stick around even after your initial illness is over; they lie dormant in the nervous system for decades, just waiting for you to become stressed. Then—hey presto!—they burst into a full-blown infection. Chicken pox, for example, can lurk in your nerve roots only to explode years later in the agonizing form of shingles when your immune defenses are low. Researchers have discovered that chicken pox and other "latent" viruses carry on their DNA a special area that responds to glucocorticoids. When your glucocorticoid levels increase, as they do in times of stress, these repressed viruses can rise again like zombies and wreak havoc on your body.[45]

Less dramatically, stress can delay wound healing, impair response to vaccines, and even clip years off your life. Such immune aspects of stress have been the decades-long research focus of Jan Kiecolt-Glaser, a professor of psychology and psychiatry at Ohio State University (OSU), and her husband, Ronald Glaser, a molecular virologist also at OSU. Together, they have shown that epinephrine, norepinephrine, and glucocorticoids—all three are part of the stress response, as you'll recall—influence the cells and chemicals needed to mount an effective immune response.

Knowing that caregivers of people with Alzheimer's disease are under severe chronic stress, the OSU researchers evaluated how thirty-two caregivers responded to a flu vaccine compared with thirty-two matched controls. On average, the caregivers produced only one quarter the protective antibodies compared with their less burdened peers. In a second study, the researchers vaccinated forty-eight medical students with Hepatitis B vaccine on the third day of three separate three-day exam blocks. They found that those students who reported the most social support and the least amount of anxiety and stress produced the quickest and best immune responses to the vaccine. Based on these studies, the researchers concluded that stress can affect how well a vaccine "takes" in both the old and the young. By inference, a stressed person's response to viruses and bacteria encountered in daily life will also be weakened.[46]

The OSU team also examined wound healing in various situations. In one series of experiments, they created mild sores—for example, a blister on the forearm—and compared healing speed in eleven dental students after exams versus after summer vacation.[47] Likewise, they compared wound healing among forty-two married couples after hostile interactions versus after enjoyable conversations about things they wanted to do together.[48] In both instances, the more stressful situation predicted slower healing. The researchers also measured immune chemicals and cells produced by each person under both conditions and found that their levels were deficient when people were under stress. These findings offer a ready explanation for the way stress impedes healing.[49]

Kiecolt-Glaser and colleagues have also examined how stress affects aging—at the cellular level. At the ends of each of our forty-six chromosomes, which house our DNA, are structures called *telomeres*. As we age, the telomeres become shorter and shorter. Once they become too short, mistakes start creeping into the way our DNA replicates, which is the leading edge of the aging process. Kiecolt-Glaser points out that there is "ample epidemiological data that stressed caregivers die sooner than people not in that role." So she and her team compared various elements of the immune response as seen in the blood, as well as telomere lengths in circulating blood cells, in forty-one caregivers and forty-one matched controls.[50] As you might suspect, not only was immune function off in the caregivers, but their telomeres were shorter. This shows that stress can age people at the very level of their cells, thereby potentially shaving years off their lives.

You may well ask what any of this has to do with TM. Well, all of these effects—on the immune system and on aging—are aggravated by stress, just like the cardiovascular effects I discussed before. It is therefore a fair bet that TM can soften the impact of stress in general.

One interesting study by Schneider and colleagues examined how TM affects quality of life in breast cancer patients aged fifty-five and older.[51] Researchers assigned 130 patients randomly to one of two groups: standard medical care by their own doctors versus standard care plus TM. Patients were followed for an average of eighteen months.

Those patients practicing TM reported a significantly higher quality of life (as measured by standardized scales) than did the controls. As for mortality, six people in the control group died during the study, compared to three in the TM group. Although this finding was not statistically significant—the groups were too small—you may recall that there were also fewer deaths by cancer in the TM-treated group in one of Schneider's previous studies (see page 73), though that result was also not statistically significant. It is too soon to say whether these intriguing but very preliminary findings will hold up once larger numbers of people are studied.

SO, WHAT'S IT WORTH TO YOU?

Setting aside the benefits to your health, how much might you (and society at large) save financially on healthcare by regular practice of Transcendental Meditation? The question takes on urgency in these times of spiraling health costs, and fortunately it has been studied.

In the 1980s, David Orme-Johnson studied health data over a five-year period from 1,450 members (the numbers varied from year to year, so this number is an average) of SCI health insurance, a Blue Cross Blue Shield plan that insured only people who had practiced TM for at least six months and who promised to continue. The meditators were compared with a database of 600,000 people insured under different plans by the same carrier.[52] The groups were matched for many demographic variables such as age, gender, and terms of insurance.

The health profile of meditators was vastly superior—and their use of health services dramatically lower. For example, meditators who were children (eighteen or younger) and young adults (nineteen to thirty-nine) had only half the number of inpatient days compared with age-matched controls. For older adults, this decrease was even greater (just under 70 percent fewer inpatient days). Outpatient visits followed a similar pattern. When the meditators were compared with members of five other insurance groups, similar results emerged. Hospital admissions were lower in meditators for many different illness categories, including heart disease (87 percent less), diseases of the nervous system (83 percent), benign or malignant tumors (55 percent), mental illness (31 percent), and infectious diseases (30 percent).

Although intriguing, these data hardly prove that TM per se made the difference. For example, people who practice TM may be more likely to pursue healthy habits (such as a diet low in animal fat) and avoid unhealthy ones (such as drinking and smoking). So TM may well account for only part of the meditator's good health. On the other hand, by reducing stress, TM may help people choose healthier habits, thereby compounding its beneficial effects. In any event, Orme-Johnson's data are certainly consistent with the well-documented health benefits of TM.

How much healthcare money could be saved if TM were widely practiced? That is a question that Robert Herron, a researcher associated with Maharishi University, asked in a retrospectively controlled study using fourteen years of medical expense data from about 2,800 people enrolled in Quebec's provincial health insurance plan.[53] Half of these people learned TM (the meditators) at some point along the way, whereas the other half (the controls) did not. Monthly payments to doctors were adjusted to account for age, inflation, and other potentially confounding factors. Before learning TM, meditators and controls had similar medical costs. After learning the TM technique, however, doctors' fees dropped steadily for the meditators while they kept rising for the controls (as you would expect with increasing age). After six years, the gap between the two groups was 55 percent—highly significant.

A FEW MODEST SUGGESTIONS

Based on the enormous potential savings in health costs, I suggest that TM training and follow-up should be offered without charge by health insurance companies purely in their own self-interest. Until that Utopia arrives, most interested people would do well to get the training at their own expense. For most people, the cost will soon be repaid—not only by improved health and quality of life, but also financially.

In my opinion, the time is right to extend the research on TM beyond cardiology and into immunology, cancer, and aging. Perhaps some medical or psychology student reading this chapter will be bitten by the research bug and pursue these areas.

Another field ripe for research is the effect of TM on the brain (and mind). I will deal with these effects in part three, "Transformation."

In closing, please reconsider the words of Hans Selye, the father of stress research, whom I quote also at the top of this chapter:

It is not stress that kills us, it is our reaction to it.

Part III

TRANSFORMATION

4

TURNING OFF THE BRAIN'S
ALARM SYSTEM

Treating Anxiety and Anger

Worry is the interest paid in advance on a
debt you may never owe.

—SOURCE UNKNOWN

IN THE LAST CHAPTER, we considered the power of Transcendental
Meditation to prevent physical illness or, in some cases, actually reverse
it. In this section, we will consider the power of TM to help people
change emotionally and spiritually. I have called this section "Transformation" because sometimes the changes that occur after a person
learns to meditate are so dramatic that those who know the meditator
say, "It's like dealing with a different person."

In the last chapter, we saw that painful and prolonged emotions
such as depression, anxiety, and anger can damage the heart and blood
vessels. For that reason alone these emotional disturbances require
treatment. But anyone who has experienced emotional upheaval, either
personally or in others, will have some sense of the anguish these disturbances can cause and will understand that they deserve to be treated
in their own right. There are, of course, established treatments for these

conditions. As a psychiatrist, I use them all the time. Unfortunately, they are not always completely effective and they sometimes cause side effects, which limit their value. Like many of my colleagues, I am always looking around for new ways to alleviate emotional suffering, and I have been delighted to find in TM a valuable new approach.

The following four chapters illustrate how TM can be helpful to people suffering from four particular types of difficulty and distress: anxiety and anger (the present chapter); problems with attention, setting priorities, and effectiveness (chapter 5); problems with mood regulation—depression and bipolar disorder (chapter 6); and drug and alcohol abuse (chapter 7). Chapters 8 and 9 deal with the value of TM in two very different emotionally challenging environments: inner-city schools and prisons.

Then in chapter 10, we will move on to consider the value of TM for personal growth—emotional, intellectual, and spiritual. In other words, TM can help transform people's lives whether or not they are suffering in specific ways. Although I have separated body, mind, and spirit artificially for the sake of organization, they are all in fact essential parts of the mysterious and wonderful jumble that is the human condition.

Before jumping into specific emotions, I want to connect the dots between the stress response that we considered earlier and emotional responses. So let's revisit for a moment our friends the buffalo, walking into an ambush set by the lions. When they catch the scent of the lions, *fear* screams, "Run! Run!" Once at a safe distance, they realize their calf is missing. They take stock of the situation, and *anger* screams, "Go, get them! Get the calf!" As to the calf, *despair* whispers, "Stay put. Don't move." Emotions and the stress response are interwoven. When they work together, they work well. Incidentally, emotions have been beautifully documented in animals, and the complex neural circuits that support and coordinate emotions have been well studied.[1]

As with the other aspects of the stress response, emotions such as anxiety or anger work best when they are directed toward a specific challenge and are of short duration. Here they can serve as crucial alarm bells, signaling a specific danger: a snake in the grass (human or otherwise); a rival for your lover—or your job; a serious loss that requires you to recalibrate and reorganize your life.[2] Such intelligent emotions are the brilliant products of millions of years of evolution and are most highly developed among mammals. We now recognize that people who have high emotional intelligence—a superb capacity to recognize emotions in themselves and others, and to govern their own emotions—are at a huge advantage, whereas people who lack these skills are sorely handicapped.

When emotions are working badly—too much, for too long, or inappropriately expressed or directed—they can be disastrous. That is why I embrace any new approach that can help alleviate emotional pain and dysfunction, especially one like TM that is essentially free of side effects. In the chapters that follow I will relate stories of such suffering and the relief that meditation has provided.

Let us begin with three distinguished men who have suffered from a common and disabling malady of our times—anxiety—a condition in which the brain's alarm bells keep on ringing, ringing, and ringing . . . long after they have served any useful function.

THREE WISE MEN

The three wise men in this section share certain demographic similarities: All in their fifties or sixties, they are highly successful professionals. All learned to meditate in the 1970s and have been meditating ever since. All suffered from some degree of anxiety before starting to meditate, and all credit TM with greatly improving their symptoms and transforming their lives. Yet their stories differ in important ways.

BILL: The Real Deal for "The Most Nervous Person I Have Ever Met"

William Stixrud is one of the most distinguished and successful neuropsychologists in the Washington, D.C., area. He has a large practice in which he supervises many other psychologists, who hold him in high esteem. I have had the good fortune to collaborate with him in my own practice and to count him as a friend. Yet his success would not have been predicted by anyone who knew him as a doctoral student in English at Berkeley. At that time he was so anxious and insecure that he flunked out in two quarters because he was afraid to turn in his work. Then he was fired from a typing job—not because he couldn't type but because his worry and restlessness made others uneasy.

Bill's anxiety came out in many physical ways. For example, at the movies "my foot was tapping a hundred miles an hour and the person sitting next to me would say, 'Could you stop that, please? It's kind of annoying.'" He also developed a facial tic. He couldn't concentrate on anything for more than fifteen minutes before he'd have to get up and distract himself. As he recalls: "I think that I've always had some social anxiety. Even though I always had a lot of friends, I never wanted to go to sleepaway camp, and I cried my whole first week of first grade. I didn't know anybody and was slow to make friends."

By the time Bill heard about TM, he was desperate. In fact, in the three months before he learned to meditate, two people independently told him, "You are the most nervous person I have ever met." Then—what felt like a miracle occurred. The very first time he meditated he felt peaceful inside and thought, "This is the real deal." He knew right away that he had discovered something vital, and he could hardly wait to get home and meditate some more. He'd wake up and look forward to his morning meditation.

After a month of practicing the technique, Bill says his foot tapping stopped and his facial tic disappeared. A few months later he noticed that he could sit down and read for two hours at a stretch, with no urge to get up and move around.

Already his life was appreciably better. Then, over the next three years of meditation, Bill became calmer and more confident until finally he felt able to return to school and pursue a different field—psychology. Bill continues to meditate twice a day and has no trouble using the term "transformation" to describe the impact of TM on his life.

I recently attended Bill's sixtieth birthday party. He was in great spirits, surrounded by family and dozens of friends. With members of his rock band, he sang some golden oldies, accompanying himself with his electric guitar. To this observer, who had a ringside seat at the performance, there was no evidence of any facial tic or foot tapping (except in time to the music). If he felt any social or performance anxiety whatsoever, it certainly escaped my clinical eye.

TIM: Treating Panic Disorder

Tim Page was the music critic for the *Washington Post* for many years, and won the Pulitzer Prize in 1997 "for his lucid and illuminating criticism." Tim first heard of TM in the late sixties but did not get around to learning it until 1975, when he was a twenty-year-old college student in a small town in Connecticut. At that time he was suffering from "terrible, terrible panic attacks," so bad that he occasionally landed in the emergency room, where they'd settle him down with intravenous tranquilizers. Wherever he was, he felt compelled to sit near the door. He could not tolerate riding a bus for more than a few moments—so although he was in college, his mother had to drive him everywhere,

which was humiliating. As with Bill, Tim's anxiety affected his body:
He walked around with his shoulders constantly hunched up so tightly
he felt they would never relax. By the time he decided to learn TM, he
was desperate—and so was his mom. She was more than happy to pay
for his instruction.

A skeptic by nature, Tim was unimpressed with the introductory
talk. It "struck me as sort of hooey." He was also "not thrilled by"
the traditional thanksgiving ceremony, in which the instructor gives
thanks to earlier meditation teachers with pieces of fruit and a hand-
kerchief. He was suspicious as to why the mantra should not be shared
(though he adds, "I've never actually said it to anybody so I'm not
going to do that now"). As he took in the first lesson, he thought,
"Well, this is not going to do much for me." He was wrong. Here is
how he describes it:

> What happened when I started doing the mantra was . . .
> my shoulders dropped. I'd been in a terrible accident shortly
> before, and I was so full of anxiety, I was just a walking panic
> attack. And as I started to let the mantra fade into the back
> of my mind, I couldn't believe it. Within a minute or two my
> shoulders dropped! I couldn't have done that by myself if
> someone had worked with me for half an hour. But all of a
> sudden it was as if I tapped into something that was so in-
> credibly natural and restful that I was just astonished.

He experienced increasing benefits of TM over the months that
followed that February day. "It was a huge deal," he says now.

> My mom was driving me to and from the campus because I
> was so afraid of having anxiety attacks that I wouldn't walk
> very far. Walking home was only about half a mile, but I

didn't think I could do it. Then all of a sudden I could. The meditation taught me how to relax myself in all kinds of terrifying situations. In only eight months I went from being a kid in Connecticut, frightened of his shadow, to living in New York City all by myself, going to college and dealing with all the subways and the chaos of the city. TM was hugely helpful in letting me relax instantly if I needed to. Sometimes I would start to meditate, actually on the subway, and I would calm down there and then. Eventually I got so I could make myself relax under almost all circumstances. I knew there was a sort of force or power that I could tune into, which would let me get through whatever chaos I was in. I used to tell people that I considered February 1, 1975, my second birthday. Though I don't mean this in a religious sense, it really felt as though I'd been reborn.

Tim still meditates twice a day, sometimes in "very weird places," like subways or taxis. He may miss a few meditation sessions in a year, but says he certainly never goes a full day without TM. When he does miss a meditation, he doesn't sleep as well as usual that night. Nowadays, he seldom uses meditation to calm acute anxiety—he doesn't need to. His general level of anxiety is manageable. Nor have his shoulders ever hunched up again since that very first day. Tim sums up the current effects of his meditation this way:

It allows me a sort of vacation from myself, to lose my egoism or whatever thing is bothering me. If I have a crazy day and have to scream and yell at people, or work on a deadline, the feeling at the end of the day of sliding into this very, very natural peace is extremely helpful. Also, in a weird way, it's an affirmation of myself.

Tim is currently a professor of music and journalism at the University of Southern California. He has either edited or written nineteen books including, most recently, a memoir called *Parallel Play*.

DAVID: Treating Anger at Its Root

David Lynch, the prominent American filmmaker, painter, and photographer, has been practicing Transcendental Meditation for so long he can hardly remember the details of how bad he used to feel before he learned to meditate.

> I was filled with worries and anxieties and I wasn't happy. I had a lot of anger and all those negative things swimming about inside me. I was in a place where I should have been so happy, but it was only a surface happiness. I had heard the phrase that true happiness is not out there; true happiness lies within. And when I saw that I should be so happy, but wasn't happy within, that's when I started to get interested in meditation.

In his book *Catching the Big Fish*, David summarizes his negative feelings as "the suffocating rubber clown suit of anger and depression" (because "it's suffocating and the rubber stinks"). He consulted a psychiatrist but when he was told that psychotherapy might damage his creative abilities (advice that I as a psychiatrist do not endorse), he decided against it. Instead he opted for Transcendental Meditation. Here is how he describes his first meditation and the feelings that followed:

> When I had my first meditation, this inner bliss revealed itself so powerfully—thick happiness came rushing in. And I said,

"This is it." There it was. And everything just started getting better—way more fun, way more joy in the doing. Everything just got better and better. I didn't think about not getting angry—the anger just lifted away. And what they say is when you start infusing this transcendence, you don't really realize that anger is going. It's other people close to you that see it first. And it just seems natural. You're happy, and there's nothing you can do about it. You just get happier.

My first wife came to me two weeks after I started meditating and she said, "What's going on?" And I didn't know what she was talking about. And she said, "The anger, where did it go?" She got the benefit of that anger lifting. So, it's just as they say—with TM, relationships improve. Maharishi was always talking about how, once you bring the transcendence up to the surface, people can still say mean things or behave badly—but all kinds of love and tolerance come out and you see the bigger picture. So you don't find yourself getting into a fight. You just don't react the way you used to. You see the way that person is and it's OK. Everything's just different.

David has no question that Transcendental Meditation has transformed his life from one of suffering to one of happiness, a transformation he compares to the healing of a sick tree.

I like the analogy of the tree. You want to turn all the little sick leaves green. But when you work on the surface, leaf by leaf by leaf, it's so difficult. By the time you get one leaf green, a bunch of others have gone yellow or brown. The secret is, the experienced gardener doesn't worry about the leaves. He knows the tree is sick, so he gets nourishment to the roots, the deepest level. And that way you transform that whole sick tree to a state of perfection. All the leaves turn green. All the branches get strong. "Water the root and enjoy the fruit" is something Maharishi said for over 50 years.

This image of the tree brings to mind work I have done over the years with patients who have a hard time managing their anger. The conventional approach to such difficulties is cognitive behavior therapy, which involves helping the patient to identify and challenge angry thoughts, feelings, and behaviors, and to recognize what triggers them. This treatment works to some extent, but many patients find the process too arduous. They tend to slack off on their homework—and, for all its benefits, this approach does have a "painting the leaves" quality to it. More recently, I have recommended TM to some of my patients with anger problems, hoping that "watering the root" will prove to be an effective and easier alternative. Preliminary feedback is encouraging and I look forward to collecting more data on this promising alternative (or complementary) anger management technique.

Wishing to share these transformative effects on a larger scale, David has set up the David Lynch Foundation, which sponsors the teaching of Transcendental Meditation to people who would not otherwise have the chance, such as inner-city schoolchildren, whom I will discuss more fully in chapter 8 and veterans with post-traumatic stress disorder (PTSD), whom I discuss below.

POST-TRAUMATIC STRESS DISORDER (PTSD)

One form of anxiety disorder that has been much in the news lately is post-traumatic stress disorder (PTSD), topical because of its alarming frequency among returning military from Iraq and Afghanistan.

The human and financial costs of PTSD are enormous. According to a recent estimate, of the nearly 1.64 million U.S. troops deployed to these two countries between 2001 and 2008, one in seven met criteria for PTSD.[3] Half of these veterans had never sought any kind of help for their symptoms, probably because of the stigma of being labeled with a psychiatric disorder. Of those who did seek help, half received inadequate treatment.[4]

Combat-related PTSD (which used to be called "shell shock") may occur in any military personnel or contractors who have experienced or witnessed a traumatic event. PTSD victims may experience a disabling cluster of symptoms, including anxiety, excessive vigilance, an exaggerated tendency to startle, nightmares, flashbacks to the traumatic event (which may be triggered by any associated memories), insomnia, outbursts of anger, and social withdrawal. Some of these symptoms may last a lifetime; I have personally seen PTSD symptoms in veterans of Vietnam. Although the recent news has focused on PTSD arising from combat, it's important to realize that the condition can result from *any* trauma, such as being raped or mugged. Many people who lived through 9/11 suffer in this way. For example, a loud popping sound can take them back to Ground Zero.

My colleagues and I recently conducted a small pilot study on how the TM technique affected PTSD in American veterans who had fought in Iraq.[5] We monitored five young men for two months after they learned how to meditate. All responded very favorably on standardized rating scales that measure the effects of trauma. Here are the stories of two of these veterans.

Todd: Drinking to Relieve Pain

Todd, a Marine, was in his early twenties when he was deployed to Iraq as a gunner on a Humvee. The job was frightening—even when all was going well—because he knew he could run over an IED (improvised explosive device) at any moment, as many of his buddies had—with effects he had seen firsthand. Once, he even had to assemble the body pieces of a Marine he had known well. On another occasion, an IED was left in a suicide vehicle; Todd's platoon was called in to clear out the dismembered bodies of Iraqi citizens. All these events took place within a seven-month period.

Then, out on a reconnaissance mission, Todd was up in the turret when his commanding sergeant ordered him to drive along a road well known as a hotbed of IEDs. Todd was angry at the sergeant for taking this unnecessary risk—and still is because, sure enough, the Humvee hit a bomb. One soldier was thrown from the truck and injured his back, while the sergeant was concussed. Fortunately, Todd himself was not harmed physically and no one was killed. Psychologically, however, that day was a turning point. Anger at the sergeant mixed with guilt, as Todd blamed himself for not having spotted the device. Memories of cleaning up body parts blurred into fears that he also might get blown up. The seeds of PTSD were planted.

As is often the case, the clinical symptoms of PTSD were delayed until after Todd returned home, when his sleep became disturbed. He would wake up drenched in sweat, heart pounding as his nightmares took him back to the battle zone. When he spent the night with his girlfriend, he would wake up and find that he had her in a choke hold, as though she were the enemy. During the day, he was jumpy and easily startled. Driving along the streets of Washington, D.C., every time his car went over a pothole, he would feel panic and terror as though he had once again hit an IED. When his mother was ill in the hospital, he could not visit. It made him physically sick because the injured people on the ward triggered memories of mutilated bodies. The bad memories were always there, as if lying in wait. To blot them out, Todd took to drinking vodka all day long, which did numb the pain but prevented him from getting on with his life.

When Todd heard about our TM program on the radio, he decided he had little to lose. He didn't have much hope, but it seemed worth a try. Todd's results? Almost immediately, the TM technique helped him calm down, feel less anxious, and sleep better. His nightmares are now rare. He is less jumpy and can now even hit a pothole without panicking. He now drinks only when others do, and his girlfriend has noticed that he is much calmer. "She admires how much more I've got my life together," he says, and their relationship has improved. Todd has enrolled at the local university as a psychology major.

Here are some of his observations about the effects of TM on his life:

> I think TM helped my relationship with my girlfriend a lot. Even beyond the PTSD symptoms, it's helped me be organized and more understanding. I guess I have an open mind now. It helps me set priorities and clear out of my head stuff that's not a priority. TM has definitely helped a lot with school. My grades have actually increased. It helped me get back on track and concentrate better in school; before, as soon as I left a class, I started thinking of other stuff. So TM has helped with organizing, prioritizing, and just being calmer overall. I just feel better. My whole body feels better.

DAVID: Becoming Numb to Protect Himself

David was deployed to Iraq with the 101st Airborne Division and arrived to find "a war-torn country with blood and blown-up vehicles all over the road, the leftovers of war, along with the chemical smell of explosives that was the first thing to stick in my mind." Then he started going out on patrol, where his squad was a target of gunfire and mortars. It was then and there that he first learned to dissociate, to go into a numb state in which he was somehow detached—intellectually aware of the daily dangers, but with little or no response to them. For example, when his squad leader was almost killed by a rocket-propelled grenade, David minimized the trauma. He said to himself, "Well at least he's alive and in good standing," and he went to sleep. Perhaps the numbness helped David continue to function, as it does for many who later suffer from PTSD, but in David's case, the numbness would not last for long.

Shortly after David's squad leader was injured, there was a huge explosion outside the barracks, "and that is when I cracked." He heard gunfire and saw a blaze of light through his closed eyelids as though he were staring directly at the sun. "I heard an explosion that sounded like death." A thousand-pound bomb had gone off about forty yards away, blowing out every window and door. "I saw my friends being carried away bloodied, with blood running down their shirts as though it were sweat. I guess it became real because I saw everybody hurt all at the same time, and this was like my whole family." From being a "very gung ho person" who always volunteered to go out on missions and fight, David now slowed down. He thought, "I just want to live. I just want to get home."

Within a few months of returning home, David developed symptoms of PTSD. Though he had always been a "nice guy," he now developed explosive and uncontrollable anger. He would attack people even for minor provocations: "I would erupt and it was insane—it was like everything I experienced in the war was starting to come out in my anger." The smells at a gas station would remind him of the smell of burning rubber and "all of a sudden out of nowhere my heart started pounding. I got tense and started looking around and freaking out." He learned that these episodes were called panic attacks. He was in a state of "continuous hyperdrive." His sleep was disrupted by every minor noise. Even the small vacuum effects created by a door being opened or shut elsewhere in his apartment building triggered memories of the huge explosion and would cause him to lie awake for hours.

David was reluctant to take the psychiatric medications that were prescribed, even though they helped somewhat. "It took my personality away," he says. "I was uncreative." But when he went off the medications, he once again felt dissociated from what was happening in his life. He experienced extreme survivor guilt ("Why me? How did *I* deserve to live?") and had a serious one-person car crash.

At about that time he entered our research study on Transcendental Meditation, with results he describes as follows:

> When I started meditating, I looked forward to the next session. So in the morning I'd be like "Oh man, I can't wait to meditate again in the afternoon"—because those would be the moments that I would be free of angst and very like myself for at least twenty minutes, and maybe ten minutes afterward. That was how I wanted to be.

After eight months of regular meditation, David is now calmer, loves life, and feels more in touch with himself than ever. He has developed a healthy type of self-love. He recognizes that in the past he was reckless and put too little value on his life. Now he is careful and wants to make something more of himself. His sleep has improved and he is less paranoid about other people's motivations. So impressed is he with TM that he has enrolled at the Maharishi University of Management, a college where meditation is part of the curriculum. He says of the technique, "It's totally given me my life back."

TOM: Coping with Overwhelming Stress

> Everything can be taken from a man but . . .
> the last of the human freedoms—to choose
> one's attitude in any given set of circum-
> stances, to choose one's own way.
>
> —VIKTOR FRANKL,
> *Man's Search for Meaning*[6]

The above quote from Viktor Frankl's classic is relevant to the subject of my next story—Tom Goldstein. Frankl was a famous Austrian neurologist who, because he was a Jew, was sent to Auschwitz and other death camps during the Second World War. As a student of the mind, Frankl pondered the question of how people manage to cope when confronted with overwhelming stress and horror. Tragically, many people died in the camps, regardless of their attitude toward life. But Frankl observed that a person's attitude *could* make the difference between life and death. It seemed to him as though some people just gave up . . . and died. Others somehow managed to survive. Somehow, in the midst of horror, they found *meaning*—a thread that kept them going and helped guide them out of the labyrinth of horror.[7]

What follows is a modern-day story of someone who was thrust into just such a labyrinth, and found his way out—in this case with the help of TM.

In 1979, Thomas Goldstein, a former Marine, was arrested for a brutal shotgun killing on the streets of Long Beach, California. Within nine months of his arrest, he was convicted, sentenced, and sent to state prison, where he remained until 2004. Had he admitted wrongdoing and shown remorse, he would probably have been paroled, but Tom wouldn't. He *couldn't*. He knew he was innocent, even if nobody believed him. "The more I'd protest my innocence, the more prison officials felt I was a sociopath who refused to accept responsibility for his crime," Tom told me. "After my appeal was denied, I realized that if I wanted to get out of prison, I'd have to do it myself. So I worked in the San Quentin law library—and I studied law. I started filing habeas petitions on my behalf, asking the court to review constitutional errors that may have occurred."

How did an innocent man land in prison? In Tom's case, the conviction rested on two pieces of evidence: an eyewitness identified him from a photo lineup, and a jailhouse informant claimed that Tom had confessed the details of the crime to him. Also, Tom lived near the scene of the crime. That was basis enough for the California court system to sentence him to life in prison.

Tom describes the appalling conditions at San Quentin in the early eighties:

> It was noisy; it was overcrowded; it was not hygienic. The daily interactions in overcrowded conditions, the shouting on the tiers at all hours of the day and night—just being in that environment created stress. Also, you're constantly watching your back and seeing who's to your right and who's to your left because there was a lot of violence in maximum security prisons back then. You're never really comfortable except when you're in your cell.

Tom filed many habeas petitions on his own behalf—all of which were unsuccessful. There were also three appeals of his conviction—all of which were turned down.

It was a lucky day for Tom when he learned TM in San Quentin in 1981. There were many people waiting to learn, but Tom jumped ahead in line because his cell mate was due to be taught, and the teacher wanted his cell mate to have a companion who also meditated. Here's what Tom says about TM.

> What I discovered is that by meditating, you can stop your chain of thoughts and reduce the stress that's generated by those thoughts. So if something happens in the yard, if someone gets stabbed or you have an argument or confrontation, it only happens once in your life, but it can happen a hundred times in your mind; it keeps going over and over: "I should have done this; I could have done that." And you get mad about it. Through meditating, you're able to stop that chain of thought.

In California, Tom explained to me, every prison locks down between 3:30 and 4:00 p.m. for the afternoon count. Tom found that to be a good time to meditate—with results that he describes as life-saving.

> I think that without meditation I would not have been able to survive the stresses of prison. I was just so overwhelmed with being disbelieved; with being in with these people whose values were so different from mine. I don't know how I could have gotten through it without a way of stopping my thoughts and having that twenty-minute period when I didn't have to think about anything else.
>
> And once I experienced that meditative state, I could take that feeling into other areas of the prison, and not be so affected by the stresses and by the disbelief of other people. When I was doing my habeas petitions and doing my appeals, there was nobody there to support me. Nobody said, "You're doing a good job. Just keep it up; you're going

to win." It was more like, "You filed it, you lost. Now do your time." Or, "You know, less than one percent of habeas petitions ever win." Or, "Yeah, sure you're innocent; everybody here is innocent." So it was really a big deal to learn that I could react differently to this sort of thing.

Slowly, Tom's luck began to change. In 1989, the Los Angeles Grand Jury began an investigation into the use of jailhouse informants, and the following year concluded that there had been a rampant misuse of these snitches for the previous ten years—which included the very years when Tom had been arrested, tried, and imprisoned.[8] The grand jury found that the Los Angeles County District Attorney's Office had deliberately procured inaccurate and dishonest testimony from snitches. The "notorious jailhouse informant" Edward Fink, a heroin addict who had briefly shared a cell with Tom and had testified against him, fit the pattern reported by the grand jury. Although Fink had sworn on the stand that he had received no benefit for testifying against Tom, he had in fact avoided two felony charges.[9]

Still, the wheels of the legal system turned slowly. In 1998, Tom's federal appointed attorneys succeeded in scheduling a habeas hearing. In 2002, the eyewitness who had "identified" Tom recanted his testimony and revealed how police had steered him to pick Tom's picture out of a photo lineup. Finally, his new lawyers showed that his original trial lawyer had not even interviewed the eyewitness—proof that Tom had not received an acceptable defense in his initial trial.[10]

Tom Goldstein was released in 2004 after twenty-four years in prison.

In 2010 he obtained an $8 million settlement against Long Beach for wrongful conviction.

Tom continues to meditate.

ANXIETY: AN ALARM BELL THAT
WON'T STOP RINGING

Anxiety, like that described by Bill, Tim, Todd, and both Davids, is common and can be disabling. When severe, it may be part of what clinicians term "anxiety disorders," which torment approximately forty million people in the United States at a cost estimated at more than $46 billion a year.[11] Indeed, treating these disorders accounts for almost one third of the country's total mental health costs.

There are different forms of anxiety disorder, which often occur together. For example, Bill sounds as if he had mostly generalized anxiety disorder. Tim suffered from panic disorder, which often leads (as in his case) to agoraphobia, fear of venturing out lest one have a panic attack. It sounds as if David Lynch had a mixture of anxious and depressive symptoms, which often go together. The two veterans, of course, had PTSD, yet another member of the anxiety disorder family.

What all these men (and anxiety disorders) have in common is an overactive alarm system. In the last section, we encountered people suffering physically from stress, which can manifest with high blood pressure and cardiovascular disease. But we know that the stress response also has a brain component (involving the amygdala), which registers emergencies and drives us to take appropriate actions—such as fight or flight. When it's working normally, the brain's alarm system is triggered by real danger, lasts only as long as necessary, and can be lifesaving. People with anxiety disorders, however, like those profiled in this chapter, have alarm systems that are on overdrive.

In Bill's case (generalized anxiety), the alarm bell rang incessantly, interfering with his ability to do simple things that were way below his intellectual ability. For Tim (panic disorder), sudden, massive, unprovoked, and overwhelming alarm sirens left him paralyzed, afraid to venture out alone. David Lynch had nasty grumbling alarm signals, which filled him with worry and prevented him from feeling happy. As for the two veterans with PTSD, it is no mystery what knocked their alarm systems out of kilter—massive trauma in Iraq. After a numbing silence, which allowed them to function on the battlefield and get their job done, their alarm sirens began to wail at all times of day and night in the form of flashbacks (triggered by ordinary events, such as hitting a pothole in the road) and nightmares of being back in the war zone.

To get a sense of the toll that anxiety takes on people, consider what would happen at a fire station if there were three-alarm warnings ringing all day long in the absence of any real emergency. That is what it is like living with an anxiety disorder. It wears you down and prevents you from using your talents and abilities to lead an enjoyable and productive life. What makes matters worse, as several of my patients have told me, is that you never know which alarm bell out of all the false alarms will be the real thing! The amygdala is like the child in the old story who cries wolf too often, which makes it hard to tell when the wolf is really upon you. As a result, a person with an anxiety disorder is on the lookout for an emergency *all the time*. It makes sense that a technique that can turn off these alarm bells most of the time and allow them to ring only when necessary and as long as is necessary would be enormously valuable.

RESEARCH ON TM FOR
TREATING ANXIETY

We learned in the last chapter how TM can quiet down the sympathetic nervous system, as evidenced by quicker recovery after unpleasantly loud noises, frightening movies, or jolts of pain. It seems very likely that TM's success for the anxious people you've met in this chapter worked in a similar way; it soothed their fight-or-flight responses, both physically and emotionally.

For anxious people—with PTSD in particular—TM may also help by a process of systematic desensitization—allowing worrisome thoughts and feelings to emerge in the context of profound relaxation and transcendent joy, thereby weakening the neural links that were forged by the trauma (see chapter 1 for a further discussion of this mechanism). Desensitization could explain in part how TM helped Todd, David, the rest of our study cohort, and a group of Vietnam vets who participated in a small but well-designed study back in the seventies.

In that study, conducted by James Brooks and Thomas Scarano at the Denver Vet Center, ten Vietnam veterans with PTSD were taught TM while eight similar veterans were treated with the conventional psychotherapy of the time.[12] At the end of three months, seven of the ten men in the TM group said that they needed no further help from the VA center for their problem, whereas the psychotherapy group showed little improvement. Despite the small numbers of patients involved, the difference between treatments was statistically significant. These earlier results, along with our pilot study,[13] are highly encouraging.

More broadly, Transcendental Meditation as a treatment for trait anxiety—the tendency to be anxious—has been amply studied, as shown by Kenneth Eppley of Stanford University and colleagues. This team performed a meta-analysis on 146 studies that examined the effects of various relaxation techniques, including TM, on trait anxiety.[14] The other techniques included biofeedback, progressive relaxation, and other forms of meditation. Their findings? While most of the non-TM techniques had similar effect sizes, Transcendental Meditation was significantly more effective than average, while meditation techniques requiring concentration were significantly less so. As you may recall, the results of a meta-analysis are often expressed in effect sizes, which take into account the magnitude of the effect as well as the variability across studies. In the Eppley meta-analysis, the effect size for TM was

0.7 (0.8 is considered large), for the relaxation techniques 0.4 (0.5 is considered medium), and for other forms of meditation 0.28 (0.2 is considered small). This review strongly suggests that TM may help people with a broad range of anxiety problems, and may do so more effectively than several other nondrug techniques.

Encouraged by stories such as those I have shared with you here, I have started recommending TM to some of my patients with anxiety disorders, such as Henry, a young man who had suffered for most of his life from disabling anxiety. Henry's symptoms responded to medications, but he did not like the side effects. When he heard about TM, he was eager to try it out. After learning TM, he felt so much better that he was able to lower the dose of his medication significantly without feeling any worse. Later on, he did what he called "my own controlled experiment." He stopped meditating for a while, became anxious again, restarted meditating, and rediscovered the benefits. (In my experience, a good many patients carry out such "experiments" to see if they really need whatever treatment they are getting.)

If the three wise men and the two veterans featured in this chapter are representative of how people with anxiety disorders might respond to TM, imagine how much suffering and expense its widespread use could save. From a solely economic point of view, Transcendental Meditation is much cheaper than many other forms of treatment because: (1) For the most part, it is self-administered. The onetime cost is the training. (2) It may be possible to avoid or minimize psychiatric drugs or other services. (3) If the patient keeps meditating, the effect continues to work—for a lifetime. In addition, the technique is flexible: TM can be practiced anywhere, in any private moment, with no special equipment or facilities.

I hope that more researchers will seek grants to use TM for emotional as well as physical disorders (where funding initiatives have been more successful). Who knows? Maybe one of you reading this book will be in a position to research these possibilities.

More urgently, I am eager to see efforts—by the Veterans Administration, funding agencies, and private charities—to make TM accessible to veterans suffering from PTSD, as part of research studies or otherwise. There are hundreds of thousands of veterans tormented by PTSD, for whom current approaches are both costly and inadequate. I suggest that it is high time to try this different, less expensive, and highly promising approach.

ANGER AND HOSTILITY

> Anger as a desire for avenging injury has cost the human race more than any plague. To govern one's mind and speech when angry is a mark of great ability.
>
> —SENECA

So far we have seen two examples where the TM technique helped people moderate their anger. In the case of David Lynch, his wife was surprised that after only two weeks of meditation, his anger had disappeared. The other David, the veteran with PTSD, had experienced uncontrollable rage that also seemed to melt away after he began to meditate. Although anger management problems are all too common, our current psychiatric classifications do not deal with anger by itself. Perhaps that is wise, as pathological anger often coexists with other emotional struggles, such as generalized anxiety, depression, bipolar disorder, or PTSD.

Like all normal emotions, appropriate anger, appropriately directed, can have value. It sometimes takes a good jolt of anger to precipitate personal growth or needed social change. Often, however, we encounter in ourselves or others exaggerated and misdirected anger.

By "hostility," psychiatrists mean a mind-set in which the whole world appears threatening. To this defensive mind-set, anger in thought and feeling seems like a necessary baseline state, simply the safe way to deal with outside threats. Anger and hostility are, of course, harmful to relationships of all kinds, wreaking havoc in marriages, families, and the workplace. As I mentioned in the last chapter, anger can be damaging to your physical health. In fact, one review panel investigating behaviors that predispose to heart attacks concluded that hostility is as damaging as (or more so than) high cholesterol, high blood pressure, and cigarette smoking.[15]

As I have listened to the stories of people who meditate, reduction of anger emerges as a common theme. Again and again, people talk about how helpful TM has been at relieving excess anger and how that, in turn, has improved their relationships and general quality of life. You might want to watch out for more examples of this pattern in the stories that follow.

One of my favorite quotes from Lewis Carroll captures the blind destructiveness of rage.

"I'll be judge, I'll be jury," said cunning old Fury.
"I'll try the whole cause and condemn you to death."

Like the Fury in the poem, fury in the real world mindlessly becomes judge and jury and rushes to judgment. By calming the mind, TM can slow down the impulse to be rageful (or even just irritable), so that we can moderate our behavior even when provoked.

5

THE SCHOOLBOY WHO PULLED OUT HIS HAIR

Attention, Priorities, and Effectiveness

> But Fidgety Phil,
> He won't sit still;
> He wriggles and giggles,
> And then, I declare,
> Swings backwards and forward,
> And tilts up his chair.
>
> —*THE LANCET*
> *(Britain's preeminent*
> *medical journal),* 1904

THE POEM OF Fidgety Phil, above, is probably the first reference in the medical literature to a problem that proves to be widespread in our schools: attention deficit disorder (ADD) or attention deficit hyperactivity disorder (ADHD). In this chapter, I will explore how Transcendental Meditation might be able to help people with these extreme difficulties in attention, concentration, and focus. Of even greater interest perhaps—at least to those who do not have ADHD—is what we can learn about the effects of TM on attention and effectiveness for almost everybody. We may be "normal" yet at times still have issues with focus, setting priorities, and effectiveness.

To start, consider the following success stories:

SAM: "TM TRANSFORMED MY LIFE"

Sam first realized he had a problem when he was in second grade. When he became excited in class, he couldn't stop himself from blurting things out. After a while, teachers would lose patience with him, throw him out of class, or send him to the principal's office. The more this happened, the less Sam felt in control of himself. In retrospect, Sam realizes he was very impulsive—unable to think through the consequences of his actions before acting. The worst part of the problem was the effect it had on his self-confidence and his feelings of worth as a person. Even today, after years of success, Sam has to battle that self-esteem problem that was ingrained in him as a child. During class he would miss most of what the teacher was saying because something else had caught his attention: he'd be daydreaming, off in his own world. A few teachers recognized Sam's gift for math, but most gave up on him as a lost cause. In the playground, Sam would impulsively get into fights with classmates, so that he had few friends. School was a nightmare for him, both in and out of the classroom.

Sam entered a downward spiral that is all too familiar to people with ADHD and their families. As he puts it, "It was a self-fulfilling prophecy. I acted out impulsively. They treated me as though I was misbehaving, so I acted out more. I started school two or three years behind in social and emotional development, and it just got worse and worse." So bad was Sam's social anxiety in his elementary school years that he didn't even want to walk the dog when the neighborhood kids were around for fear of having to deal with them.

Luckily Sam's parents understood that he had a problem and were very supportive. They switched him from school to school, took him from one professional to another, and provided him with the best care possible in an attempt to find an environment in which their son could thrive. Sam was diagnosed with ADHD in second grade and was prescribed medications, but, as he puts it, "no medication ever really fit me." Finally, in ninth grade, Sam was prescribed the ADHD drug Strattera, which helped him concentrate well enough to get through high school and into college, but it had some unpleasant side effects—insomnia, anxiety, and irritability. In addition, it did not resolve the worst problems caused by his ADHD—the lingering damage to his self-confidence and social anxiety.

After high school, Sam moved on to Georgetown, a prestigious university where the new intellectual demands are hard on all freshmen, let alone one who struggled with anxiety, insomnia, and getting along with people. Once again, Sam felt especially overwhelmed by the social challenges, "the pressure to go out, to always have a good time and be the coolest person on campus." When he resorted to alcohol, that common social lubricant on college campuses, he felt depressed and physically ill the next day. Doubtful that further medical approaches would solve his problems, Sam was looking around for something new to try when he heard about a college research program involving Transcendental Meditation and readily signed up for it.

For Sam, the benefits of meditation were by no means immediate. In fact, over the first six weeks, his anxiety actually intensified. He had developed a good relationship with his TM teacher, however, who coached him along and helped him persevere. Then something changed: He slowly became less anxious, more able to manage his academic work—and was able to converse more easily. He could now listen to others. He felt less stressed and was much less irritable. As he put it, "Being a better communicator, I became a better friend." He began to make good friends. He also became much less impulsive and developed a quiet self-confidence.

After watching him undergo four months of steady progress, Sam's doctor cautiously phased out the Strattera—without any loss of his newfound social talents. That helped, too, because although Sam had benefited from the drug, he was pleased to be rid of its side effects.

Others began to notice the changes in Sam between three and six months after he started meditating. His parents said that they felt TM had given them back their son. When he visited a previous workplace, coworkers were struck by how relaxed he was and said that he seemed like a new person. Although initially Sam felt a need to keep his meditation private, as he became increasingly comfortable with himself, he began to share with others the secret of his newfound calmness and success.

As his ability to concentrate, focus, and set priorities improved, so did his grades. He graduated from college, became a financial analyst, and was snatched up by a large financial firm. He rapidly emerged as the leading producer in his group and was in the top fifty in his firm; since then, other firms have vied to recruit him.

On the personal front, Sam was able for the first time to have a steady girlfriend, and when I last checked, they were engaged to be married. He realized recently just how far he had come when other members of the family began to argue, and he could just sit back without feeling the need to jump into the fray.

Sam says that TM has improved his health, his career, and his relationships with other people: "It has transformed my life."

SCOTT TERRY: A THERAPIST WHO PRESCRIBES MEDITATION

Scott Terry, a psychotherapist practicing near Chicago, knows first-hand how much Transcendental Meditation can help people with problems of attention and concentration. Like many people with ADHD, he has had the condition for as long as he can remember, but it really emerged as a problem in junior high school when he was thirteen.

He recalls, "I was very hyperactive. My brain was going too fast and I couldn't slow it down enough to focus." Scott was so frustrated that "I would literally sit in the classroom rocking in my chair and ripping out my hair so that every desk I sat in would be covered with hair."

Not surprisingly, Scott hated school and especially hated that nobody understood the problems he was having. The teachers often blamed him for his behavior, and his classmates would joke about his rocking. One kid who was known for using drugs asked Scott what drug *he* was taking—because Scott's behavior made it look as if he were on something stronger than anything the other kid had ever tried.

Like many people with ADHD, Scott had other problems as well, particularly the anxiety and depression that often follow ADHD. Though gifted intellectually, Scott also had learning disabilities—he struggled, for example, with spelling and grammar. Unfortunately, traditional medical approaches, like Ritalin and other stimulants, were of little help. As luck would have it, however, Scott had two elder brothers, aged eighteen and twenty at that time, with whom he had a close relationship, and these brothers had learned TM. They had an intuition that Scott might benefit from TM as well and said to him, "You really need this." So, at age thirteen, Scott learned to meditate. The results were astounding: Within a week of learning to meditate, Scott's rocking and hair-pulling completely disappeared. The anxiety and depression also soon lifted.

Scott went on to obtain a doctorate. His dissertation was titled "In Search of the Characteristics of Adults Who Are Gifted and Have a Learning Disability." Scott chose this topic because, as he put it, "My own personal struggle was a similar cognitive and educational one—a war within myself—and school was the sad battleground."

Although as an adult his problems were compounded by a head injury, he recovered and now runs a thriving group practice. He is happily married to a fellow meditator. Scott credits TM with improving his ability to stay on task and organize others. "By being able to reduce my stress and anxiety level, I became able to focus. I could say, 'I need to do this, then that' and do it, instead of getting caught up in the drama of events."

Scott currently reflects on two common thinking patterns in ADHD: the tendency to pull together disparate facts (or to get lost in them), and to hyperfocus—to zero in like a laser on something that catches one's interest. "It's both a blessing and a curse," he says. "The curse is when the disparate facts draw your attention away from where you want it to go, or when you hyperfocus on something unimportant. The blessing is to allow those thinking patterns to pull together facts in a creative and useful way, and to take that intense hyperfocus and make it work for you."

Currently, Scott recommends TM to all of his psychotherapy clients, emphasizing that it is not a panacea and needs to be accompanied by other healthy habits, such as exercise, a good diet, and adequate sleep. I echo this advice. Sometimes if people embrace a treatment expecting a miracle, they fail to appreciate a modest but very meaningful improvement. Also, as you will see repeatedly in this book, TM is usually only part of a solution, albeit an important part.

As Sam's and Scott's stories both show, people with ADHD suffer from a lot more than problems with attention. They often have associated anxiety, depression, and impulsivity. They are more likely to smoke and have a harder time quitting.[1] As we will see, people with ADHD also often have a hard time getting tasks accomplished because of their so-called "executive function difficulties" that are often part of the condition.

It is possible, of course, that Sam and Scott are just isolated success stories of the "unexplained miracle" sort that sometimes occur in medicine. Or maybe their strong desire to be well produced a powerful placebo effect. I find those ideas unpersuasive, however, for several reasons. When I hear a story such as Sam's, involving multiple treatment attempts over many years with limited success, followed by brilliant success with a different approach, I always prick up my ears. Likewise, because the behavioral changes that Scott describes are so radical and unusual, the researcher in me springs to attention. What is going on here? Above all, both turnarounds have been sustained over so many years that we really should learn more about the matter. It is certainly unlike any placebo effect that I have ever seen! Could TM help others that much and, if so, by what mechanism does it work?

As we have seen, randomized controlled studies are the gold standard by which effectiveness of a treatment is judged. Unfortunately, no such studies are available for TM and ADHD. We do, however, have one promising pilot study on ten students between the ages of eleven and fourteen. In research conducted by Sarina Grosswald, Bill Stixrud, and colleagues in the Washington, D.C., area, the students were taught TM at school; they then meditated in a group for ten minutes twice a day for three months.[2]

These children were selected because they obviously needed help: Most were already taking the stimulants typically used for ADHD, and three were on other psychiatric medications as well. So these were not easy cases and three months is not long—yet it helped.

Sarina and Bill remember two children in particular. Joe was an extremely hyperactive twelve-year-old whom his teacher described as the most challenging student he'd ever seen. Medicines were of little help to him. In an attempt to help Joe contain his excess physical energy, his mother had taken him to karate and gymnastics classes. When it came time to be tested for the study, Joe felt compelled to demonstrate his backflips and karate kicks before responding to the test questions. As Sarina puts it, "Sitting still was not part of his repertoire." It was a challenge to teach Joe to meditate, because it was hard for him even to keep his eyes closed—but eventually he succeeded. The results were remarkable: Finally he was able to sit still and read a book. His mother was overjoyed; his doctor astonished.

A second boy, Mike, age fourteen, would get into fights every day. But three weeks into meditating, he was not getting into a single fight. When provoked in the school yard, he would say, "I'm meditating now," and go on his way. Another boy told Stixrud, "Before learning TM, when someone would bump into me in the hall, I would hit him. Now I ask myself, 'Should I hit him or not?'"

Even more telling than individual stories, from a researcher's point of view, were the results of standardized psychological measures taken before and after the TM program. The researchers found significant improvements in attentional difficulties, depression, and anxiety. The decrease in anxiety was particularly impressive—50 percent! Another startling set of findings from this small pilot study is the significant improvement seen in several executive functions, as measured by a standardized questionnaire.[3] We'll discuss executive function in greater detail later in this chapter, but for now, let me say that after three months of regular meditation, the children were significantly better able to resist impulses and stop inappropriate behavior on their own; to modulate and control their emotions; to begin tasks and independently generate ideas; and to monitor their own behavior. Perhaps most important, the children's working memory improved. Working memory is the ability to hold information in mind in order to complete a task, remember something long term, or develop plans. Working memory is essential for completing tasks that involve many steps, like mental arithmetic or following complicated instructions. It is extremely difficult to improve executive functions, so any technique that offers such promise should cause educators, parents, and students—and, for that matter, all of us—to pay attention.

When Sarina Grosswald suggested the study to Bill Stixrud, he initially hesitated, recalling that in the 1970s some research using relaxation techniques had failed to help people with ADHD, whereas stimulants, by and large, had worked. Then Stixrud thought further: TM *can* be stimulating. It increases EEG coherence between different parts of the brain (as mentioned in chapter 1), and it *does* appear to improve all aspects of executive function. At the time, Stixrud was studying how stress disrupts cognitive function. Now he thought, "If nothing else, by reducing stress, TM might improve attention and executive functions."

Sometimes an early impression of how well a novel treatment works can be gleaned from the response of the staff who know the patients. For example, I recall the buzz among the NIMH ward staff when we first began to use light therapy for seasonal affective disorder. I distinctly remember one of my medical colleagues reporting to me on a patient who had been in the research study for only a week, "I don't know what treatment Joan is receiving," he said, "but she's blooming like a rose! The staff all showed a palpable excitement that some valuable new treatment was emerging—and they were right." I find it significant that Bill Stixrud had similar reactions from school personnel soon after starting his study. He says:

> It was pretty obvious going in that the staff members loved it. They thought, "Oh my God, this is life transforming!" We'd be walking down the halls of that school, and people would stop us to say that it really is different here, now that these kids are meditating. Now, I'm sure that it's never the case that everybody in a group wants to meditate every single day— but this fairly complicated group of kids who had ADHD and other problems was able to meditate twice a day, and it made enough difference to affect the whole school.

In their published paper, the members of Grosswald's team point out several important implications of their findings.[4] First, the study shows that schoolchildren with ADHD *are* capable of practicing TM for ten minutes twice a day, even if they have other emotional problems and are taking stimulants and other psychiatric medications. That in itself is impressive. The team sees TM as particularly well suited to people with ADHD because it is easy to learn and, unlike other forms of meditation, requires neither focus nor concentration. Second, TM appears to diminish the stress, anxiety, and depression that often accompany ADHD. Finally, TM may also help with the executive functioning problems so common in people with ADHD.

I agree with these conclusions and welcome, as others surely will, the possibility of a simple nondrug alternative or supplement to the current offerings for ADHD. As we saw with Sam and Scott, stimulants and other medications, which are often the first line of treatment for ADHD, may be ineffective or only partially effective. Also, some people find drug side effects hard to tolerate. As a clinician who treats people with ADHD and executive functioning problems, I am not inclined to wait for the results of controlled studies. There is very little downside to learning TM and, as you can see from these few vignettes, potentially much to be gained.

If further studies confirm the findings of Grosswald and Stixrud, the number of people who might stand to benefit is considerable. According to the Centers for Disease Control, approximately 7.8 percent of school-age children in the United States (more than four million) met criteria for ADHD in 2003, of whom over half had received medications for the condition.[5] Although estimates vary, approximately the same percentage of adults are thought to suffer from ADHD.

EXECUTIVE FUNCTIONS: KEYS TO EFFECTIVENESS

When I began writing this book, I knew that TM was a powerful technique that could transform people's lives. I had seen it happen. But the biggest surprise to me, after listening to the stories of dozens of people, was the impact of TM on their personal organization, effectiveness, and quality of thinking—in short, on their executive functions.

The term "executive functions" refers to a cluster of abilities that are essential to success in life, both personally and at work. In order to accomplish anything, you must be able to estimate how long the task will take, what materials you will need, and what matters most—your priorities. You must then be able to carry out the necessary steps in a sequence that works, and to persist until the job is done.[6] People who struggle with executive functioning may have trouble with every single one of these steps. For example, they may procrastinate and be able to start work only when they see the situation as an emergency. They often have trouble completing tasks and, over time, their homes and workplaces become littered with half-done projects.

Another set of executive functions involves the ability to respond appropriately to your own emotions. As we saw with Sam and Scott, people with ADHD often have a hard time regulating feelings of frustration, anger, anxiety, or disappointment. They become preoccupied with these feelings, unable to bring them into perspective or to set them aside and focus on a task. They may take too long with a task and be reprimanded, which upsets them so much that the work goes even slower. A vicious circle can develop, the lack of focus and the emotional instability each making the other worse. Or sometimes people who struggle with executive function will impulsively blurt out their feelings at the wrong moment. Or they may yield to knee-jerk responses rather than taking their time to think: Do I really want to do this? Is now the right time? This trait can cause problems both at work and in relationships.

Throughout this book, you will find many stories of people who report improved ability to organize themselves, set priorities, and in general function better once they've been meditating for a few months. These reports crop up everywhere, without regard to diagnosis, environment, or emotional factors. You may recall from the previous chapter, for example, Todd, a veteran with combat-related PTSD, who found that meditation helped him become more organized, which in turn helped his relationship with his girlfriend. Likewise, a number of people in our study of TM for bipolar disorder spontaneously reported similar benefits, along with improved ability to inhibit inappropriate emotional expression, such as not losing one's temper. Even when it comes to the very high-functioning people profiled in the chapter on self-actualization (chapter 10), you may be surprised to learn how many credit TM with improving their decision making, their effectiveness, and thereby their success in life.

Isn't it curious to think that a simple technique, practiced twice a day, can make successful people even more so? In order to understand how that might occur, let us consider the part of the brain that coordinates executive functions.

THE PREFRONTAL CORTEX (PFC): THE CEO OF THE BRAIN

The importance of the prefrontal cortex (that part of the brain just behind the forehead) in regulating executive functioning has been known since the mid-1800s thanks to the famous story of Phineas Gage, a construction foreman who at the time was laying railroad tracks in New England. One day, Gage sustained an accident while blasting rock: a thin metal rod shot up through his eye socket and into his brain, damaging his prefrontal cortex.[7] After the accident, Gage underwent a character transformation. Whereas previously he had been described as a shrewd, energetic businessman with a well-balanced mind, afterward he became rude, capricious, temperamental, and unable to follow up on plans or complete projects.[8] In recent years, studies confirmed that people with damage to their PFC have trouble with executive functioning.[9]

In people with ADHD, we see evidence of a more subtle type of problem in the PFC, according to Amy Arnsten, professor of neurobiology at Yale University.[10] For example, imaging studies have shown reduced size and functional activity of the right PFC in people with ADHD. Arnsten contends that the cardinal symptoms of ADHD may all arise from weakened PFC regulation of behavior and thought. The PFC has extensive connections to other parts of the brain through which it regulates attention and action, inhibiting inappropriate thoughts and behaviors and coordinating goal-directed actions.

Arnsten points out that proper functioning of the PFC is critically dependent on the presence of certain neurotransmitters in proper concentrations, notably norepinephrine (NE) and dopamine (DA). You may recall that NE is one of the primary chemicals released in response to stress (chapter 3). Studies by Arnsten and others have shown that either too much or too little release of these two chemicals in the PFC impairs its functioning.

As with Goldilocks's porridge, ideal PFC functioning requires that the concentration of NE and DA be just right. When this occurs, we are awake and interested (corresponding to the long-held observation that people learn best in a state of calm alertness). When NE and DA systems are underactive, which may occur when we are tired or (chronically) in people with ADHD, we tend to become fatigued or bored. Conversely, under stress these systems become overactive, which can result in distractibility and difficulty setting priorities—behaviors that also occur in people with ADHD. At either extreme of neurotransmitter activity, attention and executive functioning deteriorate.

Most of the stimulants and other medications that are helpful for people with ADHD boost the release of DA, NE, or both in the prefrontal cortex. Arnsten theorizes that these chemicals may be deficient in the PFC of people with ADHD, which might explain how these medications work. It may also explain why people with ADHD tend to get bored unless they are engaged in something novel or exciting.

On the other hand, under conditions of stress, the amygdala sends signals to the PFC, causing the release of large amounts of DA and NE. These high concentrations of DA and NE may impair PFC functioning, and may also result in a clinical picture that resembles ADHD.[11] Sarina Grosswald has pointed out that people who are under stress often struggle with concentration and organization, memory problems, flawed judgment, and short temper—all symptoms that will sound very familiar to someone with ADHD. Grosswald speculates that many children diagnosed with ADHD may actually be suffering from the symptoms of stress instead—which might explain why stimulants aren't always successful. In reflecting on his own anxiety and difficulties before learning to meditate, Bill Stixrud says that he behaved functionally like someone with ADHD—unable to sit still for very long without distracting himself to relieve his anxiety.

It is likely that different people with ADHD develop their symptoms as a result of different types of brain chemical and neurological disruptions. For example, some may have too little DA and NE released into their PFC, while others may have too much. Bear in mind, however, that Arnsten's pioneering work probably represents an early (though very important) attempt to explain ADHD in terms of brain chemistry and much more can be expected from future research.

Like the CEO of a company, the PFC is constantly evaluating how the brain should be allocating its attention. Which inputs should be put on hold and which deserve immediate action? Just as an effective CEO runs a company, so an effective brain governs an individual's decisions and actions. There are of course exceptions—for example, when the fire marshal sounds the alarm and tells everyone, including the CEO, to leave the building immediately. Likewise in emergencies, as when you encounter a snake, the amygdala takes control and propels you into action without you having to give the matter much thought.

As I discussed in the last two chapters, people under severe or chronic stress and those with anxiety disorders have too many false alarms going off. The PFC is overwhelmed by too much DA and NE, and the individual is unable to act properly. If these alarm bells can be modulated—for example by TM, which might reduce the release of DA and NE into the PFC—then the brain's CEO can exert a more powerful influence and govern the individual more effectively. As we saw with Sam and Scott, people with ADHD are also under a lot of stress, not just for all the ordinary reasons that make life hard for young people these days, but because they *also* have problems with attention and executive functioning. By reducing their stress and decreasing the release of these neurotransmitters, TM may help children with ADHD settle down. I recognize that I am suggesting that both boosting NE and DA activity in the PFC (for example, by stimulant medications) and decreasing their activity (for example, by TM) may be helpful to people with ADHD. This apparent paradox—if true—has yet to be resolved.

THE ADHD OF EVERYDAY LIFE

The abilities to concentrate, focus, and be effective are not all-or-nothing gifts. Like other traits, they exist on a spectrum—most of us function between the extremes. That is why many of us who might not carry an ADHD diagnosis or live in chaos would nevertheless like to be *more* attentive, focused, and effective. You might say we're all "a little bit ADHD"—which is becoming more and more "normal," given the way our lives are flooded with stimuli.

The way the human brain works, our attention gets grabbed by novelty—an excellent way to be for most of human history. You and I are here today in part because our ancestors paid more attention to a ripple in the high grass than to the grass as a whole. The ancestor who noticed a lion stalking at the very edge of his visual field might have passed on his genes more successfully than the one who focused only on the path ahead.

Nowadays, however, the prizes (at least in school) go mostly to those who "stay on task." This becomes harder and harder to do, however, as we almost all live in an environment where things constantly bleep, bling, flash, or pop up! The modern environment seems designed to forcibly grab our attention, even in our own homes.

Over two centuries ago, long before the cell phone, the Internet, or, for that matter, the electric lightbulb, William Wordsworth put it best with his prophetic words:

> The world is too much with us; late and soon,
> Getting and spending, we lay waste our powers.

Meditation helps because it gives us a break from the breakneck pace of the world. It lets the mind . . . slow . . . down . . . so that we can think more calmly and clearly. Since I started meditating, I have noticed that many things that once seemed so urgent now seem less so. This de-escalation can happen even as the gift of a single meditation session. I may sit down to meditate thinking that something is a big problem, then after a mere twenty minutes, conclude that it's not such a big deal after all. Maybe my PFC is quieting down the amygdala, which is less likely to fire off a false alarm. Whatever the reason, over months and years of meditation, I hear fewer internal alarm bells, and I have become better able to concentrate and make good decisions.

How might this happen? You may recall from the introductory chapter that during transcendence there is an increased density of alpha waves—the type of brain rhythm found during relaxation—in the frontal parts of the brain. Also, there is greater brain wave coherence in the frontal areas, meaning that the waves are working in a more coordinated way. These changes may explain how TM helps the brain's CEO to govern from the top down, rather than allowing the fire marshal to run the show.

6

HELPING THE SPIKES
AND VALLEYS
Meditation and Moods

> I have not felt my usual self since a year
> ago. The last five months since I have been
> medicated I have felt numb, emotionless
> and lethargic. I have become cynical that I
> will ever return to the person I was. This
> has left me hopeless and often suicidal.
>
> —PAUL

THE ABOVE LINES were written by Paul, at that time an aspiring filmmaker in his mid-twenties, in anticipation of his first consultation with me. Paul is the young man I mentioned in the introduction, whose persistent encouragement led me to start meditating again—and ultimately to write this book. By the time he came to me, Paul had already been whipsawed around by the mood swings of manic depression, suffering first a bout of depression, then a wild mania that landed him in jail.

Paul was transferred to a hospital, where his mania was reversed with large dosages of medications, which caused unpleasant side effects. Then the mania was followed by depression, as is often the case. Here's how Paul describes this sequence of events:

The drugs evaporated my emotions, leaving me lethargic, sedate, numb—my brain moving about as quickly as a snail on Valium with its tail stuck to a trail of molasses. When the drugs finally brought me down, all side effects failed to compare to the misery of the bipolar depressive phase—six months of no capacity for pleasure, only misery, of trying to sleep at any free moment I had, to escape the pain. Every time I would awake, a dread would sink in from the realization that I was in fact still alive. The little bit of mental energy I had was spent fighting the idea of suicide. After five years of this hell, every ounce of hope, will, faith—and every other thought or feeling that makes a human being feel there is a reason to live—had been beaten out of me. What was left was the vacant ashy remains of a body with no soul, heart, mind, or identity—like a burnt-out, decaying shell of a house that has no reason to still be standing.

When I first saw Paul, he was taking four different medications, but had become depressed again. He also worried that the medications needed to stabilize his moods would flatten out his creativity, which was one of his life's passions. A numb and lethargic life seemed hardly worth living.

Five years later, thanks to hard work by Paul and a team of professionals, his state of mind has radically improved. Here is how Paul sees it currently.

It is very clear to me now—something that I hadn't thought was possible—that every aspect of my psychological state—emotional depth, ability to connect with people, to joke around, my wisdom level, appreciation of things, overall happiness, creativity and work, in terms of intellectual and

emotional depth—is far better today than at any time before
I had bipolar disorder.

"This is all a result of very rigorous living," he adds, and pauses to
assemble a mental list.

I'm always taking medications . . . doing light therapy . . . meditating, exercising, eating well . . . sleeping at the right hours . . .
staying away from drugs—using only minimal amounts of
alcohol. And I have to listen to exactly what my doctors say
and follow their advice to the T. I've learned not to argue with
them—even when I want to resist their advice—and, of course,
I'm continually developing the ability to monitor myself. I have
to stay alert for signs of danger, like waking up at night.

Well, it took a long time to live by those rules and wait
for my optimal state to come back. It took the element of patience to wait and not live in the moment. You think that the
state you're in at the moment is the state you'll live in for the
rest of your life.

"Has all this hard work paid off?" I ask. "Oh yes," he answers without hesitation:

There have been two manias and two depressions since we
started working together, but thanks to my strict program,
there's no brain damage that anyone can detect. My latest
work is the best I've ever done, according to everyone's
opinions.

This is very important for me to remember for the future,
in case I have another mania or depression, so that I don't
fall into a pattern of cynicism that will prevent me from living

according to my healthy habits or—in the worst case—lead
to my suicide.

Managing bipolar disorder, as you may gather from Paul's regimen,
is complex and includes many elements. You might well wonder how
it is possible to tease out which parts of the patient's program are essential—or whether it all is. One of my former patients used to talk
about "adding up 5 percent improvements till we get there." Also,
each person is truly unique. People with bipolar disorder (or any other
condition, for that matter) differ in their lives, their underlying tem-
peraments, and their personal chemistries. So although research shows
we can expect some improvement from important mood stabilizers
such as lithium, in practice, "controlling" manic depression is often like
an ongoing dance. The patient and clinician work along together. We
change one thing and watch what happens. Then we try another. We
work empirically, always trying to make things better. The process may
not always meet the standards of science, but in the real world, trial
and error is often all we have. Even today, medicine remains as much
an art as a science.

Although Paul was already on several medications when he started
TM, he soon experienced some welcome changes. He went from "just
getting by" to exuberance and genuine happiness; from "a place of dry
emptiness with no juice in me" to "genuine well-being and feeling
juiced up." When he meditates regularly, Paul says, "it's like the foundation. It gets me to do the other healthy things." Conversely, whenever he skips TM, he feels "more scattered, less energized and vibrant,
less conscious of myself and my actions—not as much in control.
Things unravel." But when he gets back to his TM routine, he recov-
ers "a high quality of life and happiness." Over time, Paul has learned
to cut any slippage short. The loss of well-being just isn't worth giving
in to unhealthy temptations. Today, he's pretty much a poster boy for
TM—and for excellent control of bipolar disorder.

Inspired by this case, my colleagues and I obtained a grant to study TM in a whole group of bipolar patients, most of whom had both manic and depressive symptoms (often at the same time).[1] The study was controlled by wait-listing: Patients were randomly assigned either to receive immediate TM training (eleven people) or to go on a wait list (fourteen people). Both groups continued with their previous medical routines so that the impact of TM—the variable of interest—would be apparent.

My colleagues and I met with the TM patients regularly to monitor their clinical condition. At the same visits, another team of clinicians, who did not know the treatment condition, assessed the patients' moods by means of standardized rating scales. This is a so-called single-blind treatment design, in which the patients are aware of the treatment they are receiving (as they have to be in the case of TM), but the raters—on whose judgment the conclusions will depend—are unaware of who got what. People in both conditions were asked to call in daily to report that they were doing their meditation (in the TM group) and/or continuing to take their medications (both groups).

Paul, who had been my main source of inspiration for the study, had been of the opinion that TM had helped the most with his mania. I had therefore predicted (based admittedly on this rather slender evidence) that TM would be most effective for the manic elements of bipolar disorder. I was wrong. Although a few people reported a drop in manic symptoms, for the group as a whole there was no apparent effect, good or bad, on mania. Depression, however, did seem to respond—certainly by individual patient reports, as well as on inspection of our results.

Unfortunately, eleven patients are too few to make the results statistically significant. The strength and consistency of the change we saw, however, suggest that if the group had been larger, significant effects of TM on depression might well have emerged. In the language of drug trials, it would be fair to say that we saw "a signal" that TM might well have an antidepressant effect, but that larger numbers of patients, specifically with bipolar depression, would need to be studied to confirm (or disconfirm) this impression.

Three of our research clinicians (aside from myself) were so impressed by the changes they saw in the patients that even before the study was over, they signed up to learn TM at their own expense. You will see why as you read these comments from the patients in our study.

> Salesman in his forties: I'm much more relaxed. There's a lot less anxiety, no hyperness or elongated bouts of depression. The evening TM helps set my mind at ease, and helps me sleep and work on my studies at night.

> Intern in her thirties: I'm less angry and stressed, better able to function at work. I have better focus for longer periods and have been able to decrease my afternoon Adderall [a stimulant].

> Salesman in his fifties: Others say I've seemed calmer. A psychologist friend said if she didn't know better, she'd think I'd changed my medications.

> Retired man in his sixties: I'm much more in control of what happens to me. TM is a tranquil oasis against the self-critical and stormy thoughts I used to have upon awakening. It gives me a sense of peace. And the longer I do it, the more aware I am that I can call upon that experience during the day. My sleep has improved.

> Female massage therapist in her late forties: At the beginning of the study, I was angry and full of rage. There's defi-

nitely been a trend to more even-mindedness, as opposed to going up or down. I feel like I'm cleaning out my brain. It's been years since I've been so deeply relaxed.

Saleswoman in her late twenties: When you have many thoughts in your head, the meditation helps you pluck one out as opposed to having all of them twirling around. It helps to have a quiet place to go to. I like having that place in my head.

Jim, an engineer in his thirties: Since integrating TM into my daily routine, it has helped the spikes and valleys. Normally, if an intensely negative event were to occur, I would be a mess for a week or longer. Now, when I have a similar, al-most exact same trauma, I am out for only a day. So yes, I experience depression. But now I am able to recover much faster. I'm less irritable and much easier to be around. I can handle things more easily. Some people have noticed I'm a lot calmer. Others say I'm a lot less of a pushover. Maybe I'm more resilient. But the biggest effect is that when a stressful event occurs, I know I can take a ten- to twenty-minute break from my day, close my eyes, and meditate. And in that period of time, I'm usually able to level myself off.

TM has a metaphysical quality to it. There is a state of serenity that's fleeting, and it's a pretty decent feeling . . . but there's definitely a biological effect as well. There's some-thing going on with the body here, and it's measurable. Meditation is not just sitting and closing your eyes and then getting up out of your chair after twenty minutes. For those that say that it is a religious experience from the East, I say, "Try it for yourself before you make that kind of judgment because there is a real biological effect."

One of my colleagues' patients—Joanne—a woman in her mid-sixties, had problems reminiscent of Jim's, including bipolar disorder. Although Joanne's mood disorder was well controlled with medications, she still overreacted to other people. If someone honked at her in traffic, she would feel depressed for hours, likewise if a supermarket clerk gave her an angry look. My colleague thought TM might help—and, sure enough, it did. As Joanne points out, "Nobody likes it if someone honks at you or gives you an angry look," but, to her amazement, her depressed responses to other people's rudeness now last no more than a minute.

Another unexpected benefit of TM is that Joanne no longer feels she has to continually please people. Only now does she realize how much work she put into filtering what she said to people so as not to offend them—and how many times she just went along with things she didn't like in order to stay in their good graces. Joanne astounded herself recently when someone invited her to pet his dog, and she replied, "No thanks, I don't like dogs." Joanne compares herself to a young person who is learning how to be assertive without being needlessly offensive. In the process, however, she is having fun practicing her new skill—the ability to say what she means without constantly worrying about how others will feel about it.

Returning to our study, several patients reported increased calmness, improved focus, and improved ability to stay organized and set priorities—no surprise, given TM's known effects on the prefrontal cortex. TM helped bipolar patients improve their executive function, just as it did for people with anxiety disorders and ADHD.

If TM proves useful in managing bipolar depression, it would be of great clinical value, because studies show that people with bipolar disorder spend much more time feeling depressed than manic, yet have fewer effective treatment options.[2] I am happy to report that pharmaceutical companies have recently boosted their efforts to find new treatments for bipolar depression. Even assuming they succeed, however, TM may still fill a great need since we are often at a loss as to how to help people with bipolar depression.

All in all, despite the lack of statistical significance, our study suggests that TM might be very helpful for bipolar patients. In fact, all the clinicians who worked on the study are now referring certain of their bipolar patients, particularly those with residual depression, for TM training—*along with their other treatments*. I put that phrase in italics to emphasize that Transcendental Meditation is not a stand-alone treatment for bipolar disorder. Nor do I recommend that you "give it a try" instead of consulting a psychiatrist. Depression of any sort, whether major depressive disorder[3] or part of bipolar disorder, is a serious matter, and there are established and effective treatments that should be put in place first. If you have a bipolar diagnosis and are considering adding any intervention (including TM) that might affect your mood, be sure to check it out with your doctor first.

One important observation was how few side effects occurred. One man complained that if his meditation was disrupted by work phone calls that he was not at liberty to ignore, he would develop headaches. A few people reported "disturbing memories" during their TM training or practice. In general, however, people with bipolar disorder seem able to meditate easily and without problems.

Nevertheless, this is perhaps a good moment to address an important aspect of any treatment—side effects.

SIDE EFFECTS OF TM

Of all the treatments I recommend to my patients, TM is among those with the fewest side effects. That being said, there is *no* treatment worth anything that has zero side effects. That applies to psychotherapy, light therapy, exercise, yoga, or any other treatment you can imagine. Like these other practices, if TM is conducted properly, the frequency of side effects is very, very low.

Three categories of side effects that I have encountered in people practicing TM are: (1) headaches or dizziness if the session is interrupted and the person does not emerge from meditation gradually as instructed; (2) difficulty falling asleep, which almost always happens only when someone meditates late in the evening (meditating at night is not recommended by TM teachers); and (3) flashbacks or disturbing memories that emerge during meditation. These are rare in people without significant emotional problems. Disturbing memories may also occur in other therapy settings, such as psychotherapy. These side effects are almost always manageable within the context of the relationship between the teacher and student. If anyone reading this develops side effects during TM, be sure and contact your teacher, who should be able to help you work through it easily. People with significant emotional problems or who are under the care of a psychiatrist, or both, should discuss this with the teacher before learning to meditate. It is part of a questionnaire that new meditators are asked to complete before training begins. Where necessary, the teacher can then work with the psychiatrist to minimize the chance of side effects—or be ready to deal with them should they occur.

HOW MIGHT TM HELP DEPRESSION?

My team and I were intrigued by the unexpected finding that TM may relieve depression, and brainstormed potential explanations to account for it. As you can see from the following list, we had no shortage of ideas.

▶ As mentioned in the chapter on anxiety, TM helps people feel calmer and improves attention. Since depressed people often experience anxiety, irritability, and poor concentration, a decrease in these symptoms might help them feel less depressed.

▶ Depressed people often ruminate. TM tends to stop repetitive thoughts that loop endlessly back on themselves and may help depressed people let go of their ruminations.

▶ People report TM to be a pleasant experience, look forward to their sessions, and often notice benefits soon after starting to meditate. This offers hope and a sense of having some control over one's body and emotional reactions—a sense of control that is often lacking in depression. Being able to retreat twice a day to an oasis away from the continual sadness of depression allows depressed people to have a part of the day that they can count on for some relief, and upon which they can build a greater sense of peace.

▶ Often when people are quite depressed, they are unable to refocus their thoughts in the way prescribed by cognitive behavior therapy, a standard form of treatment for depression. TM doesn't require focusing or refocusing thoughts as it is an effortless technique that a depressed person can usually master.

▶ TM may reduce the fatigue and lack of energy so common to depressed people by inducing its well-documented state of "restful alertness."

▶ Depressed people often show signs of an increased stress response as evidenced, for example, by sleep disruptions and elevated blood levels of glucocorticoid hormones. The well-known ability of TM to reduce stress may help correct these abnormal stress responses.

▶ TM is a structured activity, and structuring the day often helps depressed people.

▶ Doing something like TM, which is generally considered to have many health benefits, may improve self-esteem, which is often low in depressed people.

Unfortunately, to my knowledge, there is currently no other research available on the effects of TM in bipolar disorder, though I hope our findings stimulate others to explore the topic. But as of the time of writing, what you read here sums up the state of our knowledge about the effects of TM on bipolar disorder.

DEPRESSION: A BEAST WITH MANY FACES

By now, most people know that when we talk about depression in a clinical context, we don't mean mere sadness. Though most depressed people are in fact sad, they also suffer many other agonies and indignities: pervasive loss of pleasure; disruptions of sleeping, eating, and sexual interest; sluggish thinking and acting; withdrawal from friends and family; impaired self-esteem; pessimism and suicidal ideas. As you can imagine, major aspects of a person's life, including work and relationships, may suffer.

Without going into detail, I want to point out that depression is a beast with many faces (Sir Winston Churchill called it his "black dog"). I have already shown you one face—bipolar depression, where the depressed symptoms occur in someone who also has had manic symptoms. But many people with clinical depression have never been manic. These people are said to suffer from major depressive disorder (MDD).[4]

This diagnosis is a bit of a grab bag, because people with MDD often differ from one another in both severity and symptom profile, which is relevant when considering whether TM might help a particular depressed person. For example, a profoundly depressed person may be too slowed down and lethargic even to speak or feed himself. Such a person probably could not learn the technique. Others, however, may be excellent candidates, particularly people who have not fully responded to medications. Look back at the list of possible ways that TM might help depressed people and you will see how TM might give that extra boost—that extra 5, 10, or 15 percent—to someone who feels partly better but not yet quite himself. I would also recommend TM for people who feel both depressed *and* anxious—two unpleasant emotions that often go together. As we saw in chapter 4, TM can often reduce anxiety. Finally, TM might help depressed people who cannot tolerate the stresses of daily life because they react so strongly. In other words, TM may help depression in those people with overactive fight-or-flight responses, such as the people we met in chapter 4.

In the first of the following two stories, anxiety was a prominent part of the landscape, while the second features a woman with marked reactivity to criticism and rejection. These features may account for their excellent responses to Transcendental Meditation.

JIM: Getting Back to Medical School

Jim Bray was a second-year medical student at Loyola University in Chicago in the mid-1970s when he dropped out because of depression:

> I found it very difficult to concentrate and do work I'd pre-
> viously had no problem with. I was sleeping a hell of a lot
> more, as many as eleven or twelve hours a day, which was
> not conducive to success at medical school. I lost my appe-
> tite and had no interest in things. I think overlying the de-
> pression was a huge amount of anxiety as well. Medical
> school is just the beginning of a very long hard haul, you
> know. The training can be so *daunting* once you see how
> much there is to know, and I got to thinking I couldn't do it.
> Like so many people who are depressed, it was building up
> for months, but I kept it hidden because of the stigma at-
> tached to depression back in those years.

Finally, Jim took leave; he went home to his family and consulted a psychiatrist, who treated him for a few months with imipramine, an antidepressant commonly used at the time. Jim developed side effects but felt no benefit. Then he happened to see an ad for TM in his hometown newspaper and signed up to learn. Here's how he describes the experience:

> The amazing thing was that the effect was almost immedi-
> ate. From the first session I felt like the depression was lifted.
> My senses were sharper. I was just filled with an internal joy
> that didn't exist before. I don't think I ever experienced any-
> thing quite like it.

On reflection, Jim believes that had he not begun to meditate, he would have dropped out of medical school. As it was, he discontinued his antidepressants, returned to school, and went on to become an obstetrician and gynecologist. He routinely recommends TM to those of his patients who are anxious or depressed, often with positive results.

His wife and five adult children have also learned TM—without his prodding. Jim says of his transcendent experiences:

> It's almost like a touch of heaven. And the nice thing about it is that the longer I meditate, the more I am able to carry that sense outside of the meditation session. So I'm fortunate in that I feel happy most of the time, almost like being in love. I think that feeling so happy is primarily because I keep meditating. It's like exercise—if you're not doing it regularly, the effect is going to wear off. But I can honestly say that I've had very few bad days in my life since 1975.

SARA: An Unhappy Fund-Raiser

Sara was a sixty-year-old fund-raiser for a nonprofit organization when she consulted a colleague of mine for depression. Besides many of the usual symptoms—sadness, lethargy, broken sleep—Sara was also agitated, irritable, and highly sensitive to rejection or criticism. When she first came for treatment, she was already on one antidepressant (Lexapro), to which my colleague added a second (bupropion). She did well on that combination for a year, but then work became more stressful. She felt unfairly treated—blamed for problems that were not her fault. Her boss was two-faced, she thought. He would support her when it suited his needs but would "throw me under the bus" when someone had to take the blame. Unfair! Unfair! Sara became irritable and defensive, firing up at even a hint of criticism. Yet when she was alone, she would sometimes brood over the problems. Perhaps she *should* have known. Perhaps it *was* her fault. Perhaps she *was* incompetent—too old to do the job. She'd better hold tight to this job, because no one would hire her. The situation was hopeless.

Although Sara's psychiatrist tried to help with both psychotherapy and medication changes, Sara kept teetering on the edge of clinical depression. Any little stress was enough to push her back down into the dumps—until finally, after eight months of juggling medications, her psychiatrist persuaded her to try TM. She had resisted the idea for months both because of the time commitment and because she could not imagine that it could help. Meditation just seemed too "flaky," not something she'd ever thought of doing.

After practicing TM for just two weeks, however, Sara was already calmer and more relaxed. She enjoyed the quiet place that her mind would go to during sessions, and despite worries about the time commitment, she made her TM sessions a priority. Soon she began to handle criticism better, responding less irritably and defensively. Sara quit doubting herself over any little thing and no longer felt like a failure. Instead, she felt more like an observer. When the office went to war, she could simply take things as they came, without getting enmeshed in the conflict. And as less blame came her way, paradoxically, she lost her desperate need to cling to her job. As her psychiatrist put it, "Six weeks of TM was able to accomplish what eight months of talk therapy and tweaking her medications could not."

Since her recovery, Sara has stayed well with no medication changes—none was needed—*and* she's left her job; she credits TM with empowering her to do so. She concluded that she had been in "a dysfunctional work situation," where the problems were not her problem.

Howard Stern's Mother

Here's a surprise testimonial to TM that you can watch on YouTube.[5] Radio talk show host Howard Stern publicly credits Maharishi Mahesh Yogi and the TM technique with curing his mother's depression and saving her life. He tells the story of how, when he was an eighteen-year-old college student, his mother became profoundly depressed, "on the edge of the envelope." She had just lost her sister, which "threw her into the worst depression I can imagine." He was concerned about her for many years.

One day, while watching the Johnny Carson show in 1973, his mother saw Maharishi Mahesh Yogi as a featured guest. She looked into TM and proceeded to learn the technique. Afterward, when she called Stern, her voice sounded different. "My life's been changed by TM," she said. When Stern went home for a visit, he found that his mother was "super happy, content, had a philosophy of life, and understood that life must go on." A lot of her physical ailments, including her insomnia, were cured. According to Stern, his mother continued to meditate and remained well.

What can we make of these three singular stories involving major depressive disorder? To me, the most striking aspect of the first two cases is how fast Transcendental Meditation began to work. With Jim, the change was almost instantaneous, while Sara was feeling better within two weeks. The story of Howard Stern's mother is, admittedly, thirdhand, but I found it moving to hear how grateful this devoted son is to the technique that made such a difference in his mother's life.

The benefits reported by these three people with major depressive disorder resemble those of the bipolar depressed people in our research study. It may be that TM can help people with many different types of depression.

I won't repeat at length all the ways my team suggested that TM might help depression (see pages 139–40), but here they are in summary: TM reduces stress and anxiety, which may be part of depression. It provides a pleasant retreat at least twice a day that breaks the monotonous gloom of depression. TM also interferes with thoughts that loop back on themselves, which helps depressed people let go of painful ruminations. It provides a structured activity and makes people feel like they are doing something helpful and positive for themselves. And it boosts energy, which depressed people lack.

Whatever TM did for these three people, its effects have been lasting. Jim has not been depressed in the thirty-five years since he first learned TM. Sara remains well.

And if Howard Stern is still talking publicly about the changes in his mother after she learned to meditate almost forty years ago, the results must have been not only transformational, but enduring.

WHAT THE RESEARCH SHOWS

Aside from my group's research in bipolar depression, no systematic studies of the effects of TM on depression have been done. That is, nobody has taken a large group of depressed patients and treated some with TM and others with a control treatment. However, there are to date at least five well-designed studies of people who were selected for reasons *other* than being depressed, but whose mood was measured as part of their overall evaluation, both before and after they learned TM.

For example, in two recent National Institutes of Health-sponsored studies of older minority men and women at risk for cardiovascular disease (eighty African American and fifty-three Native Hawaiian), Sanford Nidich and colleagues at Maharishi University compared Transcendental Meditation with health education. As part of this study, researchers evaluated the mood levels of study participants, using a standardized depression scale.[6] In both studies, meditators fared significantly better than controls with regard to depression scores over a nine- to twelve-month period.[7] In the study of African Americans, the TM group experienced twice as large a reduction in depression scores as did the health education control group (45 percent versus 22 percent less depressed), while in the study of Native Hawaiians, the TM group had a 14 percent reduction in depression scores, whereas the control group's scores actually increased by 12 percent. (In other words, overall, the TM group felt less depressed and the controls felt more depressed.)

In a third study, Nidich and colleagues divided 296 university students in the Washington, D.C., area randomly into two groups: One group received TM training while the other group was put on a waiting list for TM. Once again, compared after three months with the control group, the meditators rated as significantly less depressed.[8] Their depression scores dropped 38 percent compared with the wait-list people, whose scores remained unchanged.

A fourth study compared TM with a corporate stress management methodology in forty-four employees of a federal government agency. These people had volunteered to participate in what was described as "a three-month stress management program."[9] After three months the TM group showed greater improvement in both depression and anxiety. Interestingly, both groups were retested three years later. Even though the TM group had received no further program support or instructor contact, almost three quarters of them were still meditating—and still holding on to their gains against depression and anxiety.[10]

In a final study, Ravishankar Jayadevappa, a researcher at the University of Pennsylvania, and colleagues compared TM with a health education control in twenty-three African American patients over fifty-five years old, all of whom had recently been hospitalized for cardiac failure. After six months, the TM group scored significantly better on a standardized depression rating.[11]

Unlike many of the earlier studies on TM and mood, these five projects all incorporated important design features, specifically: (1) the use of a control group; and (2) random assignment to TM versus control groups. I find it encouraging that these well-designed studies appear to confirm earlier, less rigorous experiments showing that TM can improve the symptoms of depression. So while the pickings may be scanty, the results are consistent: TM significantly improved mood in several varied populations.

CONCLUSIONS

While I could easily retreat to that old shibboleth "More research is needed," I find the evidence for TM as an adjunctive treatment for depression to be quite encouraging, specifically:

- several promising case histories and anecdotes involving both bipolar depression and major depressive disorder

- five controlled studies in which TM improved mood in a variety of groups (though these people were not specifically selected for having clinical depression)

- many plausible explanations for how TM might alleviate the symptoms of depression

A recent meta-analysis by Jay Fournier, of the University of Pennsylvania, and colleagues stirred up a brouhaha by suggesting that antidepressants don't work at all for people with mild to moderate depression.[12] As a clinician who has been treating depressed people with antidepressants for more than thirty years, I don't share their conclusions. Richard A. Friedman of Cornell University offered a rebuttal in the *New York Times* that I found more persuasive.[13]

Nevertheless, the controversy did raise the question as to whether antidepressant medications have been oversold. Certainly that question has crossed my mind, as I am sure it must have done for many other psychiatrists. Although we depend on antidepressants as a mainstay in treating depression, again and again we see their limitations. Conversely, I believe that other forms of treatment for depression— like talk therapy, for example—have been *undersold*. When did a representative of a major corporation last come into a doctor's office with free pens and coffee mugs, asking the doctor for some time to discuss the latest form of psychotherapy? But I digress!

I suggest that TM be considered as a nondrug therapy when a person has not fully responded to conventional treatment—*not as a standalone therapy* (though it worked that way for Jim Bray). It may work as a stand-alone treatment for people who are simply down in the dumps but don't have true major depression (check note 1 on pages 286–87 for a guide in this regard). TM is easy to learn, inexpensive in comparison with other treatments, and can be practiced effortlessly anywhere and at any time without special equipment. Recommending TM for my depressed patients—and the encouraging early results that I have seen—reminds me of my experience with light therapy for seasonal affective disorder. When we began studying that treatment in the early eighties, we thought we might be dealing with a small number of special cases who might stand to benefit from a treatment that seemed wacky at the time. Yet it turns out that SAD is very common and that light therapy is widely useful. In just the same way, the people you have met in this chapter—like Jim and Sara and Howard Stern's mother—may really be the tip of a huge iceberg of depressed people who might benefit from TM. According to the National Institute of Mental Health, in any given year, 14.8 million people in the United

States suffer from major depression, and 5.7 million from bipolar disorder. If even a fraction of these people might derive some benefit from TM, we should consider it as a treatment option.

Those of us who have worked with depression for many years, as I have, know how serious it can be—life-threatening, even. So, despite my upbeat conclusion, I do need to close with a warning. If you or someone you know is not just down in the dumps, but clinically depressed, please seek (or refer that person for) professional help. Do not try TM as a substitute for conventional care—rather, save it as a supplement after conventional methods have been tried.

7

SILENCING THE BUBBLE MACHINE

Addiction and Recovery

It's not true that life is one damn thing
after another—it's one damn thing over
and over.

—EDNA ST. VINCENT MILLAY

IT IS ONE of life's great injustices—or so I am often told—that one
man can go home and enjoy a glass of wine with dinner and leave it at
that, whereas another man feels compelled to finish off the bottle . . .
then open the next. Likewise, how unfair it is—I often hear—that one
woman can take just a few tokes at a party whereas her friend walks
around in a marijuana-induced haze because she just can't get enough.
By the same token, why is it that one man comes home to his wife,
makes love, and falls happily asleep, while another, married perhaps
to an equally beautiful and loving woman, is repeatedly on the prowl?
These are some of the mysteries of addiction, the topic we will consider next.

This chapter's opening quotation is from Pulitzer Prize–winning
poet Edna St. Vincent Millay, who struggled with alcoholism and drug

addiction for years. "One damn thing over and over": The phrase captures the repetitive, obsessive, helpless quality of an addict's life.

Scientists believe that in certain people the tendency to addiction is genetic—an addictive drug or behavior can hijack the brain's pleasure centers. The addict becomes focused on one or more particular pleasures, eventually to the exclusion of all else. Whatever the addiction, over time it takes more and more to produce any pleasure, and the intervals get shorter and bleaker. Edna St. Vincent Millay wrote famously about burning her candle at both ends and enjoying the light, even though she knows the candle will not last till morning. So it is with addicts: They burn up their brain's pleasure chemicals even though they know—or ought to know—that they will have to pay for their brief pleasures in disruption and damage to their relationships, their work, their bodies, and their brains.

What can be done? Treatments are available for alcoholism and drug addiction, including medications, counseling, and twelve-step programs. Too often, however, the addicted person relapses—often several times, even among those who eventually kick the addiction. It follows that any new supplemental approach should be welcome both to those who suffer addictions and those who try to help them. Let's consider, then, what Transcendental Meditation can offer, starting with a few individual examples. Then we will consider the research on addiction.

MOBY: GETTING RID OF UNWELCOME GUESTS

The multitalented musician Moby, who sings and plays keyboard, guitar, bass guitar, *and* drums, has been called "one of electronic music's all-time biggest artists" and "one of electronica's most visible presences for nearly two decades."[1] Moby's real name is Richard Melville Hall; his nickname comes from the classic novel *Moby-Dick* by Herman Melville, a distant relative of his. As you will see from his comments, Moby is a thoughtful, intelligent, and spiritually alert man. Moby's problems with alcohol are a matter of public record, and he is willing to speak plainly about them. "My vice was always drinking," he says, "and I'm actually grateful that I never have to question whether I'm an alcoholic or not. I have the weight of evidence—a few thousand times where I tried to go out and drink in moderation, but was incapable of it."

When we spoke, Moby had been sober for a few years. He credits TM with helping him get sober, but only as one part of a healthy lifestyle that includes exercise, prayer, being part of a good community, having good friends and family, and attending twelve-step meetings. As he points out, "If someone were to be doing tons of cocaine and eating junk food and watching TV all day, doing TM twice a day probably wouldn't help too much." Yet when added to his self-care program, Moby finds that TM has had a specific effect.

> One reason I drank was that my brain would get to a level of agitation, and one thing that was incredibly effective at diminishing the agitation was alcohol. For me, TM is an effective tool at diminishing agitation. And because it was agitation that often led me to drink, its lack—the lack of restlessness—makes me less inclined to do so.

An interest in TM did not come easily to Moby: "My mother was a spiritual seeker," he explains. "And as is true for a lot of people in the sixties and seventies, there was a period when she flirted with TM. So I assumed that TM was like EST or some other strange cult, that it was for hippies who'd taken too many drugs and needed to come down somewhere." Given that mind-set, it was interesting for Moby to have TM presented by filmmaker David Lynch, a person he respected, as a "simple and effective practice."

Moby had already tried many other methods to contain his "pervasive sense of restlessness." As he observes, "We live in a culture where ostensibly the cure to restlessness is having the perfect home, perfect job, perfect girlfriend, etc. And, as I'm sure is true for most people, once you have all of these and you *still* have a sense of restlessness . . . you have to look further afield." Looking afield, he tried a number of meditative practices, including some simple mindfulness meditation, object meditation, and concentrating on various thoughts. "I would go to Whole Foods and buy different New Age magazines," he says now. "I'd read about different meditative practices and try them all."

In the end, he found that TM worked best for him because of its simplicity. "There are no bells and whistles," he says. "There is no dogma attached to it, no compulsion whatsoever. And I find the simplicity of it to be very effective."

Moby had been doing TM for about two years when we spoke, though not always 100 percent of the time. "I'm actually grateful that I've had a sporadic TM practice," he says, because it makes everything clear. "When I do it regularly, I'm more calm, less irritable, and generally a bit happier. When I'm doing it every day, the quality of my life internally just improves."

He has also noticed that TM enhances his creativity in ways he explains as follows:

> I think that TM basically turns down the craziness and noise
> that's going on in most of our heads, that we might not even
> be aware of. It gives us a sense of calm, and from that calm a
> better perspective, so that we realize whence our choices are
> proceeding. For myself, what I've learned is that a lot of my

decisions are fueled by desperation. So if I'm working on a record, sometimes I feel that compulsion or desperation that I have to make the best record *ever,* and it has to sell well, and it has to be validated by critics and fans. And I realize that's all proceeding from a place of fear and desperation. It does seem, in a lot of the actors and writers and musicians and creative people I've met, that their creativity is fueled by fear and the need to be validated. And what a good meditation does is, it just helps you remove the fear and desperation . . . and you're left with the joy of creation. When I meditate, I find I do things for more honest, more enjoyable, and healthier reasons.

So, I think of a good meditation practice like TM as turning the heat down on a pot of water. It just calms everything down. Another analogy: It's like my brain is an overcrowded party, and TM is making the unwanted guests go away. And so suddenly, instead of having seventy-five people in a room that holds fifty, after a good meditation, the unwanted guests leave and you're left with a neurological environment that's a lot more manageable.

Moby recognizes that alcoholism, like other addictions, is often a relapsing and remitting condition. Indeed, in granting me an interview, he expressed concern that should he resume drinking and this fact become public, it would somehow diminish the reader's opinion of TM—or, for that matter, the other elements of his healthy lifestyle.

This concern was wise—not because of anything particular to Moby, but because of the nature of addiction. No matter how well controlled an addiction seems, relapse is always possible—and so is abstinence. Many addicts do quit and stay clean and sober at their first try, if they are highly motivated and understand the issues. It's not uncommon, however, for people with addictions to have one or several relapses before they finally succeed—which is why, for some, a realistic goal can be fewer and fewer relapses, with longer and longer sober periods in between. Obviously the ultimate goal is no more relapses, but knowledgeable addicts recognize the danger of overconfidence—even after thirty years of healthy living—by referring to themselves as "recovering" rather than "recovered." Twelve-steppers assert on a daily basis the modest but achievable goal of abstinence "one day at a time," and they pay respect to the power of addiction by referring to the illness as "cunning and baffling."

As a psychiatrist, I can testify that humility in the face of this formidable adversary actually strengthens the person with addiction. Paradoxically, remembering the ever-present risk of relapse decreases its likelihood.

JONAH: FILLING A HOLE IN THE SOUL

Jonah, a sixty-seven-year-old man from a southern town, has been in active recovery for twenty-nine years. For twenty-eight of those he has been a certified substance abuse counselor. And, as you can imagine, when it comes to addiction, he knows what he's talking about. His is a harrowing, but all too common, tale of the ravages of addiction, both for the addict and for those who cross his path, literally and figuratively. I include it here in detail both because of the key role that TM has played in his recovery and because of his profound insight into the nature of addiction. Here is Jonah's story, in his own words.

> I believe I was born an addict, that the predisposition for the illness was always there, the characteristic of: never enough,

don't know when to quit, highly sensitive to feelings and the world. Those kinds of things were there before I ever took a substance.

Genetically speaking, my mother had an uncle who was an addict, and she was a prescription addict. On her side of the family there are eight of us in my generation who are addicts. I use the word "addict" to mean someone who continues to use a mood- or mind-altering substance in the face of negative consequences, so the substance is not relevant. There are uppers, downers, and outers, and they all have their own particular getting-high phenomena and detox phenomena. But my concern is with recovery, which is the same process for all addicts. That includes the behavioral ones such as sex and gambling.

I believe that addiction at its root is a hole in the soul, a spiritual illness. It's the need for more, more, more. And when you fill the hole with junk—alcohol, drugs, sex, whatever—the hole is temporarily sated, but it just gets worse. The drugs and behaviors are the individual's attempt to get back into balance, but we overshoot. We've got broke stoppers. I've seen people in recovery substitute one addiction for another. I say "addiction," not "drug of choice," because I don't believe an addict has a choice. Addiction is the *loss* of choice.

As the addiction grows it takes over a person's life. As someone said, "Your brain begins to make decisions without consulting you." You have no moderator, no watcher on the threshold, no observer-self. That controller gets taken over by the addiction—if it was ever there to begin with.

The first drug I used was nicotine, which I didn't think of as a problem. The next was alcohol. When I took that substance into my body, it was like I could talk, I could walk—I felt *whole*. It felt like I'd just been having an alcohol deficiency. So my first use of alcohol was already not social. I got drunk, passed out, blacked out, got into trouble. My active addiction went from age fifteen until thirty-eight, a twenty-three-year career of using.

Throughout my life until I got into recovery, whatever I was doing, once I would start, I could not predict when or how or if I would stop. Generally I would go for a month or two without using chemicals, which I would take as an indication that I didn't have problems. But the addiction was always there in the back of my head: When can I do it? How can I hide it? How can I get some money to do it? How can I cover up the last one? Who's not gonna find out? So there was a low-level obsession going on, although I was not even aware I was thinking about it. So the addiction removes you from the here and now. There's this constant thing going on in the back of your mind, a restless feeling. I always wanted to be somewhere else, doing something else, with someone else. I was never satisfied. The minute I got something, I didn't want it anymore.

We call it "the bubble machine." It's that incessant chatter that goes on in my head. It's an obsession that wears you down and breaks down all your natural barriers. According to the *Narcotics Anonymous* book, it's a fixed idea that takes us back time and time again to our drug of choice or some substitute, to recapture the ease and comfort we once knew. And the obsession is followed by compulsion, so that once I start, I cannot stop of my own free will. If I sit around and obsess about food, I will become gluttonous. If I sit around and look at women in the springtime, I will want to go online and look at pornography. If I'm in a relationship with someone and we break up, I'll want to stalk her.

My use of drugs and alcohol got me into at least twelve motor vehicle accidents. My father used to call me "Crash." One time I was in a head-on collision and the EMTs left me for dead because they couldn't find a pulse. A neighbor came by, recognized the car, and thought he saw signs of life. I was up underneath the passenger side of the car with the front of my head cut open and a huge concussion, blood all over the place. He picked me up, put me in his car, and took me to the emergency room. Now I see that as evidence of some power, some life force, bigger than myself watching over me. At the time, of course, I took credit for my survival myself. I broke the back of the woman in the other car and crippled her for life. At the time, in my addiction, I said it was her fault, that she deserved it. Now I realize that I have to make amends to her and all the others I have harmed [the ninth step of AA]. That's why there's so much passion in my life for talking about recovery and helping others. For ten years I went to the prisons, carrying the message of recovery to inmates—for free. And every day that I help another addict, I'm making amends.

Of course there were warnings, by which I mean black-outs. I'd wake up in the morning and not know how I got home; see grass on the bumper of my car and not know how it got there; go to a jazz festival in Rhode Island and wake up in a park in Boston.

An important aspect of Jonah's addictive history is his addiction to sex and love. At present, this diagnosis is not generally accepted, but having seen many people with the problem, I regard it as an illness, so its diagnosis is entirely legitimate. In fact, if you take all the criteria for alcoholism or drug addiction and substitute the words "love" and "sex" for the drug in question, many love and sex addicts would meet the same criteria as, say, alcoholics. These are people whose pursuit of love and sex is excessive. Despite the damaging consequences of their behavior, they can't stop when they should, which can ruin their lives—not to mention their partners' lives. Anyone who reads even the headlines of newspapers should be able to identify several such individuals without much difficulty.

Sex and love addicts could easily be seen as simply having character flaws—which may also be true, and that is how alcoholism and drug abuse used to be considered. With increased enlightenment, however, I predict that the uncontrollable pursuit of sex and love, along with compulsive gambling and other behavioral problems, will be officially recognized as what they are—addictions. Sex and love addiction is an equal-opportunity affliction, affecting both rich and poor, men and women. In fact, Edna St. Vincent Millay, the writer with whom I began this chapter, is known to have had many lovers, even in the years when she was married (with her husband's knowledge). Some would view this part of her history as the glamorous life of a bohemian poet. My guess, however, is that for Millay, sex had a "one damn thing over and over" quality, as suggested by the closing couplet of one of her famous sonnets:

> Pity me that the heart is slow to learn
> What the swift mind beholds at every turn.

Let's get back to Jonah, with the story of his love addiction in his own words. Warning: The details that follow are gritty and viewer discretion is advised.

My sex addiction started around age eleven when I learned to masturbate. And there again, there was that giddy experience of, "Wow, this is awesome! And I can do it whenever I want! It's mine. Nobody can take it from me, and I don't have to pay for it." Unlike other kids who masturbate, I would have marathon sessions, so much so that it would hurt before I couldn't do it anymore. It took that much to make me stop.

I married someone I never should have married, which was part of my addictive process. I think my disease picked the person I married rather than me choosing. We went to Lake Tahoe and got married while I was in a total blackout, drunk. She was a woman who had two illegitimate children by two different men. She was on welfare at the time and had been sexually abused by her father. Like others with sex addiction, I mistook pity for love, intensity for intimacy. Part of my sex and love addiction was going for the hay fire, that immediate rush, that in-love intoxicated experience of a new romance.

I have spent forty years of my life paying for my indiscretions. I had five children with my wife, none of whom did I plan to have. A couple of them happened during blackouts, and some were rapes of my wife. It was like she wanted a man who would give her children and I wanted someone who would make me look legal on job applications. So I'd get drunk at her and she'd get pregnant at me. And I wouldn't know we were gonna have a kid until I felt a lump in her belly. And that would feed my resentments. You see, addicts have got to have resentments to justify our addictive behaviors.

We say in recovery that sex and love addicts don't have relationships, they take hostages. My wife finally left me because if you live with someone in active addiction, you are being emotionally and mentally abused. By the time she left, even though I never laid a hand on her, she could not be in the same room as me without being physically sick. I was responsible for character assassination, innuendo, sarcasm. I came home one Friday night and my wife said, "How was your day?" I said, "That's it, God damn it, get off my back, leave me alone," and I went off and got drunk at her.

And then there were, of course, hundreds of women. In those days I called them relationships, though of course I was just using them. Just as I could not see myself living without drugs, I also could not conceive of myself living without being half of a couple, without having a woman in my life.

Jonah first saw Maharishi on the Merv Griffin TV show in 1973, shortly after he had joined AA, whereupon he immediately learned TM and loved it. "All my addictions went away. Everything: smoking, drinking, marijuana, sex—it just went away." He explains the effect as follows:

I'd always been seeking connection. And when I connected with things that were impermanent, I was always disappointed, got a resentment, and then would get drunk or stoned. When I transcended, I connected with something permanent, something I'd been seeking all my life, at the relative level. Now I'm finding it at the absolute level, moving the awareness to that level of consciousness. Transcendence treated the hole in my soul.

Now I need to qualify this. At the end of that year I came home one Friday afternoon and my wife had left me and taken the children. They were all gone. And in pursuing her, finding out where she was and where the kids were, I started smoking cigarettes and picked up alcohol again. I moved back into addictions. However, I continued to meditate. That was in 1974. Three years later I got off alcohol and haven't touched a drop since June 24, 1977.

One by one, Jonah's other addictions left him, so that he now leads a sober and celibate life. He is on good terms with all of his children and grandchildren and says his life is "incredibly full and rich." He continues to attend his twelve-step groups and points out that all twelve-step programs encourage prayer and meditation (Step 11) as a means of maintaining recovery. He continues to meditate regularly and routinely recommends it to his clients. "As I've aged, I've added more meditation time to my life. Whereas many people my age become cynical, I'm feeling vigorous and alive and active."

HOWARD STERN QUITS SMOKING

We last encountered radio and TV personality Howard Stern paying tribute to Maharishi Mahesh Yogi for saving his mother's life, helping her emerge from depression by means of TM. At that time, Stern told an audience, he was eighteen years old and had no interest in meditating. Nevertheless, his mother "dragged" him to the TM Center, where he learned to meditate.[2] Although he had no intention of quitting smoking, he reports that within one month of learning he spontaneously ended a three-and-a-half-pack-a-day habit; the cigarettes started to irritate him. Shortly thereafter, he broke his ankle playing basketball—the type of stress that would normally have sent him back to smoking. But this time he had no urge to do so. In addition to helping Stern quit smoking, he credits TM for helping to regulate his sleep and break a long-standing pattern of insomnia. He says it also helped him with his creativity and other aspects of his life.

Here, then, we have three powerful stories in which different types of addiction respond to Transcendental Meditation. As always, the key question is: How typical are these experiences? Do we dare draw any general conclusions?

WHAT THE RESEARCH SHOWS

In contrast to the scarcity of research on how TM affects people with mood disorders or ADD, we know a good deal about the effects of TM on people suffering from addictions. In 1994, Harvard-trained psychologist Charles Alexander and colleagues reviewed nineteen studies conducted between 1972 and 1994. For those readers interested in the details of these studies, I recommend the excellent book by O'Connell and Alexander in which they are published.[3] For the rest of you, here's how I see Alexander's conclusions:

Taken together, all but two studies showed significant reductions in the use of cigarettes, alcohol, and illegal drugs in diverse groups from different parts of the world, including students, elderly African Americans, young Swedish drug users, Vietnam veterans with post-traumatic stress disorder, and severe alcoholics. Six of these studies were rigorously designed, with participants assigned to TM or control conditions, while the other thirteen studies were less well planned. Results were similar, however: TM helped. In general, the longer people had been meditating at study's end, the better the outcome. Because of their superior design, three studies are especially noteworthy.

Geisler studied 115 young people in Germany who were using multiple illicit drugs.[4] The experimental group (76 people) received

TM training in addition to regular counseling, while the control group (39 people) received counseling only. After one year, 45 percent of the TM group had stopped taking any drugs, compared with 15 percent in the control group. After eighteen months, the quit rate for the meditators had risen again—to 89 percent.

Ann Royer prospectively surveyed 324 adult smokers who attended a TM introductory lecture, inquiring about smoking habits and motivation to quit.[5] Of these, 110 decided to learn TM (the experimental group), while the other 214 made up the control group. Two years later, 31 percent of the TM group had quit as opposed to 21 percent of the controls—a statistically significant difference.

This result is more impressive than you'd think, because tobacco is one of the hardest addictions to kick. People who have successfully quit drugs like cocaine and heroin will often tell you cigarettes are harder to give up. Until recent years, AA meetings were notorious for their ambient haze of tobacco smoke—and you can still see a haze of smoke around the outside door.

As you might expect, success within Royer's TM group varied with adherence to routine: For the smokers who meditated as instructed, the two-year quit rate was not 31 percent but 51 percent. A scholar might argue for a selection bias in this study since people chose whether to practice TM or not, as opposed to being randomly assigned. Nevertheless, baseline responses about smoking habits and motivation to quit were similar for the two groups.

In the third study, Edward Taub and colleagues randomly assigned 108 inpatients suffering from chronic alcoholism to four treatment groups: standard drug counseling alone or in combination with TM, and two other control conditions—muscle relaxation feedback and neurotherapy, a form of brainwave biofeedback.[6] They intensively followed their study participants after discharge over eighteen months, at the end of which those in the TM group did best (65 percent abstinent), followed by those receiving muscle relaxation biofeedback (55 percent), neurotherapy (28 percent), and standard counseling alone (25 percent).

As you may recall from earlier chapters, one way to make statistical sense of a grab bag of related studies of different size and design is by meta-analysis. Just to remind you, in meta-analysis, differences between the impact of experimental and control treatments are expressed as "effect sizes." An effect size is considered large at 0.8 units, medium at 0.5 units, and small at 0.2 units. When Alexander and colleagues performed a meta-analysis on the nineteen studies mentioned above,[7] they found that TM was much more effective than control treatments across the board. Transcendental Meditation showed a large effect in treating both cigarette smoking and addiction to street drugs, with other treatments examined coming in a distant second.

Alexander and colleagues present data showing that over time, the use of alcohol and cigarettes decreases in those practicing TM—a sharp contrast with many other approaches for drug and alcohol treatment, where relapse rate tends to increase over time.[8]

HOW MIGHT TM WORK?

The mechanism by which TM helps addicts is not yet clear. It stands to reason, however, that as meditators feel less stressed, anxious, angry, or depressed, they are less likely to resort to addictive substances or behaviors in order to feel better. That was the case for both Moby and Jonah. Moby told me that one reason he used alcohol was to reduce agitation, "to turn the heat down on a pot of water"—something he can now accomplish by meditating. Likewise, Jonah mentioned the power of TM to silence the incessant chatter of the "bubble machine." According to Jonah, "When I got my mantra and transcended, I was able to connect with that deep, silent, blissful, fulfilling, absolute level of life. I felt satisfied."

The mechanism by which Howard Stern decided to quit smoking after learning TM is more mysterious. Even though he had been smoking more than three packs of cigarettes a day, he says they just lost their appeal for him. Others have reported similar experiences, with both cigarettes and other drugs, once they started to meditate.

According to George Koob of the Scripps Research Institute and Nora Volkow, director of the National Institute on Drug Abuse, drug addiction, once established, is a cycle with three stages: "binge/intoxication," "withdrawal/negative emotions," and "preoccupation/anticipation," more commonly known as craving.[9] Imaging studies in both animals and people suggest that separate neural circuits mediate these three phases of the addiction. Bingeing and intoxication largely involve the brain's reward center known as the ventral tegmental area. The physical and emotional pains accompanying withdrawal are associated with the brain's alarm circuitry, the amygdala. Craving involves many parts of the brain, notably one quite familiar to readers of this book— the prefrontal cortex. The transition from "just this once" to addiction involves changes in all of these neural circuits over time, which may begin with the reward centers but ultimately damages the prefrontal cortex as well. That may explain why addicts often make such bad decisions. They lose their capacity to evaluate the relative importance of various aspects of their lives, so that their decision-making potential is hijacked by their need for their preferred drug or behavior.

In earlier chapters, we saw that beneficial effects of TM in people with anxiety or ADHD may work via the prefrontal cortex. That may also explain how TM helps people with addictions. J. Peters, a researcher at the University of Puerto Rico, and colleagues have pointed out that neural circuits for fear and addiction overlap in the prefrontal cortex.[10] He suggests that extinguishing both fear and the tendency to addiction involves these circuits.

It would be of great interest to image the brains of people suffering from addictions both before and after a period of regular TM practice. I predict that we would find changes in the prefrontal cortex (corresponding to better decision making) and the amygdala (corresponding to decreased anxiety and distress).

CLOSING THOUGHTS

You may well wonder: If TM has so much promise for the treatment of drug and alcohol abuse, why did the research on this topic stop in the mid-nineties? I suggest two major reasons—*money* and *fashion*. In America, much clinical research is driven by those with a financial interest in its outcome, notably pharmaceutical companies. There is nothing wrong with this process and I myself have participated in many such studies. At the same time, I have often wondered about the value of spending millions of dollars on, for example, a new antidepressant that is almost identical to an existing generic. In terms of the company's return on investment, I am in no position to argue. Yet this process does tend to leave nonpharmacological treatments out in the cold. After all, nobody is likely to make a fortune teaching TM on skid row. And unlike a drug, which people take every day for years, TM is taught for a onetime fee, which gives the individual a technique that can be used indefinitely.

Public funding for research does exist, of course, but the pot is relatively small and it tends to be influenced heavily by the fashion of the times. Edward O. Wilson, the famous biologist, wrote in his memoir, *Naturalist,* of a time at Harvard, shortly after the structure of DNA was discovered, when suddenly nothing in biology was of interest unless it concerned molecular genetics.[11] That position ignored many important biological discoveries, including Wilson's own work, which dealt with animals at other levels of organization, such as their social behavior.

In a similar way, research on TM for drug addiction and abuse has gone in and out of fashion, rising and falling like skirt hemlines. Given the potential importance of this research, however, I'd say it's time for research on TM and addictions—or, for that matter, on TM and all the other topics in this book—to come back into vogue.

According to the National Institute on Drug Abuse, "drug abuse is a major public health problem that impacts society on multiple levels. Directly or indirectly, every community is affected by drug abuse and addiction, as is every family."[12] The agency estimates that substance abuse costs the U.S. at least $484 billion per year—more than cancer or diabetes. So, if the few individuals profiled here are in any way representative of the millions out there using cigarettes, alcohol, or drugs, if even a fraction of the nineteen TM studies presented here have any merit, surely we should do more to study this simple, practical, and inexpensive technique.

TM is perfectly compatible with other drug treatment approaches and could easily be folded into an overall treatment program. In fact, Moby and Jonah observed that TM helped them maintain their other healthy habits, such as participation in a twelve-step program. Paul, the young man with bipolar disorder profiled in the last chapter, reported a similar benefit. His regular TM practice helped him adhere to the rest of a regimen for preventing mood swings.

I should mention one final, but very important, reason for the decline in research on TM for drug abuse and addiction in recent years: Sometimes, especially in relatively small areas of research, such as TM, a single individual can make a disproportionately large impact. One example is Fred Travis's work on the effects of TM on the brain. But when it came to researching the effects of TM on addiction, the major force was Charles "Skip" Alexander, who also played a key role in understanding the potential of TM to rehabilitate prisoners. We'll talk about that in chapter 9. Tragically, Alexander died before reaching his fiftieth birthday. I wish I had known him, but I can tell you that the impact of his eighty articles is huge, and the legacy of affection and respect that he left behind is palpable.[13]

8

AN ISLAND OF SAFETY
IN A SEA OF TROUBLE
Transformation in Schools

> These days a lot of people my age don't know
> how to sit down and be quiet and relax. You
> owe yourself that down time.
>
> —LESLIE POTTS, *age sixteen*
> *Alumna of Nataki Talibah*
> *Middle School, Detroit*

VISITACION VALLEY MIDDLE SCHOOL sits in the southernmost
part of San Francisco in a poverty pocket. The neighborhood is surrounded on one side by the county line, on two sides by a large public
park, and on the fourth side by the only freeway in and out of San Francisco. As you might expect, the community is very isolated. Many of its
residents live in a housing complex built during the Second World War
for government workers, which the *San Francisco Chronicle* has referred
to as "quite possibly the most dangerous and depressed and decrepit
area in the city."[1] The school sits on the side of a hill, overlooking the
rough neighborhood in the valley.

Jim Dierke was appointed principal of Visitacion Valley in 1999,
the day before the school year began. The superintendent gave Dierke
the news of his transfer with a backhanded compliment: "We're moving

you to Visitacion Valley Middle School," he said. "We couldn't find a suitable principal, so we thought of you." By that time Dierke had been in the educating business for twenty-eight years, often working with children whose learning disabilities were so severe that no one else wanted to teach them.

The school that Dierke encountered the next day was, he says, "a very dysfunctional place, where nothing worked and no one cared if it did or not. There was a murder a week in the neighborhood. I had to start from scratch."

Dierke is by all reports a highly effective leader and a very congenial man. Yet at Visitacion he struggled for years before a turning point came, after he attended a meeting at the Center for Wellness and Achievement in Education (CWAE).[2] There he met Laurent Valosek and James Grant, the two men heading up the CWAE. Both men were longtime meditators and TM teachers. Valosek had been CEO of three high-tech companies, while Grant had been a professor of education and had implemented meditation programs in a number of educational settings. Valosek and Grant had put out a call for principals who might be interested in a Quiet Time Program, and Dierke answered the call.

The Quiet Time Program is so named because all participants are required to be quiet for at least twelve minutes twice a day. Those who wish to learn the TM technique and meditate during that time may do so; the others either sit quietly and rest or read silently. This noncoercive approach reassures any parents or students who fear that TM may violate their religious principles. In fact, once people understand that TM involves no religious beliefs or practices, their theoretical concerns usually evaporate.

Paradoxically, Dierke says that the community's indifference to whatever went on at the school was in one way an advantage: "I was able to try out new and different things," he says. "If I had approached the school district about doing meditation in one of the more affluent schools, I would have been shown the door. Over here it was like, 'Oh, you want to do that? Okay. Sure. Give it a try.'" Dierke was drawn to the Quiet Time Program largely on the basis of a previous observation:

> One day we had to go into lockdown because there had been gunfire in the neighborhood. They were chasing people around and the kids were kind of on edge. I just got on the horn and said I wanted everyone to put their heads down on their desks and be quiet for ten minutes. And I noticed afterward that there was a profound change within the school, on that particular day, as to how people treated each other. I thought, "Gee, maybe there's something to that."

Valosek and Grant suggested that Visitacion Valley start the Quiet Time Program with all the children in the sixth and seventh grades, and compare those children with the eighth-graders, who were not yet in the program. The difference was soon apparent. Within four months, the multiday suspension rate, which reflects serious behavioral breaches, dropped by 45 percent for the sixth and seventh grades. The eighth-grade control, however, followed the usual spring pattern of *more* suspensions.

As part of instituting the program, both Dierke and the faculty also received TM training, which may explain the curious change in behavior that Dierke observed in his staff:

> In schools like this you have a large burnout among faculty. So people start taking every other Thursday off, or Mondays and Fridays off, and that sort of thing. Well, all of a sudden the teachers were taking *no* days off! It was a profound difference.

The white board outside Dierke's office, on which he would write the names of teachers absent on each day, stayed blank for days at a stretch.

Another unexpected result of the program was an improvement in Dierke's own health. After he began to meditate, his blood pressure dropped lower than it had been in four years, and his doctor saw a dramatic improvement in his diabetes control. "What are you *doing?*" the doctor asked. Dierke told him. "Keep doing it," said the doctor.

As Dierke points out, "I've been an administrator for twenty years and the biggest problem in schools for principals is the stress of the position, which has increased so much. Since No Child Left Behind, there is tremendous pressure put on principals because when outcomes don't change, they fire the principals, not the teachers or the students. So it is really good news for people like me to know there's something you can do."

Dierke has noticed other welcome shifts in his students since Quiet Time became established. In his first nine years as principal at Visitacion, he never saw the children again once they graduated. Now he finds that old students "are regular fixtures around here." As ninth- or tenth-graders, they come back to visit. Dierke believes that the TM program has somehow improved the feeling tone in the school in a way that deepens the bonds between students and faculty. Also, nearly half the children say they continue to meditate during vacations, even though there is no formal program to help them do that.

Parents see the change, too, judging from the phone calls Dierke gets since Quiet Time began. "I've noticed this change in my son," one father reported. "He doesn't come home and beat up his brother any-more. What are you doing to him?" Dierke said, "We taught him this way of controlling himself." Other parents have called to say, "This is working really well with my kids. Can you teach me how to do it, too?"

The neighborhood remains dangerous. Although the murder rate has declined, Visitacion Valley is still a scary place to live. To minimize their chance of getting shot or robbed, the children literally run from their homes to school, then run back home in the afternoon. The school itself, however, is a peaceful place—in the words of the *San Francisco Chronicle*, "an island of safety in a sea of trouble." When Dierke thinks of the children these days, the words "joyfulness" and "happiness" come to mind, and he is pleased that he took the leap of faith to embrace a program that might have been controversial.

Visitacion Valley had been labeled a "hard to staff" school, with extra pay given to those brave souls willing to work there. Despite this bonus, staff turnover was high. Between 2008 and 2010, however, after Quiet Time began, there was *no* staff turnover, and the school was removed from the district's "hard to staff" list. For his accomplishments, Jim Dierke was voted Middle School Principal of the Year for the entire United States in 2008. This prestigious award is given annually by the National Association of Secondary School Principals.

Laurent Valosek, CEO of the organization that sponsored the Quiet Time Program at Visitacion Valley, essentially agrees with Dierke that the school has been transformed, and offers another picture of how bad things had been before Quiet Time. When his team first came to the school, he says:

> The level of stress was very high. There was a lot of noise, and fighting was pervasive: skirmishes, yelling, screaming—not only by the students but also, in several cases, by teachers. One of my most vivid experiences was seeing a very large, probably two-hundred-plus-pound eighth-grader swinging a large metal trash can against the wall, right outside the principal's office, and screaming. That was characteristic of the environment. There was a lot of fighting in the classrooms, with serious fights occurring maybe once or twice a week. De-

spite the presence of two security guards and, at first, a uniformed police officer as well, many teachers would also get pulled into breaking up fights. There were just so many fights, and the general demeanor of the students was heavy. We'd look into their eyes and see heaviness, not a lot of happiness.

At one of the first faculty meetings we attended, we observed the principal, Jim, speaking to his staff. It was remarkable to me that many of the teachers were paying no attention. They were sitting in little groups, talking or even arguing, while Jim tried to talk loud enough that others could hear. It was a dysfunctional meeting.

Valosek's impressions of the change in both students and teachers are similar to Dierke's.

In the springtime, two or three months after the faculty had learned to meditate, the tone of Jim's meeting was markedly different. There was a much more buoyant atmosphere. The communication between the teachers was more harmonious, and when the principal spoke, their attentiveness was far greater. There was a sharp contrast between these two faculty meetings.

Also, the culture of the whole school is remarkably different. It's filled with buoyancy. You see a lot of smiles, a lot of friendliness between students and between students and teachers. You see so many positive things, although it's one of the most impoverished neighborhoods in the city. It wasn't like that before, even though Jim was doing a heroic job. And I'll tell you, for the first year and a half that we worked at the school—even though there were some wonderful, beautiful, and profound experiences—I didn't look forward to going there. On many days I would think, "I don't want to go into that environment." Now I enjoy going there. Now, for the first time, I believe this change is sustainable, even after Jim retires. I believe that the practice of meditation over time is actually changing the collective consciousness of the school and has become part of its culture.

Observing these results, the principal of Everett, another San Francisco middle school, also requested the Quiet Time Program, which began in fall 2008. Valosek and Grant have analyzed results for both school programs to date. Here are some of their key findings.

Everyone agrees that behavioral changes have been profound, with not only significant drops in the number of fights and suspensions but also an *increase* in daily attendance. Regular suspensions dropped by almost 50 percent at Visitacion Valley. As to attendance, there had been a downward trend at both schools, as in other district middle schools. Since Quiet Time was introduced, however, both schools have seen a 2 percent increase in average attendance, in contrast to an overall *decrease* seen in other district middle schools. In fact, no other school has seen an improvement in average attendance of more than 1 percent. In summary, the improvement in average attendance following the introduction of Quiet Time is quite out of line with that of any other middle school in the San Francisco district.[3]

In both schools, then, it seems fair to say that the practice of TM made learning possible, perhaps for the first time in years. Did more learning occur? It would seem so. After four consecutive years of declining GPAs at both Everett and Visitacion, average GPA increased at both schools (by 0.2 and 0.3 on a 4.0 scale, respectively) in the year after the program was introduced. School officials are especially pleased because for underperforming minorities, such as African Americans or Pacific Islanders, average grades improved twice as much as they did for the school as a whole—again by a highly significant margin. This is particularly exciting because closing the "achievement gap" has been such an elusive goal across the entire nation that educators refer to it as the Holy Grail of education.

Psychological well-being improved as well, as evidenced by standardized tests. Students showed significantly less anxiety and depression, and higher self-esteem. Many students attributed these psychological improvements to their practice of TM.

Faculty were helped as well. At Visitacion Valley, faculty took 30 percent fewer sick days in the second year of the Quiet Time Program.[4] At both schools, faculty reported less stress on standardized surveys, as well as better sleep and greater clarity of thought. One teacher observed, "I no longer get depressed on Sunday nights," candidly adding, "while I still have a temper, it seems to emerge less often." Another commented, "My senses are more vivid and I have a faster, more complete recovery from stressful events." And then there was the teacher who credited the program with helping her lose fourteen pounds and two dress sizes.

By all indications, the Quiet Time Program has been a success for those San Francisco middle schools that have embraced the experiment. The researchers are teaching TM to a group of San Francisco school administrators as part of a study. If the findings are as favorable as those observed to date, we can expect to see the Quiet Time Programs installed throughout the Bay Area.

GOING TO THE SOURCE

The prototype for the San Francisco program is the Maharishi School in Fairfield, Iowa. Established in 1975 to provide a meditative environment for children pre-K through twelfth grade, the school embraces what they call "consciousness-based education." This expression, according to Richard Beall, head of the school, means that a high priority is given to the student's state of mind. A student under stress, Beall reasons, cannot learn optimally. Therefore, dissolving stress and optimizing brain function are major goals of the Maharishi School, and TM, which the children practice twice daily, is the chosen means. Although the school is small (by latest count it has 190 students), it has won far more than its share of prizes in science fairs, dramatic performances, and tennis and academic contests. Here are a few noteworthy examples: As of 2010, the school has had forty National Merit Scholarship semifinalists and thirty-four finalists, much higher than the national per capita average for schools. In the international creativity contest Destination ImagiNation (DI), the school has won six state championships, leading the state in this contest; it has also won six world championships at the annual DI event. At the same time, these youngsters are not overdriven; there is a palpable happiness and excitement about the place, which I observed when I visited Fairfield for several days in 2009.

It was one of the school's theatrical performances that stimulated filmmaker David Lynch to establish a foundation to bring TM into schools around the world. Invited to attend a one-act play performed by the students, Lynch thought he was in for a long night. To his surprise and delight, however, he found the acting wonderfully fresh and the children full of a type of joy and excitement he had never encountered. If this is the effect of consciousness-based education, he thought, why should it not be available to everyone? It was the David Lynch Foundation that funded the San Francisco programs.

EARLY PIONEERS

Before David Lynch set up his foundation, two pioneering middle school principals were convinced that bringing TM into schools would pay off—George Rutherford in Washington, D.C., and Carmen N'Namdi in Detroit. Here are their stories:

George Rutherford, known to everyone as "Doc," visited the Maharishi School in the early nineties and had a reaction not unlike Lynch's. "I saw TM working in Fairfield," he said. "And I thought—I could use this in my school!" His school at that time was the Fletcher-Johnson Educational Center, located in a run-down D.C. neighborhood. TM instructor Bob Roth describes the area as "a place whose back streets are so harsh, so destitute, so crime-ridden that it is considered one of the worst areas in the country." A huge, imposing concrete building, the school looked "almost like a castle without turrets—a fortress without windows sitting at the top of a hill."[5]

As Rutherford explains:

> At that time we were at the height of the drug war. All around was nothing but fighting and shooting, and a lot of it was happening right around the school. The kids would come into school in a terrible state. It was dangerous to get to school. It was *terrible* to get to school. They were frightened, and the school was the only safe haven they had. And we had to make sure it stayed that way.

In 1993, Rutherford instituted a Quiet Time Program in his school in which fifth- to ninth-grade students meditated for twenty minutes twice a day. As with the San Francisco students, there was an immediate decrease in suspensions, better daily attendance, and improved academic achievement. Indeed, the fifth-graders won that year's award for D.C.'s highest increase on the California Test of Basic Skills. Rutherford observed changes in the students very similar to those found in San Francisco: "They are calmer, and as a result, the whole school feels better. Otherwise they come to school crazy—and stay that way all day." One of the school's teachers, Rose Phillips, who had taught TM in the inner cities for decades, added, "The most noticeable benefits from TM are that the kids are more eager to learn. They read better; they have less of an 'attitude' or edge about them. They are more polite to their teachers and get along better with their classmates. They learn faster and remember things better."

In 1997, Carmen N'Namdi and her husband, both longtime meditators, introduced the Quiet Time Program into their Detroit charter school while grieving the accidental death of their little daughter, and named the school after her—Nataki Talibah.

Cara Rosaen and Rita Benn from the University of Michigan interviewed ten of Carmen's seventh-grade students who had been meditating for a year and, in 2006, reported several improvements of the kind we have already seen: more relaxation, better emotional intelligence, and improved academic performance.[6]

Reggie and Karla Dozier went through the Quiet Time Program in eighth grade at Nataki Talibah. At nineteen and fifteen years old, respectively, when I spoke to them, they thought back affectionately on the program. Reggie remembered how it helped him stay focused, collect his thoughts, and calm down. He observed shrewdly, "When you're young, you can be all over the place." An avid sportsman in high school, he remembered "coming home from a game, sore and cranked up and tired. It was a perfect time for TM." He is now a college freshman in business management. Karla said that TM helped her be calmer and "de-escalate situations." It improved her focus and ability to remember. She still meditates every day.

Leslie Potts, age sixteen and still at Nataki Talibah when I interviewed her, said that her sleep has been better since she started meditating. She becomes less angry and less likely to snap at people. This is what she had to say about meditation.

> It drowns out your negativity, like a cleansing. Even in a hec-
> tic situation, it's about finding the calm within you, not in
> your environment. You just feel completely relaxed. TM has
> no down side. It's really great.

It would be reasonable to wonder whether Quiet Time Programs will only benefit schools under extreme stress, such as inner-city schools. That seems unlikely. As a psychiatrist practicing in the suburbs, I encounter large numbers of students from upper-middle-class families who are also under severe stress, which is hardly a surprise, given their often punishing schedules. Many students take several advanced placement classes, then play competitive sports for hours each day. By the time they are done with their homework it is bedtime—or past bedtime. A 1998 survey of sleep habits among adolescents in Rhode Island by Amy Wolfson and Mary Carskadon revealed that children get less and less sleep as they move through their teenage years from age thirteen to nineteen—with negative consequences. Reduced sleep was associated with daytime sleepiness, depressed mood, and lower grades.[7]

In my experience, there are many sources of stress in middle class and elite schools. Elementary and middle schools are increasingly seen as training grounds for high school and college. A recent survey by the American Psychological Association found that more than 40 percent of students are worried about doing well at school.[8] Good grades give schoolchildren a sense of having a future. Also, in order to qualify for certain sports, a minimum GPA is required. As Jeannie, a sixteen-year-old girl in my practice, says, "Kids stress out on tests all the time, and if their scores aren't high enough, you'll hear, 'Oh my God, I'll never get into college!'" She adds, "Parents get so mad if you're not living up to their expectations."

There is a fierce sense of competition about . . . everything. To quote Jeannie again: "There is never a time when you're not competing about something—looks, school, sports, academics." While both girls and boys are concerned about popularity and grades, girls also worry a great deal about their looks (especially about being too fat or having acne). They worry that if they're not pretty, they won't be popular, won't find boyfriends, won't get married. . . . Worries about the future readily spiral out of control, and become a *current* source of stress.

Bullying has recently been recognized as a huge problem in schools. According to the American Academy of Child and Adolescent Psychiatry, "surveys indicate that as many as half of all children are bullied at some time during their school years, at least 10% on a regular basis."[9]

Social pressures run high in middle and high school. Drugs and alcohol are rampant, and it can be hard for young people to say "no" even if nobody is pressuring them directly—because of a desire to fit in and be accepted. Social networking media have amped up social anxiety. Children worry what others will say on their Facebook wall because they are afraid to be judged and publicly embarrassed.

The pressure to conform can take unexpected turns. As Jeannie, the high school student I mentioned above, says, "Sometimes, other children in your circle of friends will lie to their parents about where they are going. If you don't lie as well, you will get *them* into trouble—so there is pressure for *you* to lie to your parents as well—even if you don't want to." She also points out the sexual pressures that girls face nowadays. Several of Jeannie's friends have expressed concerns that unless they give in to their boyfriends' sexual demands, the boys will no longer want to go out with them.

So, as you can see, even in middle-class and affluent communities, it is not easy to be a schoolchild nowadays. Although Quiet Time Programs have clearly succeeded in inner-city schools, I suggest that we consider expanding their reach to more affluent communities, where they will likely be of great value. I predict that these programs would de-stress our schoolchildren and enable them to be more flexible in their thinking—something educators routinely observe when their school adopts a program of meditation.

That is certainly the experience of Nancy Spillane, principal of Lowell Whiteman Primary School in Steamboat Springs, Colorado, which serves a middle-class conservative community. After persuading her board and faculty, she proceeded to implement the Quiet Time Program in her school, first for the faculty and then for students in grades five through eight. Although Spillane has not formally assessed the impact of Quiet Time, she is as pleased with its results as the other principals I interviewed. Besides the academic value of the program, the athletes at Lowell Whiteman have observed benefits on the playing field. According to Spillane, hockey players report having "a better sense of themselves in relation to the others on the field. They seem better able to anticipate where the puck is going and to act accordingly. It's as though different parts of their brains are working more efficiently together." Such an observation is consistent with research by Dr. Fred Travis, who has found a greater coherence in EEG patterns in different parts of the brain in people who meditate regularly.

Currently, well over a hundred schools in different parts of the world use some version of the Quiet Time Program, and wherever the program has been introduced, educators and students alike have been pleased. By the time this book is published, additional schools will no doubt have adopted the program.

What, then, can research tell us about how TM may work in schools?

CONTROLLED STUDIES OF THE TM TECHNIQUE IN SCHOOLS

The results of two studies are worth mentioning. Of the two, the second study—really a set of three studies—is particularly impressive.

All these studies were performed by researchers associated with Maharishi University.

In the first project, Sanford Nidich and colleagues studied 106 high school students (87 percent of whom were classified as "minorities"—mostly Hispanic, African American, or Native American) from four U.S. locations. Of these students, 68 learned TM, while 38 did not. The meditating students improved on standard pencil-and-paper measures of emotional well-being, including anxiety, to a greater extent than those who did not meditate. One limitation of this study is that the two groups were self-selected, not randomly assigned.[10] As you may recall, in order to be confident of the conclusions of a clinical study, the participants must be randomly assigned to the different groups.

In the second project, researchers Kam-Tim So and David Orme-Johnson conducted three well-controlled studies on 362 Taiwanese high school children, and published their results in the journal *Intelligence* in 2001.[11] The reviewers for *Intelligence*, a top journal in the field, took two years before accepting the studies for publication—and no wonder: The results are that remarkable. In summary, the researchers found that after six to twelve months of practicing TM, children were significantly less anxious and improved in a broad range of different types of intelligence, compared with three control groups: (1) a group who were encouraged to take naps; (2) a group who received no special attention; and (3) a group who practiced contemplation meditation. Considering the short duration of the study, and the highly significant improvements seen across a broad range of skills, the results are intriguing. I encourage those of you who want more information about these studies to see my comments in the notes section.[12]

Further controlled studies of the Quiet Time Program would clearly be valuable for policy makers considering introducing the program on a wider basis. Those educators who may be interested in the Quiet

Time Program for their own schools should contact the David Lynch Foundation, whose mission it is to help children learn to meditate.

In the meanwhile, educators like Carmen N'Namdi, who have seen the Quiet Time Program working wonders in the lives of their students for many years, are matter-of-fact about its values. N'Namdi regards TM as a basic health requirement. According to her, its benefits should be expected. "Of course, brushing your teeth does wonders for your teeth," she says, "but isn't it supposed to be like that?"

9

LEARNING TO LOVE YOURSELF

The Long Road Back
from Prison

> No man chooses evil because it is evil;
> he only mistakes it for happiness.
> —MARY WOLLSTONECRAFT

WHAT GOES ON behind the stone walls of a prison? Most of us (myself included) don't really give the matter much thought. To the extent that we do, our ideas are shaped by movies such as *The Shawshank Redemption*, based on a Stephen King novella, and other fictional portrayals. Such depictions, from *The Count of Monte Cristo* on down, generally tell the story of an innocent man, framed by his enemies and wrongfully imprisoned, who endures unspeakable horrors until he finally escapes, as a result of his ingenuity and derring-do, to wreak well-deserved vengeance upon those who wronged him. In real life, though innocent people are too often incarcerated, these are the exceptions. Most prisoners have in fact committed crimes, some of them violent crimes, and many prisoners are addicts. One way or another, life in prison is usually nasty, brutish, and long.

So, what should be done about prisoners? Should society lock them up and throw away the key? Or should we try to rehabilitate them (indeed, is it possible to do so)? Balancing the safety of society with the rights of prisoners is an old problem—and different solutions have been proposed. As criminologist Mark Hawkins writes, "There have been cyclic fluctuations between the use of punishment and rehabilitation in the American criminal justice system from the founding of the nation until the 1980s."[1] At this time, however, a consensus is building among experts in the field that we have *too many prisoners.*

Consider the following startling facts:

☐ Between 1980 and 2007 the U.S. population increased by 35 percent. In that same time period, the prison population increased by 373 percent[2]—more than ten times the population increase!

☐ The United States has had the highest ratio of incarceration among industrialized nations, including China, as long as records have been kept.[3] Approximately 3 percent of the adult population of the United States was under correctional supervision in 1997.[4]

☐ Overall $68 billion is spent annually on corrections systems in the United States (about $220 a year for every person in the U.S.).[5]

☐ Approximately 70 percent of released U.S. prisoners will be rearrested within three years.[6]

Clearly we need new ways to reduce this runaway financial burden without compromising public safety. We must also consider that most prisoners (around 95 percent) will be released sooner or later. When that happens, their state of mind and their risk for recidivism are highly relevant to everyone—their families and friends, their potential victims if they return to crime, and, of course, the taxpayer.

According to Tom O'Connor, currently CEO of Transforming Corrections in Salem, Oregon, rehabilitation is the only reasonable solution. O'Connor points out that every dollar spent on effective rehabilitation programs can save society (taxpayers and victim-related costs) up to almost nine dollars, depending on the type of program. Meta-analyses show that the programs currently in place to rehabilitate prisoners already reduce the nation's recidivism rate by about 10 percent. We can do even better, he says, by means of new ideas and new ways of working with people.

O'Connor compares the situation in U.S. prisons to the economic problems in Bangladesh observed by economist Muhammad Yunus in the mid-1970s. Recognizing that large-scale economic programs were failing to lift out of poverty the poorest villagers near his university, Yunus came up with the idea of microloans. He initially lent $27 of his own money to forty-two women in the village to help them buy the materials they needed for making furniture. Given this small bit of help, the women were able to launch their business and repay their loans.[7] And thus began a revolution. Today, many organizations like Kiva and the Grameen Bank lend many thousands a year, all in microloans, to help poor people start small businesses. It works! And over time, more benefits unfold. For example, now the family's children can go to school, and so on.

In an analogous way, says O'Connor, the large-scale criminal justice program of incarceration is failing to prevent crime. He argues instead for microinvestments in novel forms of rehabilitation that work with people in a different way—like Transcendental Meditation. If these can lift people out of crime, they would be repaid many times over in the form of reduced recidivism. Microinvestments in people are potentially far more effective than many of the huge investments we are currently making in building and running costly prisons.

Impressed by the body of research on the use and impact of TM in prisons and other settings, O'Connor spearheaded a collaboration within the Oregon Department of Corrections to conduct an ongoing TM research project in three of their prisons.[8] O'Connor points out that many programs that work—that is, reduce recidivism—can cost between $12,000 and $14,000 per person per year. Given the relatively low cost of training people to practice TM, O'Connor thinks that the Oregon study will offer a better return on investment. Let us examine some of the research that inspired O'Connor to motivate the Oregon prison system to undertake this venture.

CAN TM REDUCE RECIDIVISM?

To date, there have been twenty studies of the TM technique in correctional facilities: nineteen on offenders (including follow-ups) and one on correctional officers.[9] As with any body of research, the studies are uneven in strength, but most are controlled in some way. I refer those readers seeking more information to an excellent monograph, *Transcendental Meditation in Criminal Rehabilitation and Crime Prevention*.[10] For the purpose of this chapter, I will focus on studies that address recidivism, the outcome that matters most to society at large.

Three well-designed retrospective studies have analyzed recidivism. In one, Bleick and Abrams followed 259 felons released from San Quentin, Folsom, and Deuel state prisons, comparing them to 259 controls.[11] They found that parolees who had taken part in TM sessions were 40 percent less likely to be reconvicted within one year of their release from prison, and 30 percent less likely to be reconvicted within six years. Both findings were not just statistically significant but *highly* significant. This alone would be impressive.

But there's more. Maxwell Rainforth, of Maharishi University, and colleagues later found and assessed these same people fifteen years after they were released from prison—reduced by now through attrition to 120 meditators and 127 controls—and found that those who had learned TM remained 43 percent less likely to have been reconvicted.[12]

Charles Alexander and colleagues conducted a similar follow-up study of former inmates released from Walpole State Prison in Massachussets.[13] They compared 152 ex-cons who had learned TM with four other groups of inmates who had participated in prison programs— counseling, drug rehabilitation, or different forms of religious activities (Christian or Muslim). Over a six-year period the TM group was one third less likely to be reconvicted.

One of the most curious studies of recidivism was conducted in Senegal by Anklesaria and King.[14] As part of the study, TM was taught to 11,000 inmates in thirty-one out of thirty-four prisons. Although the reports were anecdotal and somewhat unsystematic, the wardens from all thirty-one prisons signed a public proclamation describing the many favorable transformations they had seen, and recommended that TM be implemented throughout the system. According to a report in *Corrections Today*, the official publication of the American Correctional Association:

> Before the program was introduced in Senegal in January 1987, inmates there returned to prison at a rate of about 90 percent within the first month. After TM had been instituted, a study of 2,400 inmates released through an amnesty in June 1988 revealed that fewer than 200 of them returned within the first six months—80 percent of those who returned did not practice the technique.
>
> Colonel Mamadou Diop, Senegal's corrections director, credited meditation with the drop in recidivism, stating that "considering that there is no structure or scheme for the re-

integration of inmates into society, nor is there any provision for work or jobs for those released, it appears that the only possible explanation for this remarkable drop in recidivism in our country is to be found in the application of (the TM) program."

Diop reported in January 1989 that as a result of reducing recidivism, Senegal had closed three prisons and eight others were idled at 6 to 30 percent capacity.[15]

How might TM reduce recidivism? Armed with knowledge from earlier chapters, you can probably venture some excellent guesses. We have already seen that after meditating for a while, people report and exhibit less anger and impulsiveness. Meditators are also less inclined to use drugs, which is probably important, given the strong relationship between drug use and crime.

Several studies, some very well designed, have examined changes in the behavior and emotional lives of inmates who had been meditating for a while. Ramirez, for example, studied sixty-eight drug-addicted prisoners in Michigan, of whom nineteen were regular meditators, fifteen were irregular meditators, and thirty-one were controls.[16] There was a strong correlation between regularity of TM practice and increased self-esteem, emotional stability, and maturity, as well as decreased aggression and suspicion. Ballou[17] studied sixty-six narcotic-addicted offenders in Minnesota and found that during a ten-month TM program, meditators incurred two thirds fewer disciplinary actions and participated significantly more in educational and recreational programs.

Considering the sheer volume of positive data, it seems strange that the TM practice has not been widely embraced as a tool for helping prisoners outgrow crime. The situation parallels that of TM for drug rehabilitation, which is also highly promising—and also neglected. I suggest the same explanations here that I did before. Fashions change, funding patterns shift, and key researchers retire or die. In addition, perhaps, meditation may seem alien to wardens who haven't actually seen it in action. In the world of lockdown, the promise of bliss, unity, and strengthening neural connections could be a tough sell.

As data accumulate, however, and state budgets shrink—while populations of addicts and prisoners keep rising—now may be the right time to propose something different. The new major study of TM now in progress in the Oregon Correctional System, as well as a recently published review titled "Meditation Research: The State of the Art in Corrections," suggest that the time is right for expanding the practice of TM in prisons. Samuel Himelstein, the author of this new review, sees TM as the most solidly researched form of meditation approaches for prisoner rehabilitation.[18]

Even though the prisoners in the Oregon study are relatively recent meditators who might be inclined to speak well of the program because they are still in prison, let us hear what some of them have to say:

> Mark, age twenty-eight, who joined the program "because they offered me $15 to participate," says: "I learned a lot about myself—how to stay calm. When I meditate, I feel like I'm out of prison. It takes all the stress out of my mind. I'm staying on task and have more confidence in myself. It has helped my ADD. Waking up is better. My attitude is better."

> Ronald, age twenty-one: "It takes me away from the prison. It's a joyful little dream for twenty, thirty minutes. I'm relaxed, free. I zone everybody and everything out. I'm more peaceful and patient, and in prison you need patience. If I miss a few days, I'm a little more cranky. If I do my meditation, everything feels right."

Spencer, twenty: "I'm more relaxed, down-to-earth, vibrant, and focused. I have less anger and fewer fights."

Fred, forty-two: "For me TM is a tool for never coming back. I have had trouble with assaultive behavior and anger issues. Now it doesn't make a bit of difference what people say to me. I'm not acting on angry impulses. I'm going home; they're coming back."

Tony, twenty-four, serving a life sentence for murder at the Oregon State Maximum Security Prison in Salem: "My mind and body feel more rested. My thoughts are more crisp and clear. I can process problems and pick out the positive aspects of them. I no longer sweat the small stuff, and the larger issues seem to figure themselves out in a timely manner. I feel more alert yet less anxious. I have a large number of transcending experiences. The one that stands out the most is after the first month I had no mantra and thoughts— just blank emptiness that had a warm comforting feeling. However, I was fully aware of the outside surroundings. I've also seen colors during transcending. I have a lot of these experiences but the feeling within this one stood out the most."

THE TEACHER AND THE FELON: AN UNLIKELY COLLABORATION

Early reports from inmates in Oregon are encouraging, but how might the benefits of TM play out over a longer interval? One story that speaks to this point involved an extraordinary relationship between a convicted murderer and a highly unusual TM teacher. The prisoner was Pat Corum, the TM teacher George Ellis, and luckily they wrote about it.[19] Corum and Ellis first met when Corum was serving time in the maximum-security Folsom State Prison in California. During a previous term of more than seven years in the California state system, Corum had seen "twenty-two psychiatrists, psychologists and counselors, spending hundreds of hours in group counseling, group therapy and individual counseling." After his release, he was reconvicted within six months for robbery and first-degree murder.

According to Corum, he had never in his life felt normal. Instead, he wrote, "My feelings of isolation and loneliness were so overwhelming that I started looking outside myself for something, anything, that would stop those feelings and the pain associated with them." Corum resorted to drugs. By his own admission, he did whatever he needed to get money for drugs and other things that made him look and feel good. He remembers telling his best friend, "I'm going to do what I want to do, when I want to do it. If people don't like it, they can kill me before I kill them." Along the way, he assaulted and shot several police officers. In exchange for pleading guilty, he was spared the death penalty, sentenced to life imprisonment, and transported to the maximum-security section of San Quentin. Later, because he stayed involved with drugs and prison gangs, he was transferred to Folsom, where security is even more intense. There he was convicted of the execution-style slaying of a lieutenant in a rival gang, which resulted in a second life sentence. Instead of taking responsibility for his actions, however, Corum writes that "the only thing that changed about me as a result of that experience was that my anger about betrayal and treachery from other human beings was off the scale."

Eventually, Corum enrolled in a prison college program, where Ellis was one of his teachers. Along with the other prisoner-students, Corum would routinely intimidate teachers into giving them good grades, and they thought it would be easy to intimidate Ellis, who was short in stature. But, no, Ellis just smiled and laughed, unperturbed, and kept coming back. Amazed that Ellis showed no fear, Corum began to watch him carefully. He writes, "I noticed that he wasn't just 'laid back,' but that he also had a lot of energy, and a clarity of mind that I had never seen in anyone else." Corum now became intent on learning TM, the "secret" to Ellis's abilities, so Ellis lent him books on the subject until finally—after Corum paid the requisite fee—Ellis taught him to meditate. After meditating regularly for a while, Corum decided to give up drugs. He began to get A's on his tests, stopped receiving disciplinary write-ups, and put on twenty pounds. He writes, "This positive change began from the inside. It had nothing to do with barbed wire or armed guards, or any other external controls."

A turning point came after Corum had been meditating for six months. Confronted by a difficult situation with another prisoner, he chose not to attack. As he writes, "Instead of just reacting to the situation, I found myself feeling calm and relaxed. I had the clarity of mind to look at the various options I had for responding. I chose the best one. I just smiled and laughed. As George Ellis had done with me and my friends, I did not react to someone else's drama, and I didn't support the drama by reacting."

Corum began to think deeply about his life—past and present: "Life, I discovered, was neither fair nor unfair. Life was what I made it. Life did not change from being ugly and nasty. I changed from being ugly and nasty." Corum went on to graduate as an attorney's assistant. He became involved in several self-help groups, including AA. After being transferred to a medium-security prison, he was eventually released. He fell in love, married, and lived happily with his wife for years. He made a career assisting attorneys with their criminal cases and was pleasantly surprised that he could afford some middle-class comforts: for example, a four-bedroom house. He was particularly happy that he could be present for his family in both good times and bad.

Ellis, who had taught many prisoners to meditate, had this to say about his protégé: "Pat Corum's experience is not unique. It is an example of what has occurred a thousand times and more in correctional settings throughout the world."

As a psychiatrist, I have learned that personal change does not occur without some motivation—it's a prerequisite. Likewise, some interest in TM is probably necessary for the technique to be effective. Can those conditions be met in prison? I believe so, and a growing body of research confirms that motivation can be fostered and developed through the right kind of empathic relationships with agents for change.[20] Might TM teachers or even fellow meditators provide this kind of mentoring relationship? I think so, especially when I consider the impact people like Ellis have on those who come in contact with them. When Corum saw Ellis's fearlessness and clarity, he wanted to understand its basis—and wanted it for himself.

In the Oregon prison study, the investigators are accepting only inmates who are *interested*. I think that is wise and may well create a viable model for TM prison programs. The subjects were assigned randomly to those who learned TM and a control group of those who did not learn TM.[21] It's easy to imagine this process developing so that as each group graduates from TM training, other inmates will notice their newfound ease and strength . . . and want in.

YOU NEED EYES IN THE BACK OF YOUR HEAD: EFFECTS ON PRISON STAFF

As with the schools program, the Oregon prison staff were taught to meditate before the program was offered to inmates. This step is important, not only to give the staff the benefits of TM, but also to help them understand and support the inmates as they in turn begin their practice.

Several staff members have observed that after their colleagues retire, they don't seem to live very long. It's as though the stress of working in prison wore them down and burned them out. According to Randy Geer, the administrator of inmate services at Oregon State, "Prisons are like pressure cookers. It's like normal life distilled to its essence. When you're in the prison, you need eyes in the back of your head. You never know which information that you're given is correct and which is not. It's an environment where dangers are hard to assess," and therefore highly stressful. Geer should know. He's a second-generation corrections officer, whose father was killed on the job by an inmate. Geer adds, "People who work in corrections tend to have a lot of emotional armor." My colleague Bob Roth, who has taught TM in a prison, says it's hard for an outsider to understand how stressful the prison environment is until you actually step into it. Roth can feel his jaw locking each time he walks into a prison.

Even in its early stages the Oregon TM program has brought staff members considerable relief. One female sergeant, after twenty years in the system, says that for the first time she feels as though she can set aside her armor and experience some peace at work—a reaction Geer finds "miraculous, almost unheard of." But the sergeant's comments are supported by the results of a TM study conducted on eighteen corrections officers in the Vermont State Prisons in the late 1980s.[22] After four months, officers reported significant reductions in hostility, paranoid anxiety, and troubled sleep.

Such changes in mind-set can be lifesaving, both for officers and prisoners. As Geer points out, "It's important for staff to find a way to release bad energy; otherwise you can contribute to prison violence because you're too stressed out." His comment reminds me of George Ellis, a short man with a super-cool temperament, who disarmed a group of dangerous inmates by his relaxed demeanor and his absence of fear.

DROPS ON A LEAF: HELPING PEOPLE MAKE BETTER CHOICES

As I listen to people like Tom O'Connor and Randy Geer, it is obvious that they see their work as much more than a job—it's a calling. Why otherwise would someone return to a working environment in which his father had been killed, as Geer did? Or make the job one's life-work, as O'Connor has done?

Tom O'Connor was drawn to TM both for personal and professional reasons. Personally, it has already enlarged his world. Although he has been trained as a deacon in the Catholic Church, he experiences prayer and meditation very differently. "I think TM is more about the self," he says, "and prayer is about God or the divine." When asked whether he transcends regularly during meditation, he's not sure. "I have very pleasant experiences and I feel like there's a lot going on, but I don't know if I could say, 'That time I was transcending. This time I wasn't.'"

The ongoing effect, however, has been very gratifying:

> TM allows me to get closer to my real self—it's like drops of water every day falling on a leaf and bending the leaf a little bit at a time. It is helping me find my own voice both personally and professionally. I have felt a shift in my own mental clarity. Noise departs. It's a kind of recalibration.

That strikes me as a beautiful image for how subtly the technique can change a person, a little at a time, so that the day-to-day changes may be almost imperceptible. Yet over time, as we have seen, the effects can be dramatic.

Both Geer and O'Connor see it as necessary to somehow break down the boundaries between staff and inmates, a very tricky thing to pull off when staff must be ever alert to stay safe and avoid being conned. They see the human connection between staff and inmates as a key to rehabilitation and self-actualization. They share a hope that TM can induce the type of shift in both staff and inmates that, in O'Connor's words, "might free up a pathway to the kind of relationships we know are essential to the change process." The result, he hopes, will be "to create an environment of healing, leading to a more effective and humane prison."

I have interviewed several men who had formerly been imprisoned, drug addicted, and homeless, but who are now leading honest and productive lives, thanks, in part, to meditation. They credit TM with helping them control their temper, and avoid fighting words or violent actions, of the kind that would previously have landed them back in prison. One such man—I'll call him Joe—emphasizes, however, that meditation does a lot more than just help to curb impulses. For several years, Joe, a powerfully built man in his forties, has supervised other formerly homeless and incarcerated men in a residential rehab facility. Having observed many of these men at close quarters, he has concluded that, like himself, they come from broken relationships and broken lives, and that if they want to heal themselves, they have to learn to love themselves. He believes that taking twenty minutes for oneself twice a day is one way to develop that love. He routinely asks his men, "Did you do your TM yet?" And if they say no, he tells them, "Well, that's self-love, to take twenty minutes for yourself." He knows from personal experience: "I kind of hit them on the head with that, but that's because I still need to be reminded of that myself."

When I think of Joe and his supervisees, I realize that in the heyday of their criminal lives, these must have been very, very scary men. Yet I marvel at the changes they have made. It is impossible to meet them and remain unmoved. Likewise, Pat Corum went from being one of the most hardened criminals inside Folsom to a fully participating, useful member of society. Both Joe and Corum found a way to use their troubled past as an asset, a special kind of knowledge that allowed them to help others. And George Ellis said that Pat Corum's story was just one of many he had witnessed as a teacher of TM. The world's prisons need more such teachers.

In O'Connor's experience, many of the men in prison are not inherently evil, not psychopaths. They have just made bad choices, which they continue to do for specific reasons, such as impulsiveness, drug use, and a distorted way of seeing their relationship to others. He is hoping that TM will give these men a tool to help them make better choices. As he reflects on his image of the leaf that is gradually transformed by drops of water, it occurs to him that he has already seen such drops at work in some of his men: notably a new ability to pause for a few extra seconds before reacting. As the stories in this chapter indicate, those few seconds can make all the difference between staying out of trouble or perpetuating whatever problem landed someone in prison in the first place. The simple ability to resist destructive—and self-destructive—impulses has enormous power: It can help a person *get* out of jail, *stay* out of jail, and acquire a whole new life.

Prisoners want the same things that all of us want, says O'Connor. They just aren't able to get it. He has seen in them moments in which their understanding shifts and they realize how much damage their behavior does to themselves and others. As he observes:

If you're not *feeling* that damage, your prefrontal cortex can't even come into play. The biggest predictors of recidivism are the people you hang out with and your attitude—having a sense of agency, the knowledge that you control your own behavior. Criminals know it's wrong to steal, but they disengage that moral reasoning and allow themselves to think, "Well, it's good to do it this time because . . ." and then they have all these rationalizations so that, in their opinion, they are choosing a good thing.

If TM can help people bring their cognitive abilities online, then there's the possibility of agency. But TM helps prisoners in other ways as well: Each day it gives them a positive experience—a way to find something good inside themselves, something that's worth accessing. Add to that the subtle but perceptible shifts in calmness, cognition, and impulse control, and you can see how this apparently simple technique can help change these people's lives.

Mary Wollstonecraft, the great British feminist and philosopher, whom I quote at the start of this chapter, wrote over two hundred years ago, "No man chooses evil because it is evil; he only mistakes it for happiness." One goal of rehabilitation is to help people avoid this mistake.

10

SELF-ACTUALIZATION—
YOUR PERSONAL BEST

> Musicians must make music, artists must
> paint, poets must write if they are to be
> ultimately at peace with themselves. What
> human beings can be, they must be. They
> must be true to their own nature. This
> need we may call self-actualization.
>
> —ABRAHAM MASLOW[1]

UNTIL NOW, we have considered how Transcendental Meditation can transform those who urgently need it. In this chapter, however, you will meet people who have pursued Transcendental Meditation not so much out of dire need as a drive to feel fulfilled. In each instance, it seems to me, TM has woven its way like a golden thread through the tapestry of their lives, subtly or radically transforming them.

Psychologist Abraham Maslow described self-actualization as the ultimate universal need, one that human beings experience after satisfying the six basic needs for food, safety, physical shelter, love, sex, and a sense of belonging. I find his concept useful, as I have witnessed firsthand how earnestly people struggle, regardless of social, financial, and professional status, to be and do the best they can. Their struggle is to actualize or make real their potential as they themselves see it—an idea that is embedded in our culture. "Be all you can be" was a U.S. Army recruitment slogan for many years. Athletes speak of their "personal best" to describe their fastest times—a phrase that acknowledges both the constraints against which they work (as do we all) and their burning need to perform right up to that limit.

I have grouped the people in this chapter into three categories, connected mainly by the fact that I find them all interesting: accomplished women, successful businessmen, and people in the entertainment industry. I have always been amazed at the way successful women juggle the demands of career and family in a world that, for all its advances, is often still harder for women. The businessmen profiled may be of particular interest to those who still see TM as a form of Eastern mysticism, a "woo-woo" hippie pursuit, unconnected to the commercial realities of twenty-first-century life. Finally, show business is intriguing to almost everybody. Yet, despite its glamour, life in the entertainment industry presents its own challenges. In this chapter, we will examine the lives of people in all these categories, focusing on how TM has helped them achieve their potential, both personally and professionally.

Creativity is an important key to self-actualization, so it would be useful to ask whether TM can foster the creativity within each of us. We have seen elsewhere in this book specific examples of creative insights arising from TM, and further examples follow. I will share with you the results of research studies that find an expansion of creativity following TM after only months of practice. We will also examine evidence from brain studies, showing how TM changes brain EEG patterns in a way that may explain its power to help people become more creative and self-actualized.

THREE WISE WOMEN

Lyn: A Transcendent Professor

Lyn, a woman in her late fifties, is a professor of mathematics at a major university, a wife, and the mother of two adult sons. In her role as professor, her duties consist of teaching, research, and administrative work that recently includes, most vexingly, rewriting the faculty manual.

> I hear about all the horrible things that are going on with the university. And the faculty manual of course is very contentious because we're defining our rules of engagement when it comes to tenure, promotion, professional obligations, and workload.

Lyn is also a recovering alcoholic, who had been sober for almost ten years when she decided to learn TM. She was acting on the eleventh step of AA—"to seek through prayer and meditation to improve our conscious contact with God." Although Lyn had previously had some benefit from other forms of meditation (breathing exercises, mindfulness, and guided imagery), she continued to seek. When I spoke to her she had been practicing TM for two years:

> What I immediately found in Transcendental Meditation that was different was its ease. In all other methods there was effort involved: effort in getting quiet; effort in redirecting thoughts or being mindful. Another difference was that in TM I felt immediate relaxation of my body. It was as if my body was sinking and my soul was rising—just peacefully

leaving my body and my body was at peace with it—calm, sort of happy I'm leaving. The body seems to sink and get still. And occasionally I can notice things about my body that I don't normally notice. Things seem to be moving better inside; my blood flows more freely. It's much more of a physical process for me than the other meditations I've done.

The most obvious changes Lyn notices since she's been meditating are that she is much calmer and less reactive:

I'm married to a very boisterous, engaging, loud, happy man—highly extroverted, just filled with life, just screaming life everywhere. And I'm more quiet. A lot of times his happy aggressiveness would be very intrusive to me. Now I find it less so. I'm calmer around him, and when he gets stirred up or excited, I don't. It's easier for me to be with him. And he notices a big difference—a pleasant difference. I don't think it was ever his intention to disturb me, and now that he sees I'm not disturbed, he's very happy. He can be himself and not be concerned.

While TM has improved Lyn's home life, it has had an even more dramatic impact on her job. Returning to that vexing staff manual, Lyn says:

I have been working with nine other staff members and we've met close to forty times in the past eight months, and some of those meetings were very, very contentious. At one point, I thought the committee was going to fracture. But through going home and meditating and getting quiet and still, I have found ways to defuse all the tensions, so that we're still operating very well as a whole. I am finding my new attitude a very calm and peaceful way to live.

Working with difficult students has also become easier for Lyn. She recalls one student who was unhappy with his grade, standing in a group outside her office.

> I heard him say, "This is not going well. I need to talk to her alone." He came in, closed the door, and told me that he absolutely hated math and that all he expected was to pass. He ranted for a while. "You know, I expect to do this. And I don't like it. And I'm only doing it because I blah, blah blah." And I listened quietly until he finally wound down and I said, "Is that it?" And he said, "Yes." And I said, "Well, that's good. You told me what your expectations are. Now let me share with you what my expectations are." And I just told him, "What you need to do is this, this, and this. And if you meet my expectations, maybe you will pass the course." And he sort of looked at the floor and he shuffled a little and he thanked me and shook my hand and walked out. I heard him telling the other students, "That didn't go well for me at all."
>
> Even though I think I've always handled my students pretty well, internally I would get stirred up and outraged. How could they do this? How dare they say that? One of the gifts of TM is the peace and calm it brings. I can say to myself, "He's in his universe, I'm in mine, and the two can come together smoothly."

Most enjoyably for Lyn, since starting to do TM, she has begun to *create* again and has written a substantial article: "I would not have gotten the article done without that help," she says.

I'm much more interested in my research and there's less noise going on in my head. I was able to say, "OK, I'm making particular choices and I'm choosing to do this. Distractions don't intrude. I can prioritize better, making better judgments about the use of my time. I can now distinguish between what is productive for my students (and myself) and what is just busywork.

Once again, we see how TM helps people distinguish the important from the urgent—that is, things that will make a difference long-term versus things that have a pressing quality but won't amount to much. Lyn's description of how TM helped her creativity echoes Moby's observation that TM helped him get rid of disruptive thoughts, which were like unwanted guests at a party. Lyn's talk of "noise in the head" is akin to the incessant chatter of the "bubble machine," described in chapter 7.

As you may know, psychologist Erik Erikson defined eight stages of human maturation. Each stage has a particular task that must be mastered in order to continue one's personal growth. In the next-to-last stage, that task is generativity—giving back to the world in full measure what one has learned over a lifetime—which is the hallmark of many a happy person. For me, Lyn embodies that sort of generativity in both her work and in her relations with family, friends, and the many young women she sponsors in AA (more than fifty—she has lost count). I think it is fair to say that TM has brought her the last few steps of the way. But beyond productivity and creativity, TM has brought transcendence into Lyn's daily life, a constant source of joy. As she describes it:

The leaves are sharper. I see more birds. I used to look for birds, but I see more of them now. It's more than that, though. For example, I'm sitting in a room now and I'm very aware of everything inside the room. It's having an exchange with me. It's that cosmic consciousness. I know when I'm moving through a room and I feel everything around me that I am one with, and I am listening to my Higher Power, that my heart is open. I am truly part of the universe. . . . Then I realize I've got to go down and do the dishes!

ELAINE: The Negative Things Simply Fall Away

Elaine, a psychologist who is now almost seventy years old, has been meditating for the past twenty-six years. She was an emotionally healthy person to begin with: a successful professional with a happy marriage, three children, and (now) grandchildren. Yet she feels that TM (which she never misses) has helped her in so many ways. She used to suffer from mild anxiety; that's gone now. So are the glasses of wine she would drink in the evening to unwind, her smoking, and other "crutches." Although her marriage was always good, she now realizes that her anxiety was often a focus of their conversations, which sometimes turned into arguments. After she started meditating, that no longer happened.

Indeed, after seeing how TM helped Elaine, her husband also began to meditate—and so, in time, did their children. Elaine is persuaded that it's good for a mother to meditate: "On a practical level, it keeps you grounded, calm, and nonreactive. And when you feel better in yourself, you have a greater ability to love and be loving." She adds, "Maharishi always said children like it when Mommy goes to meditate because then they know she'll be more patient with their mischief."

In summing up the effects of her years of experience, Elaine says:

It's as if when you do Transcendental Meditation, the negative things in your life simply fall away. You feel different
inside. Your emotional life is different. And as your perceptions start to change, the knots and stresses dissolve, and
you feel connected to yourself in new ways.

MINDY WEISEL: After the Holocaust

"My mother and father were both survivors of Auschwitz and I was
one of the very first children born in Bergen-Belsen, Germany, a concentration camp that had become a displaced persons' camp. I'm the
firstborn, in January 1947, and the only daughter to two people who
were quite intense—very, very loving but real workaholics." That is
how Mindy Weisel starts her story, and understandably so. Her parents' time in Auschwitz was the defining experience not only of their
lives, but of hers as well.

If any concentration camp survivor can be called lucky, Mindy's
father was: nine out of eleven members of his family survived Auschwitz.

My mother, unfortunately, saw her entire family killed before
her eyes. She survived because she had a rare blood type
that the Nazis used for the military and so they gave her a
little extra measure of soup.

I was three when we came to America, where my parents
bought a bakery and worked sixty, seventy hours a week. My
father had severe asthma and I was always sure that each
breath would be his last. If the phone rang for me after six
or seven o'clock in the evening, even when I was a teenager,

everyone would be upset because my father needed his sleep; he had to get up at three o'clock in the morning. So I had a very other-directed kind of youth with a very beautiful mother who insisted that her only daughter be everything: beautiful, smart . . . everything.

So I got married at eighteen, I have three daughters, I'm a painter and thank God my husband is very, very supportive of my career. I've been working as an artist for thirty years and teaching at the Corcoran College of Art and Design for eleven years. I have several books published, have had thirty-five one-person shows, and I basically believe in the survival of beauty.

Despite all that success, however, Mindy has lived "with an inordinate amount of anxiety." At age twenty-eight, she and her family moved from Los Angeles, where she had lived with her parents, to Washington, D.C.

The move was a relief.

For the first time in my life I didn't have to worry how they were feeling about anything. I had lived my whole life for my parents, to make sure they were happy. And when you are raised by Auschwitz survivors, the bar for living is very high— because how could you be sad? You're not in Auschwitz. How could you be hungry? How could you be cold? How could you be anything? So you push down your feelings.

After moving to Washington, Mindy continued to suffer severe anxiety, and had a series of "nervous breakdowns." Her anxiety took different forms over the years, but was mostly what she calls "running." As she puts it:

I don't mean running for exercise. I mean like never doing enough. You know, my parents had survived so much and did so much that I had to as well. If I did fifty-two things, I should have done fifty-four. I'd write lists in the car. Then even after I'd done something, I'd write it down on a list to see how much I did. It was a real compulsion to do, do, do, do. I had many doctors tell me not to confuse fatigue with depression, that I was really exhausted.

Mindy's running culminated in a final "nervous breakdown," an unsuccessful hospitalization, and, by good luck, a transfer to The Raj, a spa that specializes in ayurvedic (traditional Indian) medicine. That is where, at age fifty-six, Mindy learned Transcendental Meditation. She told the doctor who suggested it:

"I have tried meditating and I'm not the kind of person who can sit and meditate. I get very agitated." And the doctor said, "Yes, but you're here and you're depleted, and it's something that can be taught."

So I've been meditating ever since and I don't know how I would do without it. I take great pride in the fact that I learned how to meditate. And I feel that if I can sit still for twenty minutes and not rush out of bed and start doing eight million things, anybody in the world can do it. So the message that I would love to give anyone and everyone— and I do—is that meditation is something you can learn.

And what impact has meditation had on Mindy's life? For a start, it has done the seemingly impossible: It has slowed her down, not only long enough to meditate but in a way that quiets her mind throughout the day.

I credit TM for giving me the feeling that no matter where I am, I can quiet my mind. I've been able to block out a lot of the world, meditating in train stations, nursery schools, and on airplanes—it doesn't matter. I just feel such tremendous gratitude; I don't know what other word to use except the deepest, deepest gratitude that I learned to meditate. It's room to breathe. It's room to rest, to be quiet. It's air. It's space where I can slow down and enjoy the moment. It has been like the rope I needed to help me climb back to myself.

Besides being of direct psychological help, TM has also opened Mindy up to a completely new direction in her art.

Meditation has allowed me a certain openness and willingness. I feel now as though new things are possible, not closed off. One very, very specific thing is that I have painted all my life and never thought of myself as an artist in any other medium. Then, one day, about two years after learning to meditate, I went to a glass studio nearby—and the next day I was making glass as if I'd made it my whole life. And a year and a half later, I had a one-person show at American University with thirty-two works in glass.

TITANS OF INDUSTRY

The world of business, certainly at its upper levels, might be the last place you would expect to find people willing to take time out of their day to sit quietly, close their eyes, and think their mantra. You'd be wrong, though—the three businessmen you're about to meet not only make time to meditate, but credit meditation for a large part of their business and personal success.

Bob Jones: TM on Wall Street

Bob learned Transcendental Meditation when he was fifteen, about forty years ago. He describes himself at that time as a "B student, going nowhere." Meditation helped him improve his grades, graduate with honors, and get into Brown, an Ivy League university. In retrospect, Bob wonders whether he might have had "a little ADD—they didn't diagnose it back then." He remembers being "always anxious and moving about." With the help of TM, he was able to calm down, find focus, and do what had to be done.

A few years later, however, he became disillusioned with TM and made fun of its Eastern origins for a while. But when he stopped meditating, he lost his ability to focus and became less productive. So after a short time out, he began to meditate again and has done so ever since.

Bob has been a portfolio manager for a top-tier financial services firm on Wall Street for twenty years, developing quantitative models for institutional investors. In the stressful world of the trader, he says:

> TM helps you be calm in pressured situations and think through things in a clearheaded way. A lot of times when there are problems in the portfolio or with clients, people get all upset and flustered. They can make bad decisions when they do that. So, having a calm demeanor, being able to take things as they come and to address them in a calm and thoughtful way, is very important in any industry—but particularly in asset management.

The reason people get stressed is that they have too many things going on. Well, not all those things are important. I think meditation helps you sort it out—these are the things I need to do, while these are less important and I'll get to them if I have time. By being thoughtful and focused, you find a lot of time. I actually end up with more time than I would without meditation.

Many people who are very successful in our business feed on and enjoy stress, and maybe it makes them more effective. A lot of people can't make decisions until they're on deadline or under a gun. But in the long run, I don't think that's good for their health or even for their decision making. I find that if you collect information in a thoughtful way, and if you're more calm, centered, and focused on what you need to do, you'll end up making better decisions. Also, you'll be successful without the negatives of heart disease and early death, early retirement, burnout . . . all the other things that happen to people who admittedly are very successful but do it in a stressful way.

Over the years, TM has helped Bob in many ways. For example, he credits TM with helping him quit smoking, biting his nails, and drinking more than he should. He observes that all the people he still knows from his high school class, who learned to meditate at age fifteen, are still meditating. In summarizing the role of TM in his life, Bob says:

I would attribute a lot of my success in life to meditation. It has helped me find my center, who I am and who I want to be—being on that center and achieving better focus in life.

GEORGE CROWLEY: De-stressing a Gladiator

George Crowley, a man in his late fifties, heads up a group of entre-
preneurs who have been launching companies in telecommunications
and technology for the last twenty-five years. During that time the
group has helped launch nearly forty new companies in eight different
countries. Like Bob, George talks about the extreme stress involved in
his job.

> I call it gladiating—because we deal in many different coun-
> tries and time zones. There's a lot of travel involved and a
> significant compression of meeting schedules. The com-
> plexity of the deal structures is intense because, especially
> in emerging markets, we have issues based on local culture
> and politics that require a very high level of thoughtfulness.
> It's almost like three-dimensional chess.

George has been meditating for more than two years now. Initially, he found the benefits of TM to be "marginal," which he attri-
butes to "not really understanding the process." Here's how he explains
his misunderstanding:

> My nature is that I'm a very disciplined person, and what
> seemed counterintuitive to me was the notion that the man-
> tra is most effective when I'm not focused on it. So I was try-
> ing to force my focus onto the mantra. By trying to impose
> my will as opposed to just letting the mantra happen, I was
> actually defeating one of the most important aspects of the
> practice. Now I recognize that I should not experience the
> mantra as a singularity of focus, but rather let it innocently

enter my consciousness. And if thoughts emerge while I'm experiencing my mantra, I need to just recognize that they're there and gently return to the mantra—not try to grab it by the throat as you might if it were a business problem.

George now transcends regularly when he meditates, which he often experiences as physical sensations:

One of the ways I know I'm transcending is I begin to feel all these releases throughout my body. They're like little shocks or tingling sensations in my head—almost like when your foot or hands fall asleep. My stomach starts to gurgle. My legs feel lighter. And there have been a few times when I'll just burst out laughing because it's such an incredibly plea-surable experience by the time I get there.

Since learning to meditate effectively, George has experienced many benefits from his twice-daily practice:

I find with TM, for example, in working on a number of proj-ects in Poland, I can negotiate and multitask much more effectively and less stressfully than before. I attribute that in part to TM giving my mind an opportunity to rest from the vigorous work of the previous day. Also, when I suffer jet lag—as I often do—I now take the opportunity to meditate in the morning before starting work, and I find that it renews my energy. I have a level of energy that was uncharacteristic be-fore practicing meditation.

I believe meditation is going to be a permanent part of my daily life. I think that for any of us who live in the busi-ness world, where there are high levels of daily stress, we need to recognize that the body and mind need time to rest. By incorporating TM into my daily routine, I can allow that to happen. For me, this is an incredible tool for helping me maintain a higher level of health.

RAY DALIO: Meditation Has Been One of the Biggest Beneficial Influences in My Life

Ray Dalio is the founder and president of Bridgewater Associates, a hedge fund that he started in 1975 in the spare bedroom of a two-bedroom apartment. Bridgewater currently has more than one thousand employees, and is the largest hedge fund in the world. It is widely recognized for its innovative investment strategies, which have radically changed how institutions invest.

Now in his early sixties, Ray has been practicing Transcendental Meditation for over forty years, since he was a college student. He has thought long and hard about meditation and has contributed generously to helping disadvantaged schoolchildren and others learn to meditate. As you can imagine, he has a great deal to say on the subject. First, he emphasizes the importance of persevering, especially in the early phases:

Originally, when you start meditating, a lot of ideas go through your mind at the same time as the mantra—that was true for me—so you don't transcend. You just go back and forth between the mantra and your ideas. So it took me a while, probably months, to get to the point where I could clear my mind of thoughts and start transcending. When I did that, it was great.

Here's how Ray describes transcendence:

> It is a combination of relaxation and a very blissful experi-
> ence. That sounds more like an orgasm than it really is, but
> it is blissful in the sense that I just feel really good and re-
> laxed and in good shape. You go into a different state—nei-
> ther conscious nor unconscious. When you're meditating,
> you're just not aware. Everything disappears, in a sense. But
> unlike when you're sleeping, if a pin drops all of a sudden, it
> can reverberate through you; it's shocking.

Here is how meditation has helped him:

> At first I noticed that it produced a great deal of relaxation, so
> much so that twenty minutes of meditation could even make
> up for hours of lost sleep. Then I discovered that it changed
> the way I was thinking in two ways: It made me more cen-
> tered, and also more creative. With a more centered, more
> open state of mind, everything got better. My grades went
> up. Everything became easier.
>
> Meditation helped my creativity. I find that creative
> ideas don't come from working hard at them in one's con-
> scious state. Instead, they come when I'm very relaxed; they
> pass through my brain, and I grab them. That's very much
> like a meditative state. One of the challenges for me is that
> as meditation got better and better, my thoughts improved
> and I didn't want to put them away! I wanted to have a pad
> and pen next to me to write them down. (But if I stopped to
> write them down, I'd stop meditating.) It was like trying to
> hold on to a dream, but by putting the thoughts away, I got
> even more. So TM had a beneficial effect on my creativity,

and everything got easier as I became more settled and centered—and it was easy to continue meditating despite having to allocate time for it.

I asked Ray what he meant by being "centered," a word he used several times.

I mean being in a calm, clear-headed state so that when challenges come at you, you can deal with them like a ninja—in a calm, thoughtful way. When you're centered, your emotions are not hijacking you. You have the ability to think clearly, put things in their right place, and have good perspective.

Well-read in the area of popular neuroscience, Ray talks freely of the amygdala, the brain center that generates powerful alarm signals, and the prefrontal cortex, which governs executive functions. "When you become centered," he says, "the balance of power shifts from the amygdala to the prefrontal cortex, so that you govern your emotions rather than the other way around." I agree!

Asked whether he could think of any specific creative ideas that came to him during meditation and that went on to become winners, Ray said he hadn't meant single blockbuster ideas.

I think that the decisions people make every single day all have consequences, and that one's life depends on the cumulative quality of one's decision making. I've made a whole bunch of decisions, which have been both practical and original, and they have—in aggregate—worked out for me. But since you want a few specific examples, I will give you the most important ones—in no particular order. I love markets; they're my thing, and the approach that I came up with is like nobody else's, and it works great. The way I've made my business is also totally different from most other investment management firms. It's unique, and has produced great results for our clients and a wonderful community for our employees. Very little of what I do is cookie-cutter; it's almost all original.

When I look back at my life, I am happy to have had what most people would consider a successful life, not only in terms of business, but in my relationships and in lots of ways. Most importantly, I have been married to the same woman for thirty-five years, and we are deeply in love. Our whole family is very close, and I have great friendships. More than anything else, I attribute it to meditation—partly because of the creativity, partly because of the centeredness. TM has given me an ability to put things in perspective, which has helped a lot. I think meditation has been the single biggest influence on my life.

Here then we have it, from three businessmen at the top of their different fields, their stories shaped by the unique nature of each individual, but with powerful common themes. Transcendental Meditation relaxes them, improves their clarity and creativity, helps keep their emotions in perspective, creates a sense of "centeredness," and contributes to the quality of their day-to-day decisions. Despite their hectic schedules, all three have weighed the costs and benefits of the twice-daily meditation sessions and have concluded that the time commitment more than pays for itself.

TM AND SELF-ACTUALIZATION IN
THE ENTERTAINMENT INDUSTRY

Fame is a bee.
It has a song—
It has a sting—
Ah, too, it has a wing.

—EMILY DICKINSON

Whenever you scan a magazine rack at an airport or newsstand, you will see, staring back at you, the familiar faces of the beautiful people, smiling because they have everything—or so it seems. How easy it is to envy them! And how hard to imagine—or care about—the stresses and challenges they confront. Yet having spoken with many people from this enchanted but difficult world, I can assure you that it is stressful indeed.

The pressures of the work itself are numerous. There is a need to be "on" all the time, to keep the work fresh, to remain creative. And then, of course, there can be the stress of having no work at all— which many in this industry face for long stretches at a time. For those who *do* succeed, there are the challenges that come with fame itself.

In contemplating both the dazzling rewards and painful losses fame can bring, I can think of no wiser or more succinct comment than Emily Dickinson's, shown above. How amazing that this reclusive poet, who knew so little fame during her lifetime, understood the subject so well. Yes, fame has a song, which draws myriads of people to listen in wonder. But its sting is all too apparent. Just think of all those stars who burn themselves out with uppers to stay high and downers to sleep; or celebrities gunned down, blackmailed, conned, betrayed, or hounded by paparazzi. And yes, fame has a wing. Creativity is elusive. Fashions change. Youth passes. And sometimes fame simply loses its charm.

It is easy to forget that famous people also have to deal with the same problems that face everyone else, many of which cannot be simply solved by money. Recall filmmaker David Lynch, saying that even though he had had many of the external trappings that might be expected to make a person happy, his life had felt superficial. What he lacked was a deep-seated feeling of happiness, which he found through meditation. Electronic musician Moby told a similar story. He also observed many other people who, though famous, were nevertheless insecure and discontented. Both Lynch and Moby have found an inner peace and happiness with the help of TM.

In this chapter, we will hear from others in the entertainment industry who have found that meditation enhances the quality of their lives.

PAUL McCARTNEY and RINGO STARR

As you may recall, it was the Beatles' trip to India to visit Maharishi in the seventies that inspired so many people to learn TM, myself included. So great was the influence of meditation on Paul McCartney and Ringo Starr, the two surviving Beatles, that almost forty years later, they sang together at a benefit concert to raise money so that schoolchildren could learn to meditate.

Here are some reflections Paul shared with David Lynch about his trip to India so many years ago. He remembers Maharishi as "a very spiritual and intelligent man," adding, "But what made him so endearing to me was his infectious sense of humor." And the single most important lesson gained from his trip to India?

> Getting a mantra from Maharishi and then learning how to use it. The rest is up to yourself. So, actually, being given a mantra and being taught what to do with it was the most important aspect of the trip—the rest was great fun.

He sums up the role that TM has played in his life since that auspicious visit:

> In moments of madness, meditation has helped me find moments of serenity—and I would like to think that it would help provide young people a quiet haven in a not-so-quiet world.
>
> I think meditation offers a moment in your day to be at peace with yourself and therefore the universe—which once was thought of as a slightly silly hippie idea, but now it's much more accepted and even fits with some of the most advanced scientific thinking.

Ringo, interviewed separately, echoes some of Paul's sentiments. "I think it [TM] gives you a break from the madness," he said. "I can't put it any other way really." He adds, "What meditation is for me is . . . a moment to stop the thinking and let my heart come forward. That's how I always felt about it, because you know my thinking will drive me barmy."

Ringo acknowledges that he doesn't always meditate consistently, then points out in his characteristic upbeat style, "But you know, the joy is you can always come back to it. And it's like a lot of things that are good for you, the more you do it, the better it is."

MARTIN SCORSESE

Martin Scorsese, one of the greatest American movie directors of our time, decided to learn Transcendental Meditation in his early sixties. After hearing about TM at a benefit concert, Scorsese thought it would be helpful for himself, his wife, and his daughter, who was then eight years old.

One cost of success is that more and more work comes your way, which is true for Marty (everyone seems to call him that). When I spoke to him, he listed six separate projects in various stages of development, any or all of which might need his attention on any given day. The stress of all these demands mounted to the point that as he was finishing his 2010 movie *Shutter Island,* he began to develop panic attacks. The attacks would typically set in during the morning, and he would have to wait them out before he was able to leave the room.

Since starting to practice TM, Marty gets up a half hour earlier to meditate and starts his day on a tranquil note. When I spoke to him, he had been meditating for only five months. Nevertheless, he said, the practice had already begun to help him settle down, so that he can move smoothly from one decision to the next. When we spoke, his panic attacks were subsiding; he had experienced none in several months. If he thinks an attack is imminent, he closes his eyes and repeats his mantra quietly to himself, which seems to help.

When Marty starts to meditate, there are "a thousand thoughts, which eventually settle down into a calm, floating space. It is an extraordinary experience." During a session, creative ideas come to mind: for example, intuiting a piece of music to use in a picture about George Harrison that he's been working on for some time; or thinking of running music *and* a voice-over at the same time. Such details may be invisible to most moviegoers, but are crucial for a master filmmaker seeking exactly the right effect.

After meditating, Marty finds that calmness pervades the rest of his day. He has become noticeably more patient with others, as his wife and crew chief have both told him. Like many in this book, Marty has found that TM helps him set priorities. When he is working on two or three films at the same time, as he often is, each film progresses daily as others do their part. The machinery keeps on moving on all of these projects— but he can't handle everything at once, so setting priorities is a constant challenge. After his morning meditation, Marty says he tends to find the priority for the day and week, as well as the strength to subordinate everything else, even when that requires disappointing people.

Happily, Marty's wife and daughter also continue to benefit from their TM practice.

Laura Dern

Laura Dern is a luminous actress who has captivated millions since her early poignant roles in *Blue Velvet* and *Smooth Talk*. Now in her early forties, Laura has been practicing TM for about half her life. At one time, after her two children were born, she was so sleep-deprived that she chose sleep over meditation "because I just couldn't keep my eyes open." Now she finds that "the twenty minutes of dedicated time actually give me what feels like three more hours of sleep."

In explaining a difficulty she has encountered in meditating, Laura used two terms that, since talking to her, I have found helpful in my own meditation—to "trust the meditation" and be "judgment-less." As she puts it:

When kind of dipping into meditation, a lot of thoughts will come up. It's taken me a long time to trust that they're coming up because I need to release the anxiety that those thoughts carry instead of judging and fighting my thoughts by saying, "Oh, you're doing that. You're having all these thoughts when you're supposed to be meditating." And so I'm trusting now that anything that occurs during meditation is part of the process of meditation.

At various times when life has been difficult and friends have recommended a medication that had helped them, Laura has always opted for meditation instead and says "it never lets me down." According to Laura, meditation has helped her find "a place of serenity and breath and patience, as well as physical energy and mental focus." She adds:

I've never been diagnosed with ADD but I relate to it immensely. In the world we live in, I think it's become sort of a cultural challenge. We have so much coming at us all of the time. I feel like meditation affords me a luxurious opportunity to relieve my mind of all that unnecessary weight.

Asked how TM has helped her as an actor, Laura says:

In any art form or creative path, focus and being in the moment and listening to the other person are priorities. I feel like TM has offered me a shortcut to doing that. I know I've become a better listener while acting, and I've become braver in some of the choices I've made. For an actor the number one opportunity to be truly brave is to trust yourself. And if you're scattered and not connected to yourself and your thoughts, it is impossible to be centered as an actor on the set.

As you might expect, the same qualities—being more focused, a better listener, more centered—are also helpful in Laura's personal life. She also cites one additional gift of TM: "the willingness to be culpable."

> With the practice of TM there's a little more ease with one-self, even one's flaws, because there's more mindful peace-fulness in the moment. So when someone says, "Hey, that really hurt me that you said such and such," I'm more willing to roll with it—because I've been practicing this daily rhythm of listening, witnessing, and centering myself.

My conversation with Laura ended with a lovely description of what it feels like when she transcends.

> If I were going to talk about transcendence to someone who was not a meditator, I would probably recall lying out on the beach in the late afternoon with a breeze coming off the water. And you've had an afternoon swim, and you're lying there thinking about something that you've got to take care of. But then the moment captures you so much—the wind and the salt air and the sun—that everything just floats away and you're totally in that moment. You don't fall asleep but it almost feels like a nap because you're in that dreamy state. And that's the only experience I've had, preceding TM, that I could compare it to.

RUSSELL BRAND

Russell Brand is a hugely successful British comedian, actor, writer, and movie star. Russell's early life—as chronicled in his entertaining memoir, *My Booky Wook*—was marked by trauma, loss, and battles with drugs, alcohol, and sex addiction. Although he'd been recognized since his mid-teens for his acting abilities, it was only after Russell succeeded in getting a grip on his addictions that his career took off; he has since become famous on both sides of the Atlantic.

In the course of making a documentary called *In Pursuit of Happiness,* Russell met Bob Roth, the same TM teacher who helped me get back on track with my own meditation. Impressed by Bob and what he had to say about the power of meditation to enhance one's quality of life, Russell learned TM in September 2009 and has been practicing ever since.

Transcendence was one of Russell's specific goals in learning. He yearned to discover "the timeless—a sense of my own existence beyond a conventional understanding of self." While transcending, Russell feels "a sense of past and future melting away." He recognizes that for him, "one objective of addiction has been to annihilate the self." The idea of being able to experience annihilation without harming himself was an attractive prospect, and one that Russell has fulfilled in his meditation.

Since starting to meditate, Russell has felt a "fulfillment of sensory and psychological needs" in a new way and "access to more basic transcendent experiences" in his daily life. He acknowledges having always had a wish to stimulate himself, which is common in many people with a history of addictions. He says that in the past, he has not been "a great self-observer." He is pleased to find that now he has "an extra moment of reflection before yielding to anger, lust, and primal animalistic urges. In that moment there is the acknowledgment that we can become more self-reflective beings."

Like other people in recovery, Russell has found TM helpful in "connecting me with my motives and objectives, with acceptance, and very helpful with my recovery program. I have to be particularly patient with myself as I have to clear up a lot of psychological clutter to find tranquillity." Sometimes at the end of a meditation session, he thinks of the sixth step of AA, "We were entirely ready to have God remove all these defects of character." For Russell, that seems like a perfect moment to ask to be unburdened of old baggage.

It is clear that Russell has thought deeply about the effects of TM. As he puts it:

> It gives a narrative to my life, a different perspective on reality, a recognition of transience, that both good and bad will pass. It helps me with profound and difficult ideas like death—that death need not be feared. It is part of my program of self-maintenance. I have powerful libidinous drives, and if I don't practice self-governance and spiritual values, I can become very attached to the physical and the material.
>
> I see in myself a flickering ember of something that in future can become a fire—a way to break the spell of the attachment to material and physical things, to plug directly into the source as opposed to receiving diluted forms of experience. I still feel some attachment, but I see TM as my way out.

Talking with Martin Scorsese, Laura Dern, and Russell Brand was a moving experience for me. Each of these gifted people has achieved international fame and success, yet each spoke on the record of their ongoing human struggles, notwithstanding their accomplishments. Not least, these are very busy people, who often need to be "on." For me, it is inspiring to witness the way each one continues to take time for spiritual growth, and intriguing that they have found in Transcendental Meditation such a powerful way to do so.

CREATIVITY

You will probably have noticed throughout this book—especially in this chapter—the connection between TM and creativity. So many people interviewed have reported a flowering of creativity after starting to meditate: an ability to see things from some novel angle, to pursue new directions effectively, to innovate or change—either the world or themselves—in some meaningful way.

We know that the experience of transcendence readily occurs during a TM session. After a while, this experience moves into the everyday life of the meditator—a state known as cosmic consciousness. Likewise, people are more apt to have creative ideas during sessions and, after meditating for some time, in their daily lives.

Every once in a while, epiphanies can occur during a TM session. You may recall how David Lynch worked out key elements of his famous movie *Mulholland Drive* while meditating—how the ideas came to him "like pearls on a string." You don't have to be a famous filmmaker, however, to have such an epiphany. A therapist colleague of mine, who has long dreamed of becoming a writer, had just begun to meditate when, during a session, he went into a blissful state and emerged from it with the complete idea for a play in his mind. Over the hours that followed that session, he jotted down the skeleton of the play, which he continued to develop over the course of a year. A total novice, he went on to actually *produce* the play, something that would have been unthinkable to him before he began to meditate.

Although such epiphanies make for good stories, just as important are the many small ideas that can occur during meditation, because they tend to add up. Hedge fund owner Ray Dalio spoke of ideas that come to him often as he meditates and, since he deals with the stock market, frequently involve trading insights. Likewise, in a very different field, Martin Scorsese talked of the many minor insights that occur to him during meditation; in his case, these often involve the fine details of a movie he is directing. These strings of insight shape decision making, and as in any creative act—or in life itself, for that matter—the aggregate of many small insights and judgments makes a huge difference to the final outcome.

How is it that meditation improves our judgment and decision making, creative or otherwise? Maybe it's because extraneous thoughts and unwelcome distractions just seem to fall away. Remember Moby's wonderful comparison of the mind to a party full of guests—some welcome, others not. According to Moby, when he meditates, it's as though the unwelcome guests depart, leaving the mind joyfully open to only the best and most interesting thoughts. Also, in the unstressed meditative state, the alarm centers settle down and stop bombarding the prefrontal cortex with distracting messages that interfere with clear thinking.

We have seen how the benefits of meditation carry through into the waking state, for example, in reduced blood pressure, heart attacks, and strokes. In a similar way, the creative benefits of TM continue into everyday life. Consider Lyn, the university professor, who was able to write a creative paper for the first time in ages after starting TM. With the clarity obtained through meditation, she was able to discriminate between an important and creative professional activity and busy work. More amazing is the story of Mindy Weisel, the artist who, after starting to meditate, changed her favorite medium of expression from two-dimensional paintings to three-dimensional works in glass. When asked about the biggest gifts of TM, many people list improved creativity, right up there with "being centered" and "feeling less stressed."

Anecdotes aside, what does research say? Does it bear out people's impressions of improved creativity following TM? The strongest data come from research conducted by Kim-Tam So and David Orme-Johnson of Maharishi University.[2] I have already mentioned their three controlled studies, involving Taiwanese high school students in the chapter on TM in schools. In these studies, TM outperformed control interventions on a range of intelligence tests. One of these, the test for creative thinking-drawing production (TCT-DP) is said to measure "whole brain creativity" and to reflect such traits as comprehension, analysis, curiosity, unconventionality, synthesis, and the tendency to take chances. In all three studies, just six to twelve months of TM significantly increased scores on this test of creativity. When the three studies were combined, the effect size of TM on creativity was about 0.8, which is considered large. In fact, of all the psychological functions measured by the researchers, creativity showed the greatest increase following TM. A separate study by Fred Travis also concludes that TM boosts creativity.[3]

RESEARCH ON SELF-ACTUALIZATION

Having examined the research on TM and creativity, you may well be wondering whether there is any research on TM and self-actualization. The answer, of course, is yes. Believe it or not, there are several scales (pencil-and-paper tests) that measure self-actualization. The most widely used and best validated of these scales is the Personal Orientation Inventory (POI).[4]

The POI was developed with the help of psychotherapists, who offered opinions as to what they considered mentally healthy.[5] These opinions led to 150 two-choice statements, which present opposite points of view on a particular issue. For example: Do you feel obligated to do—or free not to do—what others expect of you? Or: Do you think it is a good idea—or conceited—to think about your greatest abilities? In American culture it is considered healthier (more self-actualized) not to feel too bound by outside influences and to be comfortable with the idea of reaching one's full potential. Although the answers to the POI questions can be divided into twelve subscales, only two of these are independent—that is, not correlated with each other—and those are the two we will consider here: Time Competence and Inner Directedness. *Time Competence* measures the degree to which one is oriented to the present rather than preoccupied by the past or anxious about the future. *Inner Directedness* measures whether a person's actions arise mainly from a sense of self or from outside influences. These two composite factors are added together to create a "self-actualization score."

The POI is not perfect. For one thing, its value depends on the notion that psychotherapists in fact know what is mentally healthy. For another, people may or may not answer the questions honestly. To this second objection, researchers agree that it is very hard, though not impossible, to "cheat" without contradicting oneself. In its defense, I can only say that it's the best test we have, and has been used in more than 1,500 published papers.

In order to evaluate the effects of TM on self-actualization, veteran TM researcher Charles Alexander and colleagues conducted a meta-analysis of eighteen studies that addressed the question.[6] Fourteen of these studies used the POI and all but one of these was controlled in some way. Overall, there was a highly significant effect of TM on self-actualization—a beneficial effect that increases over time.

In order to compare the self-actualizing effect of TM with that of other techniques, Alexander and colleagues searched the literature and found a total of forty-two studies involving three comparable types of treatment: TM (eighteen studies); other meditation (eighteen studies—six Zen, three Relaxation Response, nine others); and various relaxation techniques (six studies). Overall, the effect size for TM was on average about 0.8 (considered large), whereas for the other methods the effect size was on average about 0.2 (considered small). In other words, TM's effect on self-actualization, as measured by pencil-and-paper tests, was about four times as great as that for other meditation and relaxation techniques.

While all that self-actualization is emerging in the minds of those who meditate—such as being more centered, focused, calm, and effective—what is going on in their brains that might explain these effects?

Fred Travis has described specific brain wave changes that occur during TM, and in longtime TM practitioners these changes occur even outside of TM sessions (see chapter 1). To recap: Changes are seen predominantly in the frontal part of the brain, which is known to be important in executive functioning and decision making. Specifically, the frontal lobes of meditators demonstrate increased density (power) of alpha waves, which are associated with relaxation and inward reflection. Experienced meditators also show greater alpha coherence; in other words, the alpha wave patterns in different parts of the brain are better correlated with one another, suggesting that these regions are working together more cooperatively. To these two findings, Travis has recently added a third: a better match between the demands of a computer task and the corresponding brain response. In other words, the meditator's brain becomes better adapted to respond to different types of computer tasks. (For those with a special interest in brain physiology, I describe this research in more detail in the notes section.)[7]

To simplify matters, Travis has developed a way of combining these three brain functions (frontal alpha wave density, alpha coherence, and task-to-brain response matching) into a composite index called the Brain Integration Scale (BIS). High scores on the BIS are positively

correlated with emotional stability, moral reasoning, and inner directedness, and negatively correlated with anxiety.[8] The scale is also significantly higher in top managers compared with middle managers.[9]

Travis and colleagues had occasion to test out the BIS in a recent
well-designed study of TM in college students in the Washington,
D.C., metropolitan area.[10] In this study, fifty college students were randomly assigned to one of two conditions: an immediate meditation
group and a control group—students who were taught to meditate
after the study was over. Over the ten-week study period, BIS scores
increased in the meditating group compared to the controls. Meditators also differed in that, after ten weeks, they were less sleepy and
more readily habituated to loud noises, as reflected by changes in skin
conductance (a measure of sweating). You may recall (from chapter
3) some other studies in which meditators settled down more rapidly
after being exposed to stressful experiences.

CONCLUSION

As the stories in this chapter reveal, TM can promote transformation
not only in people with specific issues (such as anxiety or ADD) or in
specific situations, but in *anybody*—including people who are already
highly successful. These stories are supported by solid research, which
illustrates the effects of TM on creativity and self-actualization—the
highest rung in Maslow's hierarchy of needs. Brain wave patterns and
responses seen in meditators point to some basic brain mechanisms
that may explain these transformations.

Part IV

HARMONY

11

HARMONY

Coherence at Many Levels

> Harmony: 1. A combination of parts into an orderly or proportionate whole; congruity; 2. Concord or agreement in feeling, action, ideas, interests, etc.
>
> —WEBSTER'S DICTIONARY[1]

> If only the whole world could feel the power of harmony.
>
> —WOLFGANG AMADEUS MOZART

ONE GIFT OF Transcendental Meditation, both for myself and for many others, is that it makes things work better together at many different levels. It creates harmony.

Let's consider the many levels at which that happens.

HARMONY WITHIN THE BRAIN

It is intuitive to think of your brain as a single entity (which, of course, in some ways it is): sort of a mainframe computer that runs pretty much everything to do with you. On the other hand, there is something about the brain that invites models of multiplicity. We hear, for example, about the left and the right brain, corresponding to analytic versus spatial skills; or the reptilian versus the mammalian brain, corresponding to primitive urges versus more warm-blooded tendencies. Although I have marveled at the brain as a single entity, cupping one in the palms of my hands in the dissection hall, I also hold with those who view this miraculous organ as behaving like several small but powerful interlinked computers.

Consider yourself right now. You are reading this paragraph, decoding the words and thoughts with an analytic part of your brain, a highly evolved network in your cerebral cortex. At the same time, though, you may feel an urge to go grab a snack from the fridge or take a trip to the bathroom—your old reptilian brain doing its job. Or maybe you are thinking fondly about something pleasant that happened last night—or may happen tonight. Your reward centers zip into action. Or, on a less happy note, you are reminded of an exam or some other ordeal that lies ahead. Your amygdala fires off warning signals—"Enough reading! Better prepare!" And so it goes. The various regions of your brain compete for attention like a bunch of unruly children, demanding to be fed or entertained. How do you bring order to the situation?

Something I have heard repeatedly from regular TM practitioners is that their thoughts become more orderly, their priorities easier to perceive and pursue. Why? Probably because TM makes brain waves more coherent, an effect that shows up after only a few months of practice: EEG tracings taken during a session show brain waves in sync with one another, almost like the harmonies in a musical composition (see chapter 1, figure 2). In experienced meditators, high EEG coherence persists *beyond* the session, permeating the rest of the person's day. That's good, because elevated levels of EEG coherence go along with higher levels of competence. You may remember, for example, that the Norwegian businessmen who were higher on the pecking order showed more EEG coherence than those lower in the hierarchy.[2]

Another way that regular meditation may help to coordinate the brain's subunits is by freeing up the prefrontal cortex, the brain's CEO, so it's not overrun by the amygdala, the brain's fire marshal, who keeps banging on the CEO's door with false alarms. During a meditation session, the mind calms down. The alarm bells ring more softly, then stop ringing altogether. In the beautiful silence that follows, the mind is free to roam and commune with its most pleasurable parts. Unexpected, creative connections may occur. Unresolved worries may fall away. Problems may yield to solutions as simply as mislaid objects that turn up in some place that seems obvious *after* you find them.

Then the mind may experience the crown jewel of a TM session, the serene state of transcendence. Time and space are suspended as you move past ordinary states of consciousness into the mind within the mind. I would love to know what part of the brain houses this state of blissful awareness—probably lots of different parts contribute—and someday scientists will answer this question. Luckily, we don't need to wait for that day in order to enjoy and benefit from the experience.

As with brain waves, the serenity that comes from regular meditation endures beyond the meditative state. The amygdala stays quiet unless there is a real emergency. Anxious people worry less. Remember Bill Stixrud, whom acquaintances described as the most anxious person they had ever seen. After he learned to meditate, his anxiety simply fell away. He was able to return to school and become a neuropsychologist (see chapter 4). Likewise, Tim Page's panic attacks settled down and he was able to leave home and go to school in New York City. The harmonious mind is also less angry. After David Lynch had been meditating for two weeks, his first wife came to him, wondering what had happened to his anger. Where had it gone? The harmonious mind enjoys clarity when the prefrontal cortex is no longer burdened by the tyrannical hypervigilance of the amygdala. The fire marshal is dispatched to his office in the basement and the CEO can work in peace.

Although harmony begins in the brain, it does not end there, because the brain and body are intimately interrelated. Let us consider how TM promotes this connection.

HARMONY BETWEEN BRAIN AND BODY

We know that emotional distress can directly harm the body. Clinical depression is a prime example. Depressed people are much more likely to suffer and die from heart attacks and other ailments than their more cheerful counterparts. Other psychological burdens can inflict damage, too. Recently, a woman in her fifties consulted me because she was struggling to help her mother, who had been diagnosed with Alzheimer's disease. My patient was the only family member able to help her on a day-to-day basis. Unfortunately, the mother had been a difficult person even before her diagnosis—hard to please, critical, and ungrateful. Now she was more so. "I know it's taking years off my life," my patient said, tearing up. I tried to reassure her, but deep down I wondered if she was right.

William James, the leading nineteenth-century American psychologist, speculated on the nature of emotion. When we see a bear in the woods, he wondered, perhaps we run first and feel afraid only later. We now know that's not exactly correct. We have specialized brain centers, such as the amygdala, that detect fear and transmit fight-or-flight signals to the rest of the brain *and* to the body. But James was right in a sense: Mind and body do respond in unison to threat, trauma, or stress. But when stress goes on and on, its chemicals (such as epinephrine, norepinephrine, and glucocorticoids), which are necessary to mount a response to challenges, may overstay their welcome and damage our health. By modulating our fight-or-flight responses, the regular practice of TM can lower blood pressure, reduce the risk of cardiovascular disease, and prolong life.

When I sit down to meditate, the effect on my body is often immediate and palpable. My breathing slows down, which probably means my parasympathetic nervous system (that soothing network of nerves) is gaining the upper hand. Ah, relaxation! While specific physical effects of meditating vary from person to person, one universal element is relaxation of the muscles, which seem to melt into the chair or just dissolve as you move into a different state of consciousness. There is harmony between mind and body, which continues into the day. When stresses do arise, they have less impact because meditators tend to let go of hard feelings instead of dwelling on them or amplifying them.

In visiting Fairfield, Iowa, where Maharishi University is located, I was impressed by how relaxed and friendly people were. Even outside of small towns in the Midwest, however, I have found most long-time meditators to be physically relaxed in their posture, alert in their expressions, and open-minded in their attitudes. It is not surprising that this demeanor and approach to life, played out day after day over years, would make a huge difference to health, longevity, and just plain enjoyment of life.

At the next level, harmony moves beyond the individual to couples, families, and small groups.

HARMONY WITHIN GROUPS

In my observation, it is common for both members of a couple to learn to meditate. Sometimes a couple will embrace TM as an interesting new activity, or perhaps in the hope of reducing stress. Couples report finding pleasure in meditating together, creating together a zone of calm in an otherwise turbulent day. In general, shared activities of a pleasant nature tend to produce harmony for any couple, but this is especially true for TM because the activity itself reduces stress. Although discord between two people may have a basis in genuine disagreement, it can often result from—or be aggravated by—extraneous stress, which makes it hard for a couple to listen to each other. Instead, they tend to get irritable and snappy, making mountains out of molehills.

It's easy to see how meditating together can produce harmony. But what effects, if any, might one expect if only one person meditates? Could that still increase harmony in the rest of the family or group? Jim Dierke, principal of Visitacion Valley in San Francisco, told me that after the TM program was introduced into his school, the father of one of his pupils asked him, "What are you doing to my son? He's not coming home and beating up his brother anymore." So the brother was benefiting by proxy from the salutary effects on Dierke's pupil. That is one small example of something that probably happens over and over again when people learn to meditate and become less stressed. Others benefit.

It makes sense that as more people within a group begin to meditate, the impact will be greater. We have learned, for example, how the atmosphere in schools and prisons has been transformed by TM programs. A school that had been a chaotic battleground became "an island of calm in a sea of trouble." Recall the story of how a menacing class of inmates in San Quentin Prison became quiet and diligent under the even-tempered tutelage of George Ellis, the short, calm, self-confident man who smiled at their threats. Having listened to so many stories from such diverse people, I can reach no other conclusion than this: Transcendental Meditation can bring calmness and peace to any group in which one or more participants meditate—and the more who meditate, the better.

What, then, about society as a whole? Could meditation help those outside the immediate range of the person or people who meditate? That has been one of the most fascinating and controversial claims of TM.

HARMONY IN SOCIETY AND WORLD PEACE

In 1960, Maharishi hypothesized that if 1 percent of the population of a city, country, or even the whole world practiced TM there would be measurable effects on the entire population.[3] This idea has become known as the Maharishi Effect, and researchers have tested it in numerous studies. Reviewing just the thirty-three peer-reviewed publications on this topic[4] goes beyond the scope of this book; the interested reader should seek out David Orme-Johnson's website.[5] We will consider just three of the studies here.

To test Maharishi's hypothesis, Michael Dillbeck and colleagues at Maharishi University compared the crime rates of twenty-four U.S. cities in which 1 percent or more of the population practiced TM with twenty-four cities matched except for low TM participation. Over a five-year period (1972 to 1977) following the introduction of TM into these cities, the high-TM cities had a 22 percent decrease in reported crime, whereas the low-TM cities had a 2 percent rise. These changes were statistically significant, as was a correlation between the percentage of meditators per city in 1972 and the amount of crime reported in the subsequent five years. The researchers went to great lengths to find other variables that might explain these effects but came up empty-handed. Their findings were published in the *Journal of Crime and Justice*.[6]

In a more ambitious test of the Maharishi Effect, David Orme-Johnson and colleagues recruited a large group of meditators and housed them in a hotel in East Jerusalem in August and September 1983, during the second war between Israel and Lebanon.[7] The goal was to determine whether the number of people meditating in East Jerusalem on a particular day—it varied from 65 to 241 people—would influence the quality of life in Jerusalem (accidents, fires, and crime); the quality of life in Israel (crime statistics, the Tel Aviv stock market, and national mood derived from news content analysis); and the war in Lebanon (war deaths of all factions and war intensity derived from news content analysis).

All of these variables were specified ahead of time, as were composite quality-of-life indexes derived from them. Data came from public sources independent of the investigators. In order to take into account the possibility that the number of meditators at work on any given day might have a delayed influence on the variables of interest, they used a statistical method called time series analysis, which accounts for such lag effects.[8]

The researchers found significant relationships between the number of meditators and improved quality of life in both Israel and Lebanon (for more details about these findings, see the notes section).[9] The researchers concluded that even if a small percentage of the population meditates regularly, that can favorably influence the well-being of the surrounding population. The paper was published in the prestigious *Journal of Conflict Resolution* after it had been vetted by twice the usual number of reviewers, given its controversial subject matter. It has been the subject of a critical review and an equally spirited rebuttal.[10]

The last study we will consider was an even more audacious test of the Maharishi Effect. About 4,000 meditators congregated in Washington, D.C., between June 7 and July 30, 1993, to see if meditation as a group could reduce the day-by-day incidence of violent crime in this violent city during that period. Once again, the researchers used the rigorous methodology described above and once again they found a significant effect. Consistent with previous research, violent crimes decreased significantly over the seven-week course of the experiment. The maximum decrease in crime of almost 25 percent (compared with baseline levels) corresponded to the maximum number of meditators, which occurred during the final week of the study.[11]

If the Maharishi Effect truly exists, how might it operate? One possible mechanism could involve social networks. For example, there has been much recent publicity about how obesity, smoking, and happiness appear to be contagious within social networks.[12] If this is true, so perhaps are serenity and nonviolent tendencies.

Most TM researchers, however, favor a different, more complex explanation, one grounded in modern physics. Essentially, they hypothesize that during the transcendent state, the brain interacts with the unified field of infinitesimal particles now known to make up the universe.[13] These field effects are then thought to influence the brains of others. According to this theory, the more people meditate, the more this effect will grow. Moreover, as with other field effects, people closer to the meditators will be influenced more than those farther away. The researchers have hypothesized that the number of advanced meditators necessary to have worldwide effects is as few as 3 in 1,000. The team from Maharishi University is currently putting their money and effort behind this theory by building a housing project and setting up funding for 8,000 TM meditators in India.[14]

John Hagelin, director of the U.S. TM organization, holds a Harvard PhD in particle physics and can talk eloquently about the many subatomic particles that have been identified and named, along with their various spins and other qualities; about string theory and other very complex aspects of our particulate universe. Taken together, these forces and particles constitute a "unified field." I have enjoyed the privilege of a private tutorial on these matters by Hagelin, but I will not try to replicate our conversation here—which would take another book. So, in brief:

Hagelin believes that during transcendence, the meditator's mind interacts with the "unified field." More specifically, according to Hagelin and colleagues, "There's a profound qualitative and quantitative correspondence between the unified field of physics and the unified field of consciousness. . . . Indeed, they appear to be identical." I cannot claim to fully comprehend the reasoning behind these ideas, but am very willing to acknowledge that there are more things in heaven and earth than are dreamed of in my philosophy.[15] I recommend that the reader wanting more information on this subject visit Hagelin's website on the topic.[16]

To digress for a moment, there is an interesting story behind John Hagelin's career shift from physicist to TM expert. As a young man, he had been in a motorcycle accident and lived in a body cast for a year. During that year, he learned TM on the advice of his doctor. Here's his description of its benefits:

> The striking effect of meditation for me was the clarity of mind it brought, especially when grappling with new concepts of an abstract nature. And quantum mechanics is an extremely abstract subject. When you're even the slightest bit tired and you're trying to work through these thick tomes, maybe in the late afternoon, you just spin your wheels and it's tiring and frustrating; it's not very clear. If I were to stop and meditate for twenty minutes, I could open up the same page and the contents would present themselves with a lucidity that was so concrete, it was more like diving into a box of Russell Stover candies.

CONCLUSION

So, TM brings harmony at many levels: within your own mind, between mind and body, between you and your loved ones, in groups,
and perhaps within the society or even the planet at large. We don't
have all the answers, but that's OK. Knowledge is in a state of constant evolution and is not, as I perhaps imagined when I was very
young, a fixed set of precepts.

I continue to meditate, which continues to bring me joy and transcendence twice a day and in between. I have particularly enjoyed my
journey of the past year, in which I have met and listened to meditators from all walks of life: patients, friends, and colleagues; scientists
who have spent most of their professional lives researching this topic;
people who were homeless, addicted, or troubled in one way or another
(or used to be before they started TM); artists, movie stars and directors, multimillionaires. It has been a privilege to meet them all and I
have learned something from each one.

I have been astonished at the strength and scope of the research on
TM—and of the technique's potential for healing and transformation.
Perhaps some of my curiosity and wonder has rubbed off onto you, the
reader. Most of all, I have enjoyed sharing my journey with you, and
hope that I have transmitted to you—one way or another—some of
that joy and excitement.

Appendix

ANSWERS TO QUESTIONS ABOUT
TRANSCENDENTAL MEDITATION

An Expert's Perspective

IN THE COURSE of researching this book, I've found a number of questions that arise again and again. Here they are—with answers from Bob Roth, who has been teaching TM all over the world for nearly forty years.

NORM ROSENTHAL: *What exactly is the TM technique—and what is it not?*

BOB ROTH: Here is a short definition—Transcendental Meditation, as it was taught by Maharishi Mahesh Yogi, is a simple, natural, effortless mental technique which is practiced sitting comfortably with the eyes closed for fifteen to twenty minutes twice a day. The technique allows the active, thinking mind to *transcend* its internal noise and quiet down to a state of "restful alertness," in which the mind is profoundly settled, yet alert—while the body benefits from deep rest and relaxation. The technique is just that, a technique. It does not involve religion or belief of any kind; it does not require a philosophy or change of lifestyle; nor does it involve "mindfulness" or any other form of meditation based on "focus," "concentration," or "control" of the mind. You just learn the TM technique, practice it, and enjoy the results.

What is this "settled" state of the mind?

Let me explain with an analogy: Imagine a cross-section of an ocean that has choppy, at times turbulent, waves on the surface—and quiet calm at its depth. In a similar way, the surface of the mind can be active, at times frenetic, with a torrent of thoughts throughout the day. And yet there is a level, deep within the mind, that is ever silent, settled, fully expanded, and fully alert. This level of the mind goes by many names—the source of thought, the unified field of consciousness, transcendental consciousness, the Self. It exists within every human being. It was there yesterday within you, it is there right now, and it will be there tomorrow. It is deep within the structure of the mind; we have just lost access to it. Transcendental Meditation is a technique, easy and enjoyable, that gives access to this field.

How does TM work?

The Transcendental Meditation technique makes use of the mind's natural tendency to be drawn—or attracted—toward fields of greater charm or satisfaction. For example, you are sitting in a room listening to music, but the music is not very good, so you're easily distracted. Then some beautiful music comes wafting in from another room. What happens? Your attention spontaneously shifts from the not-so-pleasing music to the really good music. And it's the same with books.

If you're deep in a really great book, you could be anywhere—in a crowded airport, waiting for hours—and your attention will stay right there on the page. We infer that deep within the mind, at the very source of thought, is a reservoir of energy, intelligence, and happiness. You would logically expect that this field would be an incredibly satisfying place to "be" and it is—after all, it is your own inner Self.

When you learn TM, you learn a technique that reliably turns the attention of your mind within. It's like leaning over to dive into a pool—once you're in the right position, the movement just naturally happens. With no effort at all, your attention moves to increasingly subtle, quiet, creative, and energetic levels of the mind. How do you know this is happening? Because the mind and body are connected, and you can feel it. As the mind is settling down during TM practice, the body must likewise be gaining a state of deep rest, and the functioning of the brain must change as well. And that is exactly what the research shows. During the TM technique the body is deeply rested and the mind is settled yet wide awake. You're in a unique, yet completely natural state of restful alertness. It's far different from simply resting with your eyes closed.

How does TM differ from other forms of meditation?

As I said, the TM technique does not involve any concentration, manipulation, suggestion, or control of the mind. There's no mindfulness, no contemplation, no visualization (e.g., no: "Imagine your mind is like a calm pool"). Empirically speaking, numerous studies, including several large meta-analyses comparing the results of all peer-reviewed studies on all meditation practices available for investigation at the time, show that brain wave changes and the improvements in heart health and anxiety levels clearly distinguish Transcendental Meditation from other forms of meditation.

What is a "mantra"?

When you learn to meditate, your TM teacher will give you your own mantra—a particular sound with no meaning, therefore no tendency to distract you. We say the mantra is simply a "vehicle" that lets the mind settle down toward the source of thought. According to tradition, the mantra is a sound whose effects are "positive and life supporting, from the surface of the mind to its deepest, most powerful levels." Your TM teacher doesn't make up your mantra out of thin air. The mantras come from the ancient Vedic knowledge.

And to anticipate your next question—no, there is not a different mantra for all 6.7 billion people in the world. You could say it's a bit like blood types. Everyone has red blood cells, but there are not 6.7 billion different blood types. There are a set number of types (e.g., A, B, and O, with variations of Rh, etc.), and a trained person can determine which blood type to use for which individual.

In the same way, a certified TM teacher has spent many months in graduate-level study learning how to select the proper mantra for a particular individual; how to teach its use; and how to provide a lifetime of follow-up instruction, tailored to that person's needs.

Once you receive your mantra, what else is involved in learning the technique of TM?

The correct mantra (or vehicle) is only the beginning. The rest is learning how to use that mantra correctly—that is, in a way that allows the mind to transcend, to experience finer levels of thought while the body rests. This is why TM is always taught through personal, one-on-one instruction by a qualified teacher, initially over a four-day period.

Every person is different. Everyone learns at a different pace, and no book or tape can anticipate the questions a particular person may have, or when they'll arise. So when you learn TM, you learn it in personal instruction: to make sure that something significant takes place. We don't want you to just waste your time, daydreaming.

What is the "puja" that is done at the beginning of TM instruction?

The puja—which is done just once—is a simple, few-minute ceremony of gratitude that the Transcendental Meditation teacher performs just before beginning instruction to thank his or her own teacher and other teachers who came before. This ceremony is not religious. It is cultural, a traditional way that meditation teachers prepare to teach. It has a valuable function in that it reminds the teacher that the TM technique is not new or original—and therefore that he or she should not add or subtract anything, but simply transmit the original, effective teaching.

The TM student does not participate in the ceremony; he or she only watches, and only this one time. Furthermore, traditions of honoring are nothing new to us in the West. In graduating from medical school, each medical student recites the Hippocratic oath, acknowledging the long tradition of healing and the great healers who came before. Likewise, a martial artist bows to his opponent before the engagement begins. Once I explain this perspective to new meditators, they understand and appreciate what the ceremony signifies: that TM is authentic and that it comes in a pure form from the ancient tradition of Vedic meditation.

Utilized in the ceremony are fresh fruit, fresh-cut flowers, and a white cloth, all of which symbolize growth and new beginnings. The ceremony is in Sanskrit and involves saying the names of the great meditation teachers of the past. This is the way Transcendental Meditation was taught thousands of years ago, and that it is how it has been taught to the six million people who have learned the technique during the past fifty years.

Some people say Transcendental Meditation is a religion. How do you respond to that?

Transcendental Meditation is not a religion. There are TM teachers of all religions—some of them clergy—and others of no religion at all. You don't need to believe in anything to practice the technique and get all the benefits. In fact, you can be 100 percent skeptical about the whole thing and TM will work as well as if you "believe"—it's like gravity, in a way. You don't have to believe in gravity in order to stay on Earth and not go floating off into the atmosphere! And so it is with TM. People of every religion and no religion can and do practice TM, and all of them find that it enriches all aspects of their lives, including their religious lives.

How long have you been teaching TM?

I have been a teacher of the Transcendental Meditation technique since 1972. I have personally taught more than a thousand people—as well as helping to oversee the introduction of in-house TM programs for tens of thousands of people in schools and colleges, businesses, the military, professional athletic teams, hospitals and health clinics, and prisons.

Can you predict who is most likely to benefit
from TM? What are the characteristics?

The experience of transcendence—"restful alertness"—can benefit everyone. For example, I recently taught a great guy—a big, burly seventy-year-old Vietnam veteran—and his lovely wife of nearly fifty years. They are devoted Catholics, have lived in the same house in Brooklyn since they were married, and have raised a family of soldiers. The husband told me that he had never before, even once, considered doing anything like learning to meditate. Would he be a good "candidate" to learn and benefit from TM? At first glance, maybe not. But he and his wife were intrigued and decided to start.

Six months later, they love it—and meditate daily. He is diabetic, and his blood sugar levels tend to fluctuate, spiking when he's feeling stressed. But since he started TM, his blood sugar levels have been stable. His wife has been hypertensive and on medication for decades. After meditating for less than two months, she had a checkup at which her family doctor said her blood pressure was markedly lower— and it remains that way. So, after nearly forty years of teaching the TM technique to every type of person, I would say that everyone is a good candidate. Basically, if a person is willing to learn and practices as instructed, he or she will get results.

How does one learn to meditate?

The Transcendental Meditation technique is taught through an initial seven-step course of personal instruction by a certified TM teacher, which is followed by a lifetime of follow-up mentoring that you can access at your convenience. The first two steps are free public lectures—

about 60 minutes each—which provide a comprehensive intellectual understanding of the practice. The third step is a personal interview (10 minutes) with a certified teacher. The fourth step (90 to 120 minutes) is personal, one-on-one instruction; this is when you actually learn to meditate. Steps five through seven (60 to 90 minutes each) are follow-up meetings during which you will consolidate both your intellectual understanding and your direct experience of the technique, to ensure proper practice and good results. Fifty years of experience have shown that for a person to gain initial mastery, sessions four through seven must take place on four consecutive days (e.g., Saturday through Tuesday, or some such configuration).

After you have completed these seven steps and are enjoying your twice-daily meditation, you can continue to meet with your TM teacher as needed for the rest of your life, to "check" and fine-tune your technique. These checking sessions are free, can be scheduled at your convenience, and last twenty to thirty minutes. If you move away, there are TM teachers all over the world who can provide this support. In addition, you'll have access to an archive of recorded lectures and seminars with Maharishi and global thought leaders in every field; these recordings are offered online and through your local TM teaching center.

Does it cost money to learn TM?

Yes, you pay tuition to learn the TM technique, just as you pay to take other types of classes. There's a flat fee that covers the costs of both your initial training and the lifetime of follow-up training. The fees also help build and maintain TM centers around the world, as well as provide scholarships so that inner-city schoolkids, veterans with PTSD, homeless adults and children, and American Indians living on reservations can learn to meditate.

The tuition varies from country to country, based on the local cost of living (contact www.TM.org for a schedule of U.S. tuitions). In the U.S., the tuition also varies depending on age, occupation, and need (whether you are retired, a veteran, unemployed, a student, a child, etc.). Everything is done to keep TM affordable, while also ensuring that full-time TM teachers are properly compensated for the work they do.

We don't like to turn people away, so some grants, loans, and scholarships are available through the nonprofit Maharishi Foundation.

What do you like best about teaching TM?

I have been teaching the TM technique for nearly forty years, and what I like best today is what I liked in 1972, when I first became a teacher. I like that in just a short period of time, an hour or two each day for four days, I can pass along a powerful tool, a skill that all people can easily learn and use to improve their lives from the first day onward. And that, for me, is a very satisfying thing to do.

ACKNOWLEDGMENTS

I HAVE MANY people to thank in writing this book. My colleague and friend Bob Roth brought the project to me and helped me through each step of the process. I am deeply grateful to Paul Dalio, who encouraged me to start meditating again and to write this book, and to Ray and Barbara Dalio, who made the book possible by their generous support. My agent, Muriel Nellis, made important suggestions and led me to Mitch Horowitz, my superb editor at Tarcher/Penguin. My wise friend and masterful editor Elise Hancock was as unsparing as ever with her red pen.

Profound thanks to David Lynch for supporting this project in so many ways and for sharing with me conversations he had with Paul McCartney and Ringo Starr before the TM benefit concert.

Key experts offered their input, read early drafts, and improved them. I have included their seminal work and thank them: Fred Travis for clarifying the effects of TM on the brain, and providing EEG tracings for figures 1 and 2; Robert Schneider for providing insights into TM, stress, and cardiovascular health; Craig Pearson for sharing his ideas and research on transcendence; James Grant for giving me a sneak preview into the results of his studies of TM in schools; Tom O'Connor for explaining his work in prisons; John Hagelin for discussing his ideas about TM and the unified field; and David Orme-Johnson for his enthusiastic involvement and encyclopedic knowledge, generously shared.

Thanks also to the many people in the TM community who gave freely of their time and assistance, particularly Carla Brown, Sarina Grosswald, Linda Mainquist, Mario Orsatti, and Adam Pressman. My research assistant, Shebna Garcon, answered e-mails at all hours of the day and night. Joanne Grigas transcribed many interviews. John Bartko provided statistical advice.

The people whose names follow helped in so many ways. Some told their own stories, which appear in the book; others read early versions of the manuscript. Colleagues shared their own experiences and those of their patients (anonymously and with permission). Finally, there are those who supported me personally in the countless ways necessary for any creative process. My thanks to all: Kevin Ashley, Vernon Barnes, Ora Baumgarten, Richard Beall, Larry Blossom, Russell Brand, Jim Bray, Milton Burrill, Marilyn Caulfield, Ken Chandler, Candy Crowley, George Crowley, Deborah Dauphinais, Laura Dern, Jim Dierke, Holly Difebo, Karla Dozier, Reggie Dozier, Michelle Etlin, Nick Fitts, David George, Tom Goldstein, Josh Goulding, Joanna Green, Kay Redfield Jamison, Maggie Jardot, Bob Jones, Khursheed Khine, Janice Kiecolt-Glaser, Daniel Lachman, Wendy Lachman, Sam Lieb, Wilfred Lieberthal, Bud and Nancy Liebler, Moby, Sandy Nidich, Carmen N'Namdi, Hilda Ochoa-Brillenbourg, Janet Osborne, Tim Page, Leslie Potts, Leora Rosen, Josh Rosenthal, Jenny Rothenberg-Gritz, George "Doc" Rutherford, David Sack, Martin Scorsese, Cadi Simon, Nancy Spillane, Virginia Stallings, William Stixrud, Scott Symms, Scott Terry, Catherine Tuggle, Laurent Valocek, Jeff Warren, Thomas Wehr, and Mindy Weisel.

NOTES

Introduction | MY JOURNEY BACK

1. Herb Kern's story appears in greater detail in my book *Winter Blues: Everything You Need to Know to Beat Seasonal Affective Disorder* (New York: Guilford Publications, 2006).
2. Rosenthal NE, Sack DA, Gillin JC, Lewy AJ, Goodwin FK, Davenport Y, Mueller PS, Newsome DA, Wehr TA. Seasonal affective disorder: A description of the syndrome and preliminary findings with light therapy. *Archives of General Psychiatry,* 41: 72–80, 1984.
3. Information about how to locate the TM center nearest you can be found at www.tm.org.

1 | A RETURN TO THE SELF

1. On the 340 peer-reviewed publications, see http://www.truthabout tm.org/truth/TMResearch/TMResearchPublications/Published Research/index.cfm.

2. On dividing meditation into three categories, see Travis F, Shear J. Focused attention, open monitoring and automatic self-transcending: Categories to organize meditation from Vedic, Buddhist and Chinese traditions. *Consciousness and Cognition*, 2010, in press. In this paper, the authors credit Anton Lutz with dividing meditation into the first two categories, then suggest adding the third category, automatic self-transcending. In a table (see note 7 below), they summarize the EEG changes observed in the different types of meditation. In the next footnote taken from their paper, you will find their highly illuminating explanation of the difference between focused attention and automatic self-transcending meditation.

3. The reader may ask: Why do *focused attention* meditations and the Transcendental Meditation technique have different EEG patterns? TM can be superficially described as thinking or repeating a mantra—a word without meaning—and going back to it when it is forgotten—this sounds similar to descriptions of *focused attention* techniques. A deeper analysis reveals that the TM technique is a technique for transcending its own procedures—appreciating the mantra at "finer" levels in which the mantra becomes increasingly secondary in experience and ultimately disappears and self-awareness becomes more primary. While focused arousal involves voluntary sustained attention, TM practice involves automatic moving of attention to mental silence. During TM practice, the subject-object relation that defines customary experiences is transcended. In *focused attention* the object of experience is sustained in awareness—the subject (experience) and object coexist; they are independent but interact. In TM, the object of experience fades away—you use the mantra to lose it. When the mantra disappears, the subject, or the experiencer, as Maharishi puts it, "finds him/herself awake to his/her own existence."

4. The specific brain centers with increased activity in loving-kindness-compassion meditation included the amygdala and the insula.

Lutz A, et al. Regulation of the neural circuitry of emotion by com-passion meditation: Effects of meditative expertise. *PLoS ONE,* 3: 1–10, 2008.

5. The emotional brain region affected in this study was once again the insula (Lazar SW, et al. Meditation experience is associated with increased cortical thickness. *Neuroreport,* 16 (17): 1893–97, 2005).

6. Travis F, et al. Psychological and physiological characteristics of a proposed object-referral/self-referral continuum of self-awareness. *Consciousness and Cognition,* 13: 401–20, 2004. And Travis F, et al. A self-referential default brain state: Patterns of coherence, power and eLORETA sources during eyes-closed rest and Transcendental Meditation practice. *Cognitive Processing,* 11 (1): 21–30, 2010.

7. Table 1 (see page 276) summarizes the different meditation catego-ries and their associated characteristics and EEG changes. The table is reproduced from Travis F and Shear J (see note 2 above).

8. The slow breathing that occurs during TM is orchestrated by cells in the peribrachial nuclei of the brain stem, the same part of the brain stem responsible for sleeping, waking, and dreaming. In con-trast to the cells that regulate ordinary breathing (which are lo-cated higher up in the brain stem and respond to the buildup of blood carbon dioxide levels), these cells respond to decreased blood oxygen levels. The response patterns of these two different types of brain stem cells are also different, which accounts for the slow breaths that occur during TM as compared with the sharper more distinct breaths that occur during waking.

9. Travis F, et al. Patterns of EEG coherence, power, and contingent negative variation characterize the integration of transcendental and waking states. *Biological Psychiatry,* 61: 293–319, 2002. Although Fred Travis has been a dominant figure in the field of EEG stud-ies in TM for years, it is appropriate also to acknowledge other re-searchers who have pointed out the effects of TM on EEG coherence since 1974, when physicist Paul Levine, taking the lead from Maha-

Table 1 (Chapter 1): Summary of meditation categories and associated EEG frequency bands (left column), characteristic elements of each meditation category (middle band), and meditation practices that fit into each category as determined by the published EEG patterns

Meditation category and EEG band	Elements of these categories	Different meditation practices
Focused attention Gamma (30–50 Hz) and Beta2 (20–30 Hz)	• Voluntary control of attention and cognitive processes	• Loving-kindness-compassion (Lutz, Greischar, Rawlings, Ricard, & Davidson, 2004): increased frontal-parietal gamma coherence and power Other studies with single group or case study designs ◦ Qigong (Litscher, Wenzel, Niederwieser, & Schwarz, 2001) ◦ Zen-3rd ventricle (Huang and Lo, 2009) ◦ Diamond Way Buddhism (Lehmann et al., 2001)
Open Monitoring Theta (5–8 Hz)	• Dispassionate, non-evaluative awareness of ongoing experience	• Vipassana meditation (Cahn et al., 2010): decreased frontal delta, increased frontal midline theta, and increased occipital gamma power • Zen meditation (Zazen) (Murata, Koshino, & Ormari, 1994): increased frontal midline theta • Sahaja Yoga (Afranas and Golocheikine, 2001): increased frontal midline theta and frontal-parietal theta coherence • Sahaja Yoga (Baijal & Srinivasan, 2009): increased frontal midline theta and coherence • Concentrative Qigong (Pan, Zhang, & Xia, 1994): increased frontal midline theta • Transcendental Meditation technique (Dillbeck & Bronson, 1981): increased frontal alpha coherence
Automatic Self-Transcending Alpha1 (8–10 Hz)	• Automatic transcending of the procedures of the meditation practice	• Transcendental Meditation technique (Travis et al., 2010): increased frontal alpha1 power and decreased betal and gamma power; increased alpha1 and betal frontal coherence; and increased activation in the default mode network • Transcendental Meditation technique (Travis & Wallace, 1999): increased frontal coherence in the first minute of TM practice and continued high coherence throughout the session • Transcendental Meditation technique (Travis, 2001): higher frontal alpha coherence during transcending • Transcendental Meditation technique (Travis & Arenander, 2006): higher frontal alpha1 coherence (cross-sectional design) and increasing frontal alpha coherence (1 year longitudinal design) • Transcendental Meditation technique (Hebert, Lehmann, Tan, Travis, & Arenander, 2005): enhanced anterior/posterior alpha phase synchrony Other case study ◦ Qigong (Qin, Jin, Lin, & Hermanowicz, 2009)

Note: All studies reported here used non-equivalent or matched control group designs, except for the first four studies on practice of the Transcendental Meditation technique, which used random assignment designs.

Table Reference: Travis F, Shear J. Focused attention, open monitoring and automatic self-transcending: Categories to organize mediation from Vedic, Buddhist and Chinese traditions. *Consciousness and Cognition*, 2010, in press.

rishi, was the first to study this association. David Orme-Johnson, who was the first to correlate EEG coherence with transcendental consciousness and creativity, points out the important early role of Keith Wallace. More information on these connections and this early history can be found in Orme-Johnson's website: http://www.truth abouttm.org/truth/Home/AboutDavidOrme-Johnson/index.cfm.

10. On the study of Norwegian managers, see Travis F, et al. Brain integration, moral reasoning and higher development in top-level managers: Testing a unified theory of leadership. Personal communication.

11. On high levels of brain integration in world-class Norwegian athletes, see Harung HS, et al. Towards a brain measure of performance capacity in sports. *Scandinavian Journal of Exercise and Sport*, in press.

12. Marcus Aurelius. *The Meditations*. Translated by G. M. A. Gruber (Cambridge, Mass.: Hackett Publishing Company, 1983), Book 4.

2 | THE MIND WITHIN THE MIND

1. James W. *The Varieties of Religious Experience* (New York: Touchstone, 1997; first published in 1902).

2. Maitri Upanishad. Translation by Juan Mascaro, Penguin Books, 1965.

3. Wehr TA, et al. Conservation of photoperiod-responsive mechanisms in humans. *American Journal of Physiology*, 265 (*Regulatory, Integrative and Comparative Physiology*, 34): R846–57, 1993.

4. Ekirch, AR. *At Day's Close: Night in Times Past* (New York: W. W. Norton, 2005).

5. Nathaniel Hawthorne. *Tales and Sketches* (New York: American Library, 1982).

6. Robert Louis Stevenson. *The Cevennes Journal* (Edinburgh: Mainstream Publishing, 1978), 79–83.

7. Warren J. *The Head Trip Adventures on the Wheel of Consciousness* (New York: Random House, 2007), 83.

8. Wehr TA. Effect of seasonal changes in day length on human neuroendocrine function. *Hormone Research,* 49: 118–24, 1998.

9. Jevning R, et al. Plasma prolactin and growth hormone during meditation. *Psychosomatic Medicine,* 40 (4): 329–33, 1978.

10. Orme-Johnson DW. EEG coherence during transcendental consciousness. *Electroencephalography and Clinical Neurophysiology,* 43 (4): E 487, 1977.

11. Maitri Upanishad. Translation by Juan Mascaro, 1965.

12. Henry David Thoreau. *The Selected Journals of Henry David Thoreau,* ed. Carl Bode (New York: New American Library, 1967), 33–34.

13. H. D. Thoreau: A Writer's Journal, ed. Laurence Stapleton (New York: Dover, 1960), 38–39.

14. Travis F, et al. Patterns of EEG coherence, power, and contingent negative variation characterize the integration of transcendental and waking states. *Biological Psychiatry,* 61: 293319, 2002.

15. Pearson, Craig. *The Supreme Awakening: Higher States of Consciousness—Cultivating the Infinite Potential Within* (Fairfield, Iowa: Maharishi University of Management Press, 2011).

16. According to Vedic tradition, there are seven states of consciousness. Three include waking, sleeping, and dreaming. Beyond those three are:

    Transcendental consciousness is the experience of the transcendent—the Self—in the silence of meditation.

    Cosmic consciousness is the experience of the transcendent in activity. The light of the transcendent, or Self, is maintained naturally throughout the waking state as well as in sleep and dream states of consciousness.

    Refined cosmic consciousness emerges through a process of development of the senses and the heart (emotions). Here you experience the finest levels of your environment. Your love, compassion, and appreciation for friends, family, all of humanity, and the whole manifest world are at their maximum. At this stage, the Vedic maxim "The world is my family" becomes a living reality.

Unity consciousness, Maharishi has said, is the state of full self-actu-alization, full enlightenment. In this state you experience the transcendental reality not just within yourself, but within everyone and everything.

17. Paul McCartney took the opportunity of the TM benefit concert to unveil the song "Cosmically Conscious," an excerpt of which had appeared as a hidden track on his 1993 album *Off the Ground*.

3 | DECOMPRESSION

1. On the "Battle at Kruger," see http://www.youtube.com/watch?v= LU8DDYz68kM.

2. Merz CNB, et al. Psychosocial stress and cardiovascular disease. *Behavioral Medicine*, 27: 141–47, Winter 2002. For those interested in the six different ways that psychological stress can kill via the sympathetic nervous system, here they are: (1) by promoting traditional risk factors, such as eating unhealthy food, smoking, failure to exercise, or other forms of self-neglect; (2) by damaging the inner lining of the arteries, which may then inappropriately constrict and deprive an important organ of blood, or fail to dilate when necessary to provide key organs with the extra blood needed under stress; (3) by increasing the heart rate and blood pressure, which may cause the need for blood to outstrip the supply, resulting in insufficient oxygen to the heart; (4) by causing a piece of atherosclerosis (a plaque) to rupture and block blood flow down the line; (5) by promoting inappropriate coagula-tion through action on blood-clotting elements, such as platelets, preventing blood from reaching the tissues; and (6) by interfering with cardiac rhythm in ways that can be instantly fatal if you don't

have an automatic defibrillator readily at hand. Normally the cardiac rhythm is the result of a delicate dance between the sympathetic and parasympathetic nervous systems. Too much sympathetic and too little parasympathetic activity can fatally disrupt this dance.

3. From the American Heart Association website: http://www.american heart.org/presenter.jhtml?identifier=3025147.

4. Rozanski A, et al. Impact of psychological factors on the pathogenesis of cardiovascular disease and implications for therapy. *Circulation*, 99: 2192-2217, 1999. And Rozanski A, et al. The epidemiology, pathophysiology, and management of psychosocial risk factors in cardiac practice: The emerging field of behavioral cardiology. *Journal of the American College of Cardiology*, 45: 637–51, 2005.

5. Kaprio J, et al. Mortality after bereavement: A prospective study of 95,647 persons. *American Journal of Public Health*, 77: 283–87, 1987.

6. Rozanski et al. The epidemiology, pathophysiology, and management of psychosocial risk factors in cardiac practice.

7. Lesperance F, et al. Five-year risk of cardiac mortality in relation to initial severity and one-year changes in depression symptoms after myocardial infarction. *Circulation*, 105: 1049–53, 2002.

8. Rozanski et al. Impact of psychological factors on the pathogenesis of cardiovascular disease; and Rozanski et al. The epidemiology, pathophysiology, and management of psychosocial risk factors in cardiac practice.

9. Anda R, et al. Depressed affect, hopelessness, and the risk of ischemic heart disease in a cohort of U.S. adults. *Epidemiology*, 4 (4): 285–94, July 1993.

10. Tindle HA, et al. Optimism, cynical hostility, and incident coronary heart disease and mortality in the Women's Health Initiative. *Circulation*, 120 (8): 656–62, August 25, 2009.

11. Nabi H, et al. Low pessimism protects against stroke: The Health and Social Support (HeSSup) prospective cohort study. *Stroke*, 41 (1): 187–90, January 2010.

12. Everson SA, et al. Hopelessness and 4-year progression of carotid atherosclerosis. The Kuopio Ischemic Heart Disease Risk Factor Study. *Arteriosclerosis, Thrombosis, and Vascular Biology*, 17 (8): 1490–95, August 1997.

13. One useful way to combine the results of several small studies is by a technique called meta-analysis (Hunter JE and Schmidt FL. *Methods of Meta-analysis* [New York: Sage, 1990]). This approach applies statistical methods that analyze and combine results from independent studies, taking into account all pertinent information. The pooled data are usually measured as "effect sizes," which reflect the overall magnitude of what you are looking for—in this case the degree to which anxiety predicts subsequent cardiovascular disease. Researchers often employ meta-analysis to combine the results of clinical trials and report effect sizes to describe the difference between experimental and control treatment conditions. In behavioral sciences, an effect size is considered to be large at 0.8 units or more, medium at 0.5 units, and small at 0.2 units (Cohen J. *Statistical Power Analysis for Behavioral Sciences* [New York: Academic Press, 1977]).

14. Roest AM, et al. Anxiety and risk of incident coronary heart disease: A meta-analysis. *Journal of the American College of Cardiology*, 56 (1): 38–46, June 29, 2010.

15. Janszky I, et al. Early-onset depression, anxiety and risk of subsequent coronary heart disease: 37-year follow-up of 49,321 young Swedish men. *Journal of the American College of Cardiology*, 56 (1): 31–37, June 29, 2010.

16. Rozanski et al. Impact of psychological factors on the pathogenesis of cardiovascular disease.

17. Ibid.

18. Ibid., and Rozanski et al. The epidemiology, pathophysiology, and management of psychosocial risk factors in cardiac practice.

19. Nishiyama K, Johnson JV. Karoshi—death from overwork: Occu-

pational health consequences of Japanese production management. *International Journal of Health Services*, 27 (4): 625–41, 1997.

20. Rozanski et al. Impact of psychological factors on the pathogenesis of cardiovascular disease.

21. Muntner P, et al. Trends in blood pressure among children and adolescents. *Journal of the American Medical Association*, 291 (17): 2107–13, 2004.

22. Barnes VA, et al. Stress, stress reduction and hypertension in African Americans: An updated review. *Journal of the National Medical Association*, 89 (7): 464–76, 1997.

23. Barnes VA, et al. Impact of transcendental meditation on ambulatory blood pressure in African-American adolescents. *American Journal of Hypertension*, 17 (4): 366–69, April 2004.

24. Barnes VA. Impact of stress reduction on negative school behavior in adolescents. *Health and Quality of Life Outcomes*, 1 (10): 1–7, 2003.

25. Anderson JW, et al. Blood pressure response to transcendental meditation: A meta-analysis. *American Journal of Hypertension*, 21: 310–16, 2008.

26. Rainforth MV, et al. Stress reduction programs in patients with elevated blood pressure: A systematic review and meta-analysis. *Current Hypertension Reports*, 9: 520–28, 2007.

27. Castillo-Richmond A, et al. Effects of stress reduction on carotid atherosclerosis in hypertensive African Americans. *Stroke*, 31: 568–73, 2000.

28. B-mode ultrasound is a technique in which the machine scans a plane through the body, which can be viewed as a two-dimensional image on the screen.

29. Castillo-Richmond et al. Effects of stress reduction on carotid atherosclerosis in hypertensive African Americans.

30. Schneider RH, et al. A controlled trial of effects of stress reduction on left ventricular mass in hypertensive African Americans. Presented at the 21st Meeting of the International Society of Hypertension, October 2006, Fukuoka, Japan.

31. M-mode ultrasonography. This form of ultrasonography, in which M stands for motion, involves a rapid series of B-mode scans and is one method that has been used for ascertaining left ventricular mass.

32. Paul-Labrador M, et al. Effects of a randomized controlled trial of transcendental meditation on components of the metabolic syndrome in subjects with coronary heart disease. *Archives of Internal Medicine*, 166: 1218–24, 2006.

33. Heart rate variability. When we inhale, the heart rate tends to slow down and when we exhale, it tends to speed up. The variation of the heart rate with breathing is orchestrated by the vagus nerves, which govern the parasympathetic nervous system. Named after the Latin word for wanderer, this nerve is extensively distributed all over the body, helping us relax and slow down when we need to do so—for example, when we are digesting a big meal. The degree of heart rate variability is therefore an index of the strength of parasympathetic function.

34. Schneider RH, et al. Long-term effects of stress reduction on mortality in persons $\geq$ 55 years of age with systemic hypertension. *American Journal of Cardiology*, 95: 1060–64, 2005.

35. Ibid.

36. Schneider R, et al. Effects of stress reduction on clinical events in African Americans with coronary heart disease: A randomized controlled trial. *Circulation*, 12: S461, 2009.

37. Nidich SI, et al. A randomized controlled trial on effects of the Transcendental Meditation program on blood pressure, psychological distress and coping in young adults. *American Journal of Hypertension*, 12: 1326–31, 2009.

38. The Serenity Prayer, attributed to theologian Reinhold Niebuhr, is commonly recited at meetings of Alcoholics Anonymous and other twelve-step programs. The best-known form of the prayer is: "God, grant me the serenity to accept the things I cannot change; courage to change the things I can; and wisdom to know the difference."

39. Orme-Johnson DW. Autonomic stability and Transcendental Meditation. *Psychosomatic Medicine*, 35 (4): 341–49, 1973.

40. Goleman DJ, Schwartz GE. Meditation as an intervention in stress reactivity. *Journal of Counseling and Clinical Psychology*, 44 (3): 456–66, 1976.

41. Orme-Johnson DW, et al. Neuroimaging of meditation's effect on brain reactivity to pain. *Neuroreport*, 17 (12): 1359–63, 2006.

42. The brain region that showed significantly decreased activity in long-term meditators was the thalamus, a major way station for processing painful stimuli. The brain as a whole also showed a significant decrease in activity.

43. In the controls, after five months of meditating, the brain regions that showed significant decreases in activity were the thalamus and the prefrontal cortex (an area that is important for making judgments and decisions). The brain as a whole also showed a significant decrease in activity.

44. Sapolsky RM. *Why Zebras Don't Get Ulcers* (New York: Henry Holt and Company, 2004).

45. Ibid., and Bonneau RH, et al. Stress-induced modulation of the primary cellular immune response to herpes simplex virus infection is mediated by both adrenal-dependent and independent mechanisms. *Journal of Neuroimmunology*, 42 (2): 167–76, February 1993.

46. Glaser R, et al. The influence of psychological stress on the immune response to vaccines. *Annals of the New York Academy of Sciences*, 840: 649–55, 1998.

47. Marucha PT, et al. Mucosal wound healing is impaired by examination stress. *Psychosomatic Medicine*, 60 (3): 362–65, 1998.

48. Kiecolt-Glaser J, et al. Hostile marital interactions, proinflammatory cytokine production, and wound healing. *Archives of General Psychiatry*, 62 (12): 1377-84, 2005.

49. Webster Marketon JI, Glaser R. Stress hormones and immune function. *Cellular Immunology*, 252 (1–2): 16–26, 2008.

50. Damjanovic AK, et al. Accelerated telomere erosion is associated with declining immune function of caregivers of Alzheimer's disease patients. *Journal of Immunology*, 179 (6): 4249–54, 2007.

51. Nidich SI, et al. A randomized controlled trial of the effects of transcendental meditation on quality of life in older breast cancer patients. *Integrative Cancer Therapies*, (3): 228–34, September 8, 2009.

52. Orme-Johnson D. Medical care utilization and the Transcendental Meditation Program. *Psychosomatic Medicine*, 49 (1): 493–507, 1987.

53. Herron RE, Hills SL. The impact of the Transcendental Meditation program on government payments to physicians in Quebec: An update. *American Journal of Health Promotion*, 14 (5): 284–91, 2000.

4 | TURNING OFF THE BRAIN'S ALARM SYSTEM

1. Panskepp J. *Affective Neuroscience: The Foundations of Human and Animal Emotions* (New York: Oxford University Press, 1998).

2. Rosenthal NE. *The Emotional Revolution: Harnessing the Power of Your Emotions for a More Positive Life* (New York: Citadel Press, 2002).

3. Tanelian T, Jaycox LJ, eds. *Invisible Wounds of War: Psychological and Cognitive Injuries, Their Consequences, and Services to Assist Recovery* (Santa Monica, Calif.: RAND Corporation, 2008).

4. Hoge CW, et al. Combat duty in Iraq and Afghanistan, mental health problems, and barriers to care. *The New England Journal of Medicine*, 351 (1): 13–22, 2004. And National Center for Posttraumatic Stress Disorder. How common is PTSD? Fact sheet. 2007. Retrieved from www.ncptsd.va.gov, 10/9/07.

5. Rosenthal JZ. Effects of Transcendental Meditation in veterans of Operation Enduring Freedom and Operation Iraqi Freedom with post-traumatic stress disorder (PTSD): A pilot study. *Military Medicine*, in press.

6. Frankl, Viktor. *Man's Search for Meaning* (Boston: Beacon Press, 2006; originally published in 1946).

7. Ibid.

8. Bloom RM. *Criminal Justice Magazine,* 18 (1): Spring 2003.

9. *Goldstein v. Harris, Warden,* 82 Fed. Appx. 592, CA 9 (California), Appeal of a Habeas Corpus.

10. *Goldstein v. City of Long Beach, et al.* 603 F. Suppl. 2d 1242 (2009), Motion for Disclosure of Grand Jury Materials.

11. Dupont RL, et al. Economic costs of anxiety disorders. *Anxiety,* 2 (4), 1996.

12. Brooks JS, Scarano T. Transcendental Meditation in the treatment of post-Vietnam adjustment. *Journal of Counseling and Development,* 64: 212–15, November 1985.

13. Rosenthal. Effects of Transcendental Meditation in veterans of Operation Enduring Freedom.

14. Eppley KR, et al. Differential effects of relaxation techniques on trait anxiety: A meta-analysis. *Journal of Clinical Psychology,* 45 (6): 957–73, 1989.

15. Review Panel on Coronary Prone Behavior and Coronary Heart Disease. Coronary Heart Disease: A Critical Review. *Circulation,* 65: 1199–25, 1978.

5 | THE SCHOOLBOY WHO PULLED OUT HIS HAIR

1. Gray KM, Upadhyaya HP. Tobacco smoking in individuals with attention-deficit hyperactivity disorder: Epidemiology and pharmacological approaches to cessation. *CNS Drugs,* 23 (8): 661–68, 2009.

2. Grosswald SJ, et al. Use of the Transcendental Meditation technique to reduce symptoms of attention deficit hyperactivity disorder (ADHD) by reducing stress and anxiety: An exploratory study. *Current Issues in Education,* 10 (2): 2008.

3. Behavior Rating Inventory of Executive Function (BRIEF): Isquith PK, et al. at http://www4.parinc.com/Products/Product.aspx?Product ID=BRIEF.

4. Grosswald et al. Use of the Transcendental Meditation technique to reduce symptoms of attention deficit hyperactivity disorder.

5. Taken from: http://www.cdc.gov/ncbddd/adhd/data.html.

6. Brown TE. *Attention Deficit Disorder: The Unfocused Mind in Children and Adults* (New Haven, Conn.: Yale University Press, 2005).

7. Damasio H, et al. The return of Phineas Gage: Clues about the brain from the skull of a famous patient. *Science*, 264 (5): 1102–5, May 20, 1994.

8. Damasio AR. *Descartes' Error: Emotion, Reason and the Human Brain* (New York: Grosset/Putnam, 1994).

9. Arnsten AFT. Toward a new understanding of attention-deficit hyperactivity disorder pathophysiology: An important role for prefrontal cortex dysfunction. *CNS Drugs*, 23 (Suppl. 1: 33–41), 2009.

10. Hains AB, Arnsten AFT. Molecular mechanisms of stress-induced prefrontal cortical impairment: Implications for mental illness. *Learning and Memory*, 15: 551–64, Cold Spring Harbor Laboratory Press, 2008.

11. Ibid.

6 | HELPING THE SPIKES AND VALLEYS

1. Bipolar disorder and other forms of depression: Just to clarify the use of different terms related to bipolar disorder and depression, bipolar disorder refers to a condition that has elements of both depression (see below for clinical criteria for depression) and mania or hypomania. Mania is a state of hyperactivity of thought, speech, and action. During mania, a person may feel inappropriately euphoric but is often angry and irritable instead (or as well). People with mania have a greatly reduced need for sleep. They are often gran-

diose, opinionated, and readily become enraged when people try to thwart their goals (or they perceive this to be so). Manic people often show poor judgment and are at risk of making bad decisions financially, romantically, and socially (see below for clinical criteria for mania). People with hypomania have many of the symptoms of mania but to a lesser degree. Whereas people with mania often need to be hospitalized for their own protection, people with hypomania can generally be treated as outpatients.

People with both depression and mania are said to suffer from bipolar I disorder, whereas people with both depression and hypomania are said to suffer from bipolar II disorder. Mania (or hypomania) and depression may occur at different times as separate states or they may coexist, in which case the person is said to be in a "mixed state." People with bipolar disorder who become depressed are said to be suffering from "bipolar depression," whereas people who become depressed but have never had either a manic or a hypomanic episode are said to be suffering from major depression or major depressive disorder (MDD). Bipolar depression and major depression are recognized as somewhat different in their features and responses to treatment; some regard these two conditions as separate disorders.

The standard criteria (DSM-IV) for major depressive disorder and mania are shown at the end of this chapter's notes. These criteria are published in the *Diagnostic and Statistical Manual of Mental Disorders*, fourth edition, Washington, D.C., American Psychiatric Association, 1994.

2. Calabrese J. One-year outcome with antidepressant treatment of bipolar depression—is the glass half empty or half full? *Acta Psychiatrica Scandinavica,* 112 (2): 85–87, 2005.

3. See note 1 above.

4. Ibid.

5. For Howard Stern talking about Maharishi, his mom, and TM, see http://www.youtube.com/watch?v=bxvwmL7ns24.

6. Center for Epidemiological Depression Studies (CES-D) scale.

7. Nidich SI. Reduced symptoms of depression in older minority subjects at risk for cardiovascular disease: Randomized controlled mind-body intervention trials. Presented at the 31st Meeting of the Society of Behavioral Medicine, Seattle, Washington, April 9, 2010.

8. Nidich SI, et al. A randomized controlled trial on effects of the Transcendental Meditation program on blood pressure, psychological distress, and coping in young adults. *American Journal of Hypertension,* 22 (12): 1326–31, December 2009.

9. In this study, the Profile of Mood States (POMS) was used to measure depression.

10. Sheppard WD, et al. The effects of a stress management program in a high security government agency. *Anxiety, Stress and Coping,* 10: 341–50, 1997.

11. Jayadevappa R, et al. Effectiveness of Transcendental Meditation on functional capacity and quality of life of African Americans with congestive heart failure: A randomized controlled study. *Ethnicity and Disease,* 17: 72–77, Winter 2007. As in a few of the studies mentioned above, this study also used the CES-D to measure depression.

12. Fournier JC, et al. Antidepressant drug effects and depression severity: A patient-level meta-analysis. *Journal of the American Medical Association* 6: 303 (1): 47–53, 2010.

13. Friedman RA. Before you quit antidepressants . . . *New York Times,* January 11, 2010.

CRITERIA FOR MAJOR DEPRESSIVE DISORDER

A. Five (or more) of the following symptoms have been present during the same 2-week period and represent a change from previous functioning; at least one of the symptoms is either (1) depressed mood or (2) loss of interest or pleasure.

1. Depressed mood most of the day, nearly every day, as indicated by either subjective report (e.g., feels sad or empty) or observation made by others (e.g., appears tearful). Note: In children and adolescents, can be irritable mood.

2. Markedly diminished interest or pleasure in all, or almost all, activities most of the day, early every day (as indicated by either subjective account or observation made by others).

3. Significant weight loss when not dieting or weight gain (e.g., a change of more than 5% of body weight in a month), or decrease or increase in appetite nearly every day. Note: In children, consider failure to make expected weight gains.

4. Insomnia or hypersomnia nearly every day.

5. Psychomotor agitation or retardation nearly every day (observable by others, not merely subjective feelings of restlessness or being slowed down).

6. Fatigue or loss of energy nearly every day.

7. Feelings of worthlessness or excessive or inappropriate guilt (which may be delusional) nearly every day (not merely self-reproach or guilt about being sick).

8. Diminished ability to think or concentrate, or indecisiveness, nearly every day (either by subjective account or as observed by others).

9. Recurrent thoughts of death (not just fear of dying), recurrent suicidal ideation without a specific plan, or a suicide attempt or a specific plan for committing suicide.

B. The symptoms do not meet criteria for a Mixed Episode.

C. The symptoms cause clinically significant distress or impairment in social, occupational, or other important areas of functioning.

D. The symptoms are not due to the direct physiological effects of a substance (e.g., a drug of abuse, or a medication) or a general medical condition (e.g., hypothyroidism).

E. The symptoms are not better accounted for by Bereavement—i.e., after the loss of a loved one, the symptoms persist for longer than 2 months or are characterized by marked functional impairment, morbid preoccupation with worthlessness, suicidal ideation, psychotic symptoms, or psychomotor retardation.

CRITERIA FOR MANIC EPISODE

A. A distinct period of abnormally and persistently elevated, expansive, or irritable mood, lasting at least 1 week (or any duration if hospitalization is necessary).

B. During the period of mood disturbance, three (or more) of the following symptoms have persisted (four if the mood is only irritable) and have been present to a significant degree:

　　1. Inflated self-esteem or grandiosity.

　　2. Decreased need for sleep (e.g., feels rested after only 3 hours of sleep).

　　3. More talkative than usual or pressure to keep talking.

　　4. Flight of ideas or subjective experience that thoughts are racing.

　　5. Distractibility (i.e., attention too easily drawn to unimportant or irrelevant external stimuli).

　　6. Increase in goal-directed activity (either socially, at work or school, or sexually) or psychomotor agitation.

　　7. Excessive involvement in pleasurable activities that have a high potential for painful consequences (e.g., engaging in unrestrained buying sprees, sexual indiscretions, or foolish business investments).

C. The symptoms do not meet criteria for a Mixed Episode.

D. The mood disturbance is sufficiently severe to cause marked impairment in occupational functioning or in usual social activities or relationships with others, or to necessitate hospitalization to prevent harm to self or others, or there are psychotic features.

E. The symptoms are not due to the direct physiological effects of a substance (e.g., a drug of abuse, a medication, or other treatment) or a general medical condition (e.g., hyperthyroidism).

7 | SILENCING THE BUBBLE MACHINE

1. *Time Out New York*, 718, July 2–8, 2009, at http://newyork.timeout.com/articles/clubs/75984/moby-wait-for-me-interview.
2. Stern H. Howard Stern talks about TM, his mom, and Maharishi Mahesh Yogi. YouTube, LLC, 2008, at http://www.youtube.com/watch?v=bxvwmL7ns24.
3. Alexander C, et al. "Treating and Preventing Alcohol, Nicotine, and Drug Abuse Through Transcendental Meditation: A Review and Statistical Meta-Analysis," in O'Connell D and Alexander C, eds. *Self Recovery: Treating Addictions Using Transcendental Meditation and Maharishi Ayur-Veda* (New York: Harrington Park Press, 1994).
4. Geisler M. Therapeutische wirkungen der Transcendentalen meditation auf drogenkonsumenten (Therapeutic effects of Transcendental Meditation in drug abusers). *Zeitschrift fur Klinische Psychologie*, 7: 235–55, 1978.
5. Royer A. The role of Transcendental Meditation technique in promoting smoking cessation: A longitudinal study. *Alcoholism Treatment Quarterly*, 1995.
6. Taub E, Steiner SS, Smith RB, Weingarten E, Walton KG. Effectiveness of broad spectrum approaches to relapse prevention: A long-term, randomized, controlled trial comparing Transcendental Meditation muscle relaxation and electronic neurotherapy in severe alcoholism. *Alcoholism Treatment Quarterly*, 1995.
7. Alexander et al., "Treating and Preventing Alcohol, Nicotine, and Drug Abuse."
8. Ibid.

9. Koob GF, Volkow ND. Neurocircuitry of addiction. *Neuropsychopharmacology*, 35 (1): 217–38, 2010.

10. Peters J, Kalivas PW, Quirk GJ. Extinction circuits for fear and addiction overlap in prefrontal cortex. *Learning and Memory*, 16 (5): 279–88, 2009.

11. Wilson EO. *Naturalist* (Washington D.C.: Island Press, 1994), 218–37.

12. NIDA (National Institute for Drug Abuse), National Institutes of Health, at www.drugabuse.org.

13. Orme-Johnson D. An overview of Charles Alexander's contribution to psychology: Developing higher states of consciousness in the individual and the society. *Journal of Adult Development*, 7 (4): 199–215, 2000.

8 | AN ISLAND OF SAFETY IN A
SEA OF TROUBLE

1. *San Francisco Chronicle*, February 4, 2008.

2. The Center for Wellness and Achievement in Education is funded by the David Lynch Foundation.

3. Statistics from San Francisco Schools Program were provided by James Grant. Personal communication.

4. Ibid.

5. Roth R. *A Reason to Vote* (New York: St. Martin's Press, 1999), 151, 155–56.

6. Rosaen C, Benn R. The experience of Transcendental Meditation in middle school students: A qualitative report. *Explore*, 2 (5): September/October 2006.

7. Wolfson A, Carskadon M. Sleep schedules and daytime functioning in adolescents. *Child Development*, 69 (4): 875–87, August 1998.

8. "Stress in Children Today," American Psychological Association, 2010, conducted by Harris Interactive.

9. http://aacap.org/page.ww?name=Bullying&section=Facts+for +Families.

10. Nidich S., et al. Reduced psychological distress in racial and ethnic minority students practicing the Transcendental Meditation program. Personal communication.

11. So K-T, Orme-Johnson D. Three randomized experiments on the longitudinal effects of the Transcendental Meditation technique on cognition. *Intelligence*, 29: 419–40, 2001. For details of this study, see the next note.

12. All three experiments in this paper used the same five tests to measure various aspects of intelligence, as well as the Spielberger State-Trait Anxiety Inventory (STAI), which yields two measures of anxiety—state (the mood of the moment) and trait (a more stable index). The tests measuring intelligence were: (1) the Cultural Fair Intelligence Test (CFIT), said to be a measure of "fluid intelligence," which correlates with executive control functions governed by the prefrontal cortex; (2) the Inspection Time (IT), thought to assess the speed of information processing at the step at which a stimulus is transferred to short-term memory; (3) the Constructive Thinking Inventory (CTI), designed to assess "practical intelligence," which is thought to predict success in love, work, and social relationships; (4) the Group Embedded Figures Test (GEFT), a well-known test of field independence, which predicts academic achievement, controlling for fluid intelligence; and (5) the Test for Creative Thinking-Drawing Production (TCT-DP), said to measure "whole-brained creativity." The various tests are generally uncorrelated with one another, suggesting that they tap into different psychological functions.

In Experiment I, 154 students of average age 16.5 years were divided into three groups: TM, napping (for an equal amount of time), and those with no interest in learning TM. The first two groups were randomly assigned from those who had expressed an interest in learning TM. After six months of TM practice, those in the TM group significantly outperformed the nappers on six out of seven measures (remember, the STAI yields two measures of anxiety), and the no-interest group on seven out of seven measures.

In Experiment II, 118 slightly younger female students (average age 14.6 years) were randomly assigned to three groups: TM practice, contemplation meditation, and no-treatment controls. After six months, the TM group outperformed the no-treatment control on seven out of seven measures, and the contemplation control on five out of seven measures (including state and trait anxiety). The contemplation group outperformed the no-treatment students on two out of the seven measures. Besides replicating the findings of Experiment I, this experiment is one of the few clear demonstrations that not all types of meditation produce equivalent results. Interestingly, the contemplation meditation was taught by someone highly committed to the technique, who had believed it would be as effective as TM.

In Experiment III, 99 male vocational guidance students (average age 17.8 years), majoring in technical drawing, were randomly assigned to two groups: TM or no-treatment. After one year of TM practice, the TM group outperformed the no-treatment control group on all seven measures.

In a final analysis, the researchers pooled the effects of all these studies to calculate the effect sizes for the different measures tested. Effect sizes for TM versus controls ranged in magnitude from 0.77 to 0.34, with the order of effect size being from highest to lowest: creativity (0.77); practical intelligence (0.62); field independence (0.58); state anxiety (0.53); trait anxiety (0.52); inspection time (0.39); and fluid intelligence (0.34). You may recall that in behavioral sciences, an effect size is considered to be large at 0.8 units or more, medium at 0.5 units, and small at 0.2 units (see chapter 3, note 13). So, overall, after six to twelve months of TM practice, there was a large effect on creativity; a medium effect on practical intelligence, field independence, and state and trait anxiety; and a small-to-medium effect on inspection time and fluid intelligence.

I discuss these results further in "Creativity" in chapter 10 (see pages 242–43).

9 | LEARNING TO LOVE YOURSELF

1. Hawkins MA, et al. Re-enlivening and fulfilling the criminal justice rehabilitative ideal through Transcendental Mediation and TM-Sidhi programs: Primary, secondary and tertiary prevention. *Journal of Social Behavior and Personality,* 17 (1): 443–88, 2005. And Cullen FT, Gilbert KF. Reaffirming rehabilitation. Anderson, 1982.
2. Austin J. Reducing America's Correctional Populations: A Strategic Plan. U.S. Department of Justice National Institute of Corrections, Washington, D.C., 2007.
3. Kurian GT, ed. *The Illustrated Book of World Rankings* (Armonk, New York: Sharpe Reference, 1997).
4. Maguire K, Pastore AL, eds. *Sourcebook of Criminal Justice Statistics* [online] (Washington, D.C.: U.S. Department of Justice Statistics, 1999), 462. Available at www.albany.edu/sourcebook.
5. Retrieved from U.S. Bureau of Justice Statistics at http://bjs.ojp. usdoj.gov/content/glance/tables/exptyptab.cfm.
6. Retrieved from Bureau of Justice Statistics, Recidivism at http://bjs. ojp.usdoj.gov/index.cfm?ty=tp&tid=17.
7. See http://en.wikipedia.org/wiki/Muhammad_Yunus.
8. The ongoing Oregon prisons project is taking place in three out of the state's fourteen prisons—a maximum, a medium, and a minimum security prison. Two of these prisons hold male prisoners, and one holds female prisoners. Other parties involved in this collaboration are Sanford Nidich and the Maharishi University of Management, and the David Lynch Foundation.
9. For a comprehensive table of all studies of TM in correctional set-

tings performed to date, I refer the interested reader to note 2 above or to CW Alexander et al., eds., *Transcendental Meditation in Criminal Rehabilitation and Crime Prevention* (New York: Haworth Press, 2003), 53–64.

10. Alexander, *Transcendental Meditation in Criminal Rehabilitation*.

11. Bleick CR, Abrams AI. The Transcendental Meditation program and criminal recidivism in California. *Journal of Criminal Justice*, 15: 211–30, 1987.

12. Rainforth MV, et al. Effects of the Transcendental Meditation program on recidivism among former inmates of Folsom Prison: Survival analysis of 15-year follow-up data. *Journal of Offender Rehabilitation*, 36: 181–204, 2003.

13. Alexander CN, et al. Walpole study of the Transcendental Meditation program in maximum security prisoners III: Reduced recidivism. *Journal of Offender Rehabilitation*, 36: 161–80, 2003.

14. Anklesaria F, King M. The Transcendental Meditation program in the Senegalese Penitentiary System. *Journal of Offender Rehabilitation*, 36: 303–18, 2003.

15. Murray DM. A powerful cure? Transcendental Meditation can offer peaceful road to rehabilitation. *Corrections Today*, 53 (7): December 1991.

16. Ramirez J. The Transcendental Meditation program as a possible treatment modality for drug offenders: Evaluation of a pilot project at a Milan Federal Correctional Institution. In R. A. Chalmers et al., eds. *Scientific Research on Maharishi's Transcendental Meditation and TM-Sidhi Program: Collected Papers*, vol. 2 (Vlodrop, The Netherlands: Maharishi University Press, 1989), 1118–34.

17. Ballou D. The Transcendental Meditation program at Stillwater Prison. In D. W. Orme-Johnson and J. T. Farrow, eds. *Scientific Research on the Transcendental Meditation Program: Collected Papers*, vol. 1 (Rheinweiler, Germany: Maharishi European Research University, 1977), 713–18.

18. Himelstein S. Meditation Research: The state of the art in correctional settings. *International Journal of Offender Therapy and Comparative Criminology*, in press, 2010.

19. Ellis GA, Corum P. Removing the motivator: A holistic solution to substance abuse. In D. F. O'Connell and C. N. Alexander, eds. *Self Recovery: Treating Addictions Using Transcendental Meditation and Maharishi Ayur-Veda* (New York: Harrington Park Press, 1994), 274–80.

20. Bogue B, et al. Combining officer supervision skills: A new model for increasing success in community corrections. *Perspectives: The Journal of the American Probation and Parole Association*, 32: 31–45, 2008. And Miller WR, Rollnick KS. *Motivational Interviewing: Preparing People for Change*, second edition (New York: Guilford Press, 2002).

21. As of the time of writing, over 100 prisoners are taking part in the Oregon studies. You can see a short video about their experiences at http://dlf.tv/2010/freedom/.

22. Gore S, Abrams A and Ellis G, 1984. Vermont State Prisons, in Alexander, *Transcendental Meditation in Criminal Rehabilitation*, 56.

10 | SELF-ACTUALIZATION—YOUR PERSONAL BEST

1. Maslow AH. *Religions, Values, and Peak-Experiences* (New York: Penguin Group, 1976).

2. So K-T, Orme-Johnson DW. Three randomized experiments on the longitudinal effects of the Transcendental Meditation technique on cognition. *Intelligence*, 29: 419–40, 2001.

3. Travis F. Creative thinking and the Transcendental Meditation technique. *Journal of Creative Behavior*, 13 (3): 169–80, 1979.

4. Shostrom, EL. An Inventory for the measurement of self-actualization. *Educational and Psychological Measurement*, 24 (2): 207–18, 1964.

5. Tosi DJ, Lindamood CA. The measurement of self-actualization: A critical review of the personal orientation inventory. *Journal of Personality Assessment,* 39 (3): 215–24, 1975.

6. Alexander CN, et al. Transcendental Meditation, self-actualization, and psychological health: A conceptual overview and statistical meta-analysis. *Journal of Social Behavior and Personality,* 6 (5): 189–247, 1991.

7. The third element of the Brain Integration Scale involves two computer challenge tests, administered repeatedly to a subject whose EEG is being simultaneously monitored. Both tests involve two images presented on the computer screen, with 1.5 seconds in between, to which the subject is required to respond. The first test is the simpler; image #1 simply lets the subject know that image #2 is about to appear. When it appears, the subject is required to make a simple response, such as pressing the space bar on the keyboard. A state of readiness, reflected by a *higher* amplitude of the EEG recording following the appearance of image #1, favors a quicker response. Seasoned meditators show a greater increase of EEG amplitude, reflecting a higher degree of readiness, than their nonmeditating counterparts. In the second test, images #1 and #2 are both numbers. Depending on whether the number in image #2 is greater or less than that in image #1, the subject is required to press one key or another on the keyboard. In the second task, the appearance of image #1 gives no information as to when image #2 is going to appear on the screen. In this instance, a *lowering* of EEG amplitude following the appearance of image #1 favors a more efficient response, as the person is less likely to act prematurely. In the second challenge test, seasoned meditators show lower EEG amplitude (which could be construed as greater equanimity or less tendency to react prematurely) than their nonmeditating counterparts. These EEG deflections are averaged over a large number of trials. The composite score that results is then combined with the alpha wave power and coherence to form the Brain Integration Scale.

8. Travis FT, et al. Psychological and physiological characteristics of a proposed object-referral/self-referral continuum of self-awareness. *Consciousness and Cognition,* 13: 401–20, 2004.

9. Travis F, et al. Higher development and leadership: Toward brain measures of managerial capacity. *Journal of Business and Psychology,* in press.

10. Travis F, et al. Effects of transcendental meditation practice on brain functioning and stress reactivity in college students. *International Journal of Psychophysiology,* 71: 170–76, 2009.

11 | HARMONY

1. *Webster's Deluxe Unabridged Dictionary* (New York: Simon & Schuster, 1983).

2. Study of Norwegian managers. Travis F, et al. Brain integration, moral reasoning and higher development in top-level managers: Testing a unified theory of leadership. Personal communication.

3. Hagelin JS. Maharishi Effect, at http://www.mum.edu/m_effect/ hagelin/index.html.

4. Orme-Johnson DW, Oates RM. A field-theoretical view of consciousness: Reply to critics. *Journal of Scientific Exploration,* 23 (2): 139–66, 2009.

5. From website of David Orme-Johnson, one of the leading researchers on the Maharishi Effect, at http://www.TruthAboutTM.org/ truth/Home/AboutDavidOrme-Johnson/ConsciousnessandConflict Resolution/index.cfm.

6. Dillbeck MC, et al. The Transcendental Meditation program and crime rate change in a sample of forty-eight cities. *Journal of Crime and Justice,* 4: 25–45, 1981.

7. Orme-Johnson D, et al. International peace project in the Middle East: The effects of the Maharishi technology of the unified field. *Journal of Conflict Resolution,* 32 (4): 776–812, 1988.

8. Ibid.

9. The researchers observed highly significant statistical effects of number of meditators on war intensity and war deaths, and significant effects for crime in Jerusalem and Israel as a whole. Interestingly, there was no effect on the number of fires or car accidents. Effects on composite indexes for quality of life in Jerusalem, Israel, and Lebanon were all highly significant. The data were analyzed by two Box-Jenkins ARIMA time series methodologies. These are complex statistical techniques. Even sophisticated readers would be hard pressed to evaluate the appropriateness and accuracy of the statistical procedures. Nevertheless, the high quality of the journal in which the article was published and the peer-review process to which it was submitted are important quality-control elements, which strengthen my confidence in the accuracy of the results.

10. Fales E, Markovsky B. Evaluating heterodox theories. *Social Forces,* 76: 511–25, 1997. See also website of David Orme Johnson.

11. Hagelin JS, et al. Effects of group practice of the Transcendental Meditation program on preventing violent crime in Washington, D.C.: Results of the national demonstration project, June–July 1993. *Social Indicators Research,* 47: 153–201, 1999.

12. Christakis NA, Fowler JH. *Connected: The Surprising Power of Our Social Networks and How They Shape Our Lives* (Boston: Little, Brown, 2010).

13. Here is how John Hagelin, director of the U.S. TM organization and Harvard-educated particle physicist, explains the unified field: "Modern physics has explored progressively deeper (i.e., smaller and smaller) layers of creation, from the macroscopic to the microscopic worlds of the atom, the nucleus, and subnuclear particles. This inward exploration has culminated in the recent discovery of the unified field, or 'superstring field.' The unified field is a unified, universal field of energy and intelligence at the foundation of the physical universe—the origin of all the fundamental particles and forces, and the source of the vast order displayed throughout the universe."

14. Details of this project can be found at GlobalPeaceInitiative.net.

15. The quote is, of course, from *Hamlet* (Hamlet talking to Horatio after observing the ghost of his father). On a separate but related note, however, I have long been interested in the physical phenomenon called entanglement, first hypothesized by Einstein and now pretty much accepted by physicists. According to this idea, which Einstein called "spooky action at a distance," particles very far from each other can be connected in such a way that if a change happens to one of the particles, a corresponding change instantaneously occurs to the other. An allied idea, called teleportation, which posits that information about one molecule can be communicated to another molecule over long distances, has also been accepted. For a lucid and very readable account of this phenomenon and the history of quantum mechanics, I refer the reader to *Entanglement* by Amir D. Aczel (New York: Plume, 2001).

16. See http://www.mum.edu/m_effect/hagelin/index.html.

INDEX

ABOUT THE AUTHOR

 **Dr Norman Rosenthal** was born in Johannesburg, South Africa, and attended the University of the Witwatersrand, where he obtained his medical degree with high honours. He moved to the United States and was resident and chief resident at Columbia Presbyterian Hospital and the New York Psychiatric Institute. He conducted research at the National Institute of Mental Health for over 20 years. It was there that he led the team that described Seasonal Affective Disorder and pioneered the use of light therapy to treat it.

Dr Rosenthal has maintained a private practice in the Washington, DC Metropolitan area for over thirty years, where he treats a wide variety of psychiatric problems using many forms of therapy. Dr Rosenthal was awarded the prestigious Anna Monika Foundation Research prize for his contribution to research in treating depression. He has been listed as one of the Best Doctors in America and as one of this country's top psychiatrists.

He is the author or co-author of over 200 professional articles and five popular books, including *Winter Blues*, *The Emotional Revolution*, *St. John's Wort* and *How to Beat Jet Lag*.

Dr Rosenthal currently serves as medical director and CEO of Capital Clinical Research Associates in Rockville, Maryland, where he directs clinical trials in both pharmaceuticals and complementary and alternative medicine.

www.normanrosenthal.com